PAT METHENY:
The Way Up Is W

Ken Trethewey

Jazz-Fusion Books

First published, December 2008
This second edition, February 2012

Jazz-Fusion Books
Gravesend Cottage
Torpoint
Cornwall PL11 2LX
United Kingdom

©2008, 2012 Ken Trethewey
ISBN: 978-0-9570092-1-9

All rights reserved. No part of this publication may be reproduced, stored in a retrieval system, or transmitted in any form, or by any means, electronic, mechanical, photocopying, recording or otherwise, without the prior permission of Jazz-Fusion Books.

*For Chris, Joe and Helen, my musical family,
who love music as much as I do,
and
for Graham,
who played me that first Pat Metheny album in 1981.*

Pat Metheny playing *The Way Up* gig at the Hammersmith Apollo in London, 12 June 2005. He is playing his Roland G303 guitar synthesiser. Photo: Ken Trethewey.

Contents

- Contents 6
- Foreword 9
- Pat Who? 11
- Pastorius Metheny Ditmas Bley: *Jaco* – 1974 (**) 14
- The Gary Burton Band 15
- Gary Burton Quintet with Eberhard Weber: *Ring* – 1974 (***) 16
- Gary Burton Quintet: *Dreams So Real: The Music of Carla Bley* – 1976 (***) 18
- Gary Burton Quartet with Eberhard Weber: *Passengers* – 1976 (***) 20
- Pat Metheny: *Bright Size Life* – 1976 (***) 21
- Pat Metheny: *Watercolors* – 1977 (***) 24
- Pat Metheny Group: *The Pat Metheny Group* – 1978 (*****) 26
- Pat Metheny: *New Chautauqua* – 1979 (***) 30
- Pat Metheny Group: *American Garage* – 1979 (****) 32
- Joni Mitchell: Shadows and Light – 1980 (*****) 34
- Pat Metheny: *80/81* – 1980 (***) 36
- Pat Metheny and Lyle Mays: *As Falls Wichita, So Falls Wichita Falls* – 1981 (****). 39
- Pat Metheny Group: *Offramp* – 1982 (*****) 40
- Pat Metheny Group: *Travels* – 1983 (****) 45
- Pat Metheny Trio: *Rejoicing* – 1984 (***) 47
- Pat Metheny Group: *First Circle* – 1984 (*****) 49
- Pat Metheny Group: *The Falcon and the Snowman* – 1985 (***) 52
- Pat Metheny and Ornette Coleman: *Song X* – 1986 and 2005 (*) 53
- Pat Metheny Group: *Still Life (Talking)* – 1987 (*****) 54
- Michael Brecker: Michael Brecker – 1987 (***) 56
- Pat Metheny Group: *Letter From Home* – 1989 (****) 57
- Pat Metheny Trio: *Question and Answer* – 1990 (***) 58
- Gary Burton: *Reunion* – 1990 (****) 60
- De Johnette, Hancock, Holland, Metheny Live in Concert – 1990 (***) 63
- Pat Metheny Group: The Road to You – 1991 (****) 65
- Pat Metheny: *Secret Story* – 1992 (*****) 67
- Gary Thomas: Till We Have Faces – 1992 (***) 72
- Joshua Redman: Wish – 1993 (***) 74
- Joshua Redman Quartet: Blues for Pat – 1995 (*) 75

Bruce Hornsby 76
John Scofield, Pat Metheny: I Can See Your House from Here –1994 (****) 76
The Dark Side 79
Pat Metheny Group: *We Live Here* – 1995 (*****) 80
Pat Metheny Group: *Quartet* – 1996 (**) 88
Michael Brecker: Tales From the Hudson – 1996 (****) 88
Tony Williams: *Wilderness* – 1996 (****) 89
Pat Metheny: *Passaggio Per Il Paradiso* – 1996 (***) 92
Kenny Garrett Quartet: *Pursuance: The Music of John Coltrane* – 1996 (****) 92
Charlie Haden and Pat Metheny: *Beyond the Missouri Skies* – 1997 (****) 94
David Liebman: *The Elements: Water* – 1997 (**) 96
Pat Metheny Group: *Imaginary Day* – 1997 (*****) 97
Pat Metheny Group: *Across the Sky* – 1998 (***) 101
Burton Corea Metheny Haynes Holland: *Like Minds* – 1998 (****) 101
Marc Johnson: *The Sound of Summer Running* – 1998 (***) 104
Pat Metheny: *A Map of the World* – 1999 (**) 106
Jim Hall, Pat Metheny – 1999 (***) 107
Michael Brecker: *Time is Of the Essence* – 1999 (***) 110
Pat Metheny *Trio: 99-00* – 2000 (***) 111
Pat Metheny: *Pat Metheny Trio Live* – 2000 (***) 113
Michael Brecker: *Nearness of You – The Ballad Book* – 2001 (***) 114
Pat Metheny Group: *Speaking of Now* – 2002 (****) 116
Pat Metheny: *One Quiet Night* – 2003 (****) 120
Pat Metheny Group: *The Way Up* – 2005 (*****) 120
Michael Brecker: *Pilgrimage* – 2006 (****) 128
Pat Metheny and Brad Mehldau: *Metheny Mehldau* – 2006 (****) 129
Pat Metheny and Brad Mehldau: *Metheny Mehldau Quartet* – 2007 (***) 132
The Tao of Physics 133
Pat Metheny Trio: *Day Trip* – 2008 (****) 136
Pat Metheny Trio: *Tokyo Day Trip Live* (EP) – 2008 (****) 139
Pat Metheny, Anna Maria Jopek: *Upojenie* – 2008 (****) 140
Gary Burton, Pat Metheny, Steve Swallow, Antonio Sanchez: *Quartet Live* – 2009 (***) 142
Pat Metheny: *Orchestrion* – 2010 (****) 144
Pat Metheny: *What's It All About* – 2011 (****) 146

Some Other Stuff 147
Pat's Guitars 148
Concluding Remarks 150
    Pat's vision for the art of guitar playing 150
    The formula for PMG fusion 152
    The band 156
    Breadth 157
    Desire to play 158
    Pat, the guitarist 159
    Pat, the composer 161
    Coda 162
References 164
Discography 166
Index 191

Foreword

Perhaps it sounds trite or exaggerated to say that my life has been significantly changed by Pat Metheny's music. Nevertheless, it is true. The music of the Pat Metheny Group has penetrated deep into my soul and given me more long-lasting satisfaction than any other musician or group. Clearly, there is a strong motivation for writing this book, especially since I know of no other book about Pat. It is also true to say that I am not alone in my personal experiences with this special kind of jazz-fusion music. Many of my friends have been similarly affected and, unusually for a jazz musician, the effect seems equally pronounced on women as on men.

In writing this series of books on jazz-fusion, it has never been my intention to write detailed biographies, but to assist readers to get a better understanding of the music that is available on disc. Likewise, since jazz musicians are quite prolific in their output of recorded material, I have concentrated on the jazz-fusion rather than the jazz mainstream. In Pat Metheny's case, this is especially true because of the effect that Pat Metheny's self-invented style of fusion has had on me. I am not (and never have been) affected in the same way by his extensive forays into mainstream jazz, good though they are. Pat can rightly claim that his contributions to mainstream jazz are as good as any of the electric guitar greats, such as Jim Hall, Wes Montgomery or Barney Kessel, for example; his scope is definitely more wide-ranging. However, although he is a guitarist of the premier league, it is not just his guitar playing that is the most remarkable feature of his creativity but his immense skills in the creation of a form of music that is unrivalled in its ability to move the souls of his listeners.

In writing this book my goal has been to describe Pat Metheny's recorded works to date, concentrating on the output from his band, The Pat Metheny Group (PMG), but covering his other works as much as possible. I intend to describe the music and to explain why I believe some of it is amongst the best in recorded jazz. Of course, such opinions are subjective, but my arguments are supported by some indisputable facts. Pat is one of the biggest selling jazz artists of all time. It could be argued that this proves nothing and that musical quality is not a pre-requisite for large sales. However, Pat does not work in the commercial field of music. He has achieved his successes by nothing short of extreme hard work, immense creativity and craftsmanship in a musical genre that, since the popularity swing from jazz to rock 'n' roll from the 1950s, has struggled to find popular support. Pat's achievements have also been recognised by his peers in terms of Grammy awards, with Pat at the top of the tree for jazz artists. Additionally, almost all of the top jazz musicians acknowledge his gifts in jazz composition. All this, and a wonderful guitarist too!

Pat Who?

During an edition of *The Late Shift* on UK TV's Channel 4 in 1987, Vivienne Goldman and Charlie Giddick introduced the video of Pat Metheny Group's 1982 performance at the Montreal Jazz Festival. The following is an edited extract of their conversation.

Charlie: I've just discovered that he's called Pat 'Meth-ee-nee' [rhymes with weenie] not Pat Meth-uh-nee [as in Bethany].

Vivienne: Yes, Pat Meth-ee-nee

C: He's a jazz guitarist who now plays what is called 'Fusion' which is to me a dubious concept, but I think you're quite happy with the concept of fusion?

V: Well, you know, to me just about anything is fusion because as Aristotle said, "There's nothing new under the sun", so everything – even on to "The Late Shift" – is a fusion of other shows that have gone before. Reggae, for instance is a fine example of a fusion of R&B etc etc. Pat Metheny is just another kind of fusion.

C: What you describe is a mixture of all kinds of things, which is quite natural. If you go back to Elvis Presley, then it's gospel and country, but fusion implies one thing, in this case, jazz, mixed with another thing, rock, and it's (to me) a bit like ice cream and curry. It's two things, which are fine on their own, but you jam them together and – ugh!

V: Ah, but when you think of curry and yoghurt – that works! Personally I find that this fusion of Pat Metheny's, although he's very mega – we'll come to that in a minute – leaves me a bit cold, but I wouldn't say that about all fusions...

C: ...such as?

V: ...well, Grover Washington is pretty groovy...

There has been a lot of ill-informed comment about jazz-fusion over the years, most of it by people who either have their own axes to grind or who have no significant knowledge of the subject. Had this conversation taken place ten years earlier, it might just be forgivable. Charlie might have been lamenting the loss of the great Miles Davis to fusion from pure jazz and in his ignorance thinking that this music was in some way comparable. It is remarkable that such people can be paid to indulge themselves in such a way, but sadly typical of large swathes of the media world. By the time these observations were being made, I had been a fan of Pat Metheny for six years and it was clear that the music of the Pat Metheny Group was something very special. At that time, no-one could have predicted just how powerful it would be so I suppose we must, indeed, forgive these two poor individuals for their ignorance.

I should say at this point that, unlike John McLaughlin, who is entirely happy to call himself an exponent of jazz-fusion, Pat, like Herbie Hancock, has been rather less enthusiastic about labels, preferring to think of his work as just *music*. Nevertheless, it is undeniable from the listener's point of view that, because of his work in his band, Pat Metheny Group (PMG), Pat is a leading practitioner of jazz-fusion music, even if that means a little explanation of what exactly that means. Good though that is, it is a very narrow description of him as a jazz musician because Pat is also a major artist across the whole range of jazz styles.

Beginning his career in the mid-1970s, Pat himself was unimpressed by some of the fusion of the time. "Most of the guitar gigs involved playing loud in a rock-oriented context and involved soloing over one chord. Even now, I am not interested in vamps." [1] Pat's description was exactly the formula being served up by many musicians at that time. It was a formula devised by Miles Davis and Joe Zawinul who saw the new jazz-form as being dominated by white guitarists. They both wanted to include elements of black R&B, and gospel music. As a man from the mid-western USA, Pat Metheny's personal inclination was to create his own version of jazz-fusion, although I'm sure he did not think of it that way at the time.

I am going to argue that Pat Metheny is now one of the foremost jazz musicians ever. My arguments will take the length of this book to develop. However, a simple count of the number of Grammy awards Pat has received lends immediate, if superficial, support. The Metheny/Mays partnership has been awarded no less than ten Grammys – the record industry's equivalent of the Oscars. Pat himself has received eighteen – more than any other jazz musician alive or dead, and more than most rock/pop musicians, such as Sting (16), Eric Clapton (16), Paul McCartney (13), Michael Jackson (13), Herbie Hancock (10), Frank Sinatra (9), Eminem (9), Wynton Marsalis (9), Miles Davis (8), Barbra Streisand (8), Madonna (6) and Billy Joel (5). Leader of the pack is Quincy Jones with 27, much of that success due to his work with Michael Jackson. Few other artists lie between him and Metheny. I argue that, as an all-round musician, Pat's achievement is greater, and in the following pages I intend to explain why, especially if, like Charlie and Vivienne, you have barely heard of him.

Born into a musical family in Kansas City on August 12, 1954, he grew up in the small town of Lee's Summit, Missouri, a short distance southeast of Kansas City. He started on trumpet at the age of 8, but switched to guitar at the age of 12. "I saw *Hard Day's Night* a dozen times, and the guitar was the one instrument banned from the house – how could I resist it?" He loved music of all shades and hues and never thought of himself as a lover of rock or jazz – to him, it was simply music. His progress on the guitar was astonishing and during his early teens he was playing with top local bands and receiving valuable on-the-bandstand experience at an unusually young age. A trumpet player called Gary

Sivils led one band. Pat used to sit alongside the band's pianist Paul Smith who explained the music voicings and harmonies by playing them, rather than by use of written music. Only later (mostly with jazz vibraphone player, Gary Burton) did Pat learn the intricacies of written music. [1]

Graduating in 1972 from high school by the skin of his teeth, (Pat described it as a 'mercy' graduation [1]) he was offered a scholarship at the University of Miami on the basis of his musical abilities. He left after a couple of weeks because he simply felt out of his depth at normal academics. Almost immediately he found the local jazz clubs and started to hang out with the young virtuoso bass player Jaco Pastorius who was just over two years older. However, because of his strong background in live performance, the University of Miami employed him to teach guitar for a year whilst he was still only 18. It was a fantastic year. Amongst other activities up and down the Miami hinterland, he played in a 13-piece band called Baker's Dozen alongside Jaco and a trombone player called Peter Graves, who was to be Jaco's long-time friend and musical arranger. Another bass player called Mark Egan, who took occasional lessons from Jaco, would sometimes substitute for Jaco when he was unavailable, and one of the drummers used in the band was Danny Gottlieb. These last two men were to form half of Pat's first band some four years later in 1977.

In these early years, Pat considered Gary Burton's band to be "the most important band of the late 60s" and he followed all of the band's records very closely. In the early 1970s, Pat had begun to take part regularly in an annual gig at the Wichita Jazz Festival. There, one year, he met a young keyboard player called Lyle Mays who was to become his long-time friend and collaborator when Mays moved to Boston. After Pat had begun teaching at the University of Miami, he went back to Wichita for the 1972 event where he expected to play a couple of tunes with Gary Burton. Pat knew that Gary would be attending, but without his own band. Sure enough, Pat and Gary met and discussed what they would play. Pat: "I picked a couple of his tunes that were really hard, weird tunes, and I could see that he was sceptical that I really knew them. And then when I *could* play them, that's what we wound up playing. Then in the summer of '73 he was teaching on a jazz festival camp that I also was asked to teach on. He heard me play more – I think he was interested in me as a possible member of his band – and then he offered me a job to teach at Berklee. So I came to Berklee and started teaching there, and then, within a month or so, he offered me a place in his band." [2]

In Boston, much of the jazz action took place in Copley Square, where there were two clubs, *The Jazz Workshop* and *Paul's Mall* where Weather Report had played their first gigs in 1970. In the nearby Kenmore Square was a jazz haunt called *Pooh's Pub*. Pat would frequently get Jaco to come up from Florida and join with another friend, drummer Bob Moses, who was also a member of Gary

Burton's band. As a trio, when their other commitments allowed, Pat, Jaco and Bob were often to be found gigging in these Boston clubs. [3]

Pastorius Metheny Ditmas Bley: *Jaco* – 1974 (**)

In the winter of 1973, Jaco Pastorius formed a friendship with New York-based pianist Paul Bley who, with his musician wife Carla, already had a reputation in the world of *avant-garde* jazz. The next summer Bley invited Jaco to join him for a month-long gig in New York alongside drummer Bruce Ditmas and guitarist Ross Traut. For reasons that are not quite clear, Pat Metheny took over the gig from Traut; perhaps Pat sat in on one occasion and blew him away. The quartet, now with Pat in the guitar seat, became established for a month or so and many people saw the music they created as being of the highest quality for that time. Bley had his own record label called *Improvising Artists*, and on 16 June 1974 he took the band into a New York studio to record an album called *Jaco* that appeared later that year. It was the first album for both Metheny and Pastorius and, according to Milkowski, was a great success, both commercially and artistically, yet it soon disappeared from the shelves of the music stores. [4] Pat was still not yet 20. Later, after Jaco's death in 1987, the album became highly sought after and was fortunately reissued in Japan by fans searching for anything Jaco had recorded. It is clear, both from the title and the music itself, that Bley was unselfishly intending the album to showcase Jaco's outstanding talents.

Inspection of the notes indicates that the album is a mix of pieces of variable length, ranging from the 30-second burst of *King Korn* to the ten minutes of the opener, *Vashkar*. However, whilst the first three tracks stand alone, the final six tracks are run together without breaks and appear to form a suite. My own assessment is that the music is strongly influenced by Miles Davis's *Bitches Brew*, for the substantial tracks are essentially extended improvisations on minimalist themes with very few chord changes. We now know that this type of playing to extended sections over a single chord – a style of play called a vamp – does not interest Pat, but I'm sure that at the time he was glad of the opportunity to belong to this type of headline project. It was his first record, after all. Leaving aside the sound of Jaco's bass, the textures and tones of this record are very reminiscent of the early phase of jazz-fusion, for that is exactly what this was intended to be. Part of the reason for this, of course, is that electric keyboards were still quite new and there was not a wide range of sounds to be obtained from them. From the mid-1970s, the capabilities of keyboards changed greatly and so the sounds of the recorded music did too. Here, Bley is playing 'electric piano' and the sound is quite typical of contemporary recordings. Wholly electric, apart from the drums, this record would have created quite a stir amongst those hearing it in the early 1970s and is still highly regarded by those who continue to like this kind of music. My own conclusion is that the album is of historic interest at the very least, and fans of Pastorius will not be disappointed with his contributions. As a record of his stage of development at this very early point in his career, the album is exciting, but from our standpoint today, the album has been left behind by the developments of other jazz-fusion artists, not least by Pat himself. The album is still interesting, however, because Pat's playing is quite unlike anything on the other albums I discuss here. There are significant amounts of quite free improvisation, little sign of themes or melody or planned structure, and there is not much sign of the forthcoming Metheny 'sound'.

The Gary Burton Band

Pat's time in Boston was an important stage in his career. The College at Berklee was a strong attraction to the nation's best young jazz musicians and Pat, as a teacher of guitar, was in the thick of their company. Gigs were plentiful and the musical environment was as stimulating as it could possibly be. And then there was Professor Gary Burton, with whom Pat had made his mark. Burton had been so impressed that he gave Pat the job of teaching the top thirty guitarists from the hundred or so that were studying there. Of course, these were young people, but some were older than he was. At 19, he had become the youngest teacher ever at the Berklee College of Music (from which he received an honorary doctorate more than twenty years later in 1996). Mike Stern was one of those guitarists, and he studied with Pat for six years in total.

Besides his job as an academic, Pat played in Burton's band as the sorcerer's apprentice from late 1973 to 1976. Burton was an established star of the jazz world, a member of a small group of players who chose to play the vibraphone, but an extravagant virtuoso who changed the way the vibraphone was played. Until Burton came along, players used a single mallet in each hand. Burton changed everything by holding two in each hand, a technique that, by doubling the number of notes that could be played at any one time, greatly enriched the sound but was extraordinarily difficult to achieve. As with all great players, Burton made it look easy.

Burton had made his reputation by playing vibraphone in the straight-ahead jazz environment of the Stan Getz Quartet in 1963/4. However, as a 1960s young gun, he was eager for change, as were most other members of his post-war generation. As soon as he could, he threw aside the lounge suits, collars and ties that were the traditional dress on the jazz bandstands in favour of denims and other casual clothes. He grew his hair long and listened to rock music. Soon he could imagine ways of incorporating some of the ideas from rock into jazz, especially when played alongside the electric guitar – the foundation of all rock music. Many observers point to his albums with electric guitarist Larry Coryell as being some of the earliest examples of jazz-fusion. Coryell had had similar thoughts, turned into music on *Free Spirits* (1966). He joined forces with Burton, Steve Swallow and Bob Moses for the album *Duster* (1967) and with

Burton, Swallow and Roy Haynes for *Lofty Fake Anagram* (1967). But these albums were very much experiments at this early stage of the fusion process. Today's listener is presented more with the sound of the *avant-garde* with its frequently pretentious ornaments and new harmonies that ranged from curious to hideous, than with easily recognisable jazz-fusion. It was not until Burton's startling album *Good Vibes* (1970) with Richard Tee, Jerry Hahn, Eric Gale, Chuck Rainey, Steve Swallow, Bernard Purdie and Bill LaVorgne that Burton began to find the best formula for fusion, demonstrated by the stunning fusion track *Vibrafinger*. But it seemed that, although he enjoyed the trappings of the rock musician lifestyle, Burton was not ready to abandon the purer versions of jazz and immerse himself in jazz-rock music.

Burton's philosophy was to play quality music, whether that involved the latest that fusion had to offer or whether it was mainstream or *avant-garde*. Burton was playing exactly the style of music that interested young Pat Metheny. In the same way that the myriad of colours that comprised the electromagnetic spectrum of light fused into white, the combination of all the styles music could offer seemed the most promising way up for Pat. Burton spent many hours teaching Pat all he knew about composition and harmony. He was the perfect Zen master for Pat and the Gary Burton band environment played a big influence in Pat's musical development far beyond just playing guitar.

Gary Burton Quintet with Eberhard Weber: *Ring* – 1974 (***)

Pat Metheny appeared on three albums with Gary Burton's bands, all on the ECM label and all recorded in Ludwigsberg, Germany. The first was *Ring* (1974). The band had an unusual line-up with bassist Steve Swallow augmented by guest Eberhard Weber (b1940), a uniquely talented German musician. Weber created his own highly distinctive sound, first on electrified double bass and then from the early 1970s on a specially designed solid body electric double bass (that is, played in the upright position, rather than the horizontal style of the electric bass guitar). Burton was by now well aware of the type of sound that could be achieved with a bass as a lead instrument, rather than just as a rhythm machine. Weber gave him the perfect opportunity to try this out. Weber's style was firmly planted in the European classical school of playing and entirely unrelated to anything that might be required in jazz-fusion. In addition, the influence of the *avant-garde* school must never be underestimated at this point in the history of jazz. So, not only were there two bass musicians, but also two electric guitarists as Pat was invited to play alongside Burton's old friend Mick Goodrick. His remit was to try to sound different from Mick, and Gary had in mind Pat's frequent use of 12-string electric guitar to do just that. With Bob Moses on drums the line-up was able to create a most original sound playing wholly original pieces on electrified instruments. It is important to realise that, with the likes of Miles Davis, John McLaughlin's Mahavishnu Orchestra, Chick Corea's Return to Forever, and Herbie Hancock's Head Hunters all active in the new jazz-fusion genre, Burton's music was targeted in an entirely different direction. It aimed to break down a new set of boundaries that represented the state-of-the art in jazz at that moment.

Oddly, for all Burton's virtuosity and creativity, he was not a noted composer of jazz pieces. So, if Burton was to create a new niche in his genre, he needed not only the best musicians alongside him, ideally in an unusual combination of instruments, but also access to the best-written material. For someone deep inside the honeypot of talented Berklee musicians, that was no problem at all. Three of the six tracks on the album *Ring* – *Unfinished Sympathy*, *Tunnel of Love* and *Intrude*, were compositions by jazz composer Mike Gibbs. *Mevlevia* was by Goodrick, *The Colours of Chloe* was by Weber and *Silent Spring* was by Carla Bley.

Mevlevia is a curious piece, with a 5/8 metre based on a sequence of falling chords that conveys a mysterious, far-off land. It's like some hypnotic muse that entrances me to continue to listen to the rest of the album because, anticipating what was to come, I would probably have turned it off. *Unfinished Sympathy* is clearly written to some kind of modal design, but is terribly dull. *Tunnel of Love* is slightly more understandable – an abstract painting in a slow 7/4 metre, as if we are being paddled into a dark cave with water dripping from the roof. However, there's not much of a feeling of love in this piece and the motion of the boat seems to have made Weber seasick.

Intrude begins with a drum solo that leads into a group improvisation. Burton may have thought this music was still at the sharp end of jazz, but Weather Report had moved past this particular design and Herbie Hancock's Mwandishi band was about to give it up in favour of the Head Hunters' jazz-fusion. The soul that was so evidently missing from the spine of the album finally comes oozing out in the last two tracks. Bley's *Silent Spring* is a welcome relief from the robotic Gibbs pieces and I get the distinct impression that I am listening to something special, even if I still feel rather cold about the experience. *Colours of Chloe* was the title track from Weber's first 1973 album for ECM and suddenly the warmth returns in full as the piece moves through several intriguing phases to its joyous climax.

Goodrick's composition is a carefully crafted and played piece with a deceptively simple structure, but the kind of unusual harmonies that have, like formaldehyde, acted as a kind of musical preservative. Yet, somehow, this piece is still typical of its time. Gibbs' pieces, on the other hand, definitely belong to the *avant-garde*, eminently suited for the repertoire of a group of jazz academics. Multi-award winning composer Gibbs was widely regarded as a leading jazz composer soon after his graduation from Berklee in the 1960s, but these compositions are like algorithms – fragmented sections of code from stand-alone computer software whose 'do-loops' iterate and increment. They produce transitory sensory impacts, but which emanate from nowhere and have no termination. Their stonehearted architect allows scope for the superimposition of individual improvisations over their repetitive computations, but this is an artificial world of binary notation in which silicon supersedes soul. Oh for a return to the carefree mayhem of *Tanglewood '63* (1969) or the spectral colours of *Fanfare* (1969).

There were many driving forces at work in the culture of jazz of the late 60s and early 70s, besides those behind the scenes of jazz-fusion. First there was the Miles Davis high-art jazz of the period from 1965-68 and his inviolable law that good jazz should be cliché-free. Then there was George Russell's exhortation to dispense with the usual European harmonies in favour of modes, and the widespread fashion to adopt free-form constructs and unusual time signatures. This was a time of license to create music the like of which had not been heard before. It was therefore an ideal learning opportunity for the young Pat Metheny whose contribution to the record is modest and only clearly attributable to him when he plays his distinctive electric 12-string guitar. This album was very specifically about the music itself, rather than a demonstration of the skills of the musicians playing it. This was a notable feature of jazz performance that Pat was to adopt and incorporate into his own brand.

Most people enjoy the sound of Burton's vibes, but Weber's sound is – like some hot Eastern spice – an acquired taste that is not instantly palatable. Pat does not shine on this disc and spends his time mostly strumming his electric 12-string guitar in the right channel of the mix. Mick Goodrick takes more of the lead guitar role and solos in *Chloe*. Moses is proficient and does what he is asked to do. Swallow is however, subdued, possibly because of the recording quality.

This kind of stuff may well be technically clever and played with much artistry, but there is nothing here to penetrate the soul. That was a special gift that Pat was to develop over coming years.

Gary Burton Quintet: *Dreams So Real: The Music of Carla Bley* – 1976 (***)

Carla Bley (b1936) had made a big impact, also in the field of *avant-garde* jazz, with her magnum opus *Escalator Over the Hill* (1971) and was to become one of the most widely respected composers in jazz. Not surprisingly therefore, the adoption of her music proved to be a successful venture for the Burton group. The band's second album (without Weber) was *Dreams So Real: the Music of Carla Bley* (1976).

The title track, *Dreams So Real*, is a remarkable, rich melodic narrative that puts everyone in a zone of warmth and comfort. The exquisite tones of Gary Burton's vibes are a joy to hear. I wish I had dreams as nice as these. It's the same band as on the previous album, but without Weber, which, for me, is a bonus because now there is no distraction from Steve Swallow's beautiful electric bass. So often on records of this vintage – especially where acoustic bass is used – the instrument disappears into a mushy background. This could be because of poor recording equipment or techniques, or a deficiency on the part of the engineer. It could also be a poor pressing of the disc. None is true in this case as the bass resonates strongly throughout the entire album with crystal clarity.

The second track is a very well constructed medley of three pieces: *Ictus*, *Syndrome* and *Wrong Key Donkey*. Its strong *avant-garde* nature will be unpalatable to many listeners, but there's a lot here to make the experience interesting. The head of the piece lasts for twenty seconds and consists of an AABA structure in which the band plays the main idea very loosely. From 0.20, Gary continues to improvise loosely over one of the fastest backings from bass and drums you are likely to hear. There is structure here too, with bass and drums laying down a stretched out version of the first idea and Gary tries to follow their lead, although without precision. Eventually, the head lines return and at 2.38 move into the second piece, *Syndrome*. Again, there is a brief theme before Pat takes the lead on electric 12-string in the left channel (as he is throughout the album). The pace is still fast, but less than before and in time as they play a straight-ahead 12-bar cycle. After seven minutes, the theme returns before the band go straight into the last piece, which begins as a comic four-way conversation between Pat, Gary, Steve and Mick. There follows a pair of good solos from Steve and Mick before the piece ends formally where it started.

Jesus Maria is a vibraphone solo that seems to describe the duality of male and female. For significant parts of this music, Gary's vibes have a curious contrast between left and right hand that may be the idea represented by the title. The voice of humanity, *Vox Humana*, is like an expansive mural by an Old Master. Beautifully conceived, the music is executed perfectly in two solos, first by Mick Goodrick on electric guitar (in the right channel) and then by the Young Master of harmony, Gary Burton. *Doctor* is another loose harmonisation that appears fairly chaotic but is undoubtedly significantly orchestrated. Pat plays a strong solo in this one. Finally we have *Intermission Music*, a name that conveys nothing to me. Once again, Pat is a prominent soloist. The harmonies here are frustrating and like playing a game of tag: just as you think you can reach out and touch the target, it turns away out of reach.

From my 21st century vantage point, I find it curious that this kind of record was being made at the mid-point of the 1970s when jazz-fusion was booming and the kind of *avant-garde* music that had been so prominent in the 1960s was on the wane. As one of the first to experiment with jazz-rock fusion – seen by many as a dumbing-down of a high art form – Burton had taken the decision to continue to develop his music on a higher intellectual plane. This album has many admirable qualities, not least is that it is a very fine example of a band that is completely together, whilst playing music that challenges players and listeners alike, and it makes a strong case for the high quality of Carla Bley's music. There are some truly beautiful moments on this disc, possibly assisted by its reissue in a bright new 2008 edition, as part of an ECM series entitled *Touchstones*.

Gary Burton Quartet with Eberhard Weber: *Passengers* – 1976 (***)

When *Passengers* was recorded in November 1975, the band was a quartet, once again with Eberhard Weber as guest. The first track was Chick Corea's *Sea Journey*, a lively and imaginative tune that featured some lovely playing from Burton and a Weber solo. We note now with interest that Pat Metheny contributed three tracks of the six: *Nacada, The Whopper* and *B&G (Midwestern Nights Dream)*. This was the first real sign of Pat's strong compositional drive and was to set him on the road to becoming one of the great composers in jazz.

Nacada is an extremely slow tune that is an exercise in band harmonics with no obvious chord centre. Pat's playing is in the low register of his instrument and very conventional throughout with little indication that he was trying to establish a brand on this track at least. *The Whopper* is in stark contrast, with Weber, Metheny and Burton all taking the melody in unison in places. The last of the Metheny compositions had already appeared on Pat's debut album, *Bright Size Life*, without the *B&G* in the title. I much prefer the other version, for this is a meandering meaningless piece that is simply too long.

Weber's own composition is *Yellow Fields*. A free introduction is used for Weber to demonstrate his 'sound'. Sadly, it pales in comparison to what we know Pastorius was doing and entirely fails to capture the excitement and resonance of Jaco's fretless. Weber is, of course, playing electrified double bass and the sound is therefore quite different. Perhaps it is the recording quality that fails to realise the potential of both the musician and his instrument, but then that would sound like the old 'bad workman' adage. When the band joins in there are some journeyman solos but the track goes absolutely nowhere.

The last track is *Claude and Betty* from the pen of Steve Swallow, an imaginative slow warped blues that is kinky and cool and by far the best track on the album, even allowing for the Corea piece at the start. I feel good about saying that, for it would have been easy for Swallow to be eclipsed by the superstar amongst them. The sound of the two basses soloing is a highlight. Swallow was obviously not intimidated by Weber's presence.

My impression throughout this album is that the band is taking care not to tread on the boss's toes by occupying his register during the ensemble work. Pat is frequently playing low, as, of course is Weber, leaving the lead resonances free for Burton's vibraharp. Inevitably, the recording seems restrained and lacking in consideration for the kind of sounds that might have been possible with this mix of instruments.

Pat openly admits to learning a great deal from Burton. He would offer a great deal of instruction as to how to play, both before and after gigs. It was during his time with the band that he first appreciated the necessity to communicate with the audience. "You have to render in sound something that is meaningful to you as an individual that might be of interest to someone else," he said.

By 1977, Pat was ready to move on. Initially Pat set out to join another band as a sideman, but he found that with a lot of monochordal jazz-rock fusion dominating the field, he simply didn't want to play that style of music. He was forced into starting his own band. Pat intended from the start to continue to keep all his musical options open, a strategy that has paid great dividends later in his career. Eicher, his sponsor, would almost certainly have encouraged this approach, for it was very much part of ECM's house-style to present a purer form of jazz than the hybrid fusion that was Pastorius' goal. The style of fusion that Pat would develop was still embryonic.

Pat Metheny: *Bright Size Life* – 1976 (***)

In December 1975, Pat was in Ludwigsberg Germany with Bob Moses recording *Passengers* with Gary Burton. At last, the time had come for him to record an album of his own. Pat brought Jaco Pastorius to Germany to join him and Bob and record an album that would be called *Bright Size Life*. The three had gelled brilliantly during their Boston gigs and were offered the chance to record for ECM owner and executive producer, Manfred Eicher. Pat was not sure about whether to use Jaco or not. He had been under pressure to use an acoustic player like Dave Holland because this was to be a 'jazz' record and Jaco was perceived not to be a jazz player – yet another example of the bad press that fusion was receiving. The ECM house style was a much purer form of jazz and electric bass was considered an unsuitable instrument played only by rockers. It was Moses that finally persuaded Pat to hire Jaco and Eicher did not intervene. Pat told his interviewer, Mark Small, that most of the music on *Bright Size Life* was written as exercises for his Berklee guitar students. [1]

The album begins with the title track and Pat on six-string electric guitar with his 'normal' or 'standard' guitar sound in the style Montgomery or Hall. The song is a development of an idea based around the music interval called the perfect fifth. The two notes are separated by five of the notes in a conventional European major scale where the lower of the two notes is the tonic. The perfect fifth is well known to be one of the most attractive and appealing intervals to the human ear. Consequently the tune is light, the tempo lively and the content very pleasant. Solos continue in the style of the melody and the pleasing effect of the melody is thus prolonged. Moses plays gently and Jaco provides a solid but unrestrained bass accompaniment as well as one of his Jaco-type solos replete with chords and harmonics. Funk is never far away from his rhythm as Pat imaginatively explores the melody.

The second track is *Sirabhorn*, in which Pat double-tracks his six- and twelve-string guitars. He starts out with an unusual intro on twelve strings before Jaco and Bob join him. The harmonic structure of this tune is much more creative than before. From 1.00, after the heads of the piece, he plays on with six-string guitar, the second track continuing behind to add colour. Moses is on brushes and Jaco follows Pat's chart to remain harmonically compatible. Given his rein, Jaco solos and copes very well indeed with the unusual chord structure, though he has presumably had plenty of practice during the Boston gigs.

Unity Village is a duet of Pat with himself, on six string guitars. Apart from the continuation of sound and harmonic strategy, Pat's playing is quite traditional and thoughtful and he delivers a sweet melody. Orchestrated as a conventional jazz quartet, and with a gentle Latin lilt, this piece would raise no eyebrows, but would still please many. However, in this form, with two guitars and a sprinkling of unusual chord changes, it comes across as sounding very different indeed.

Missouri Uncompromised is a very different proposition, an up-tempo number that requires Moses to play up at last. It has a fine yet quirky (I'm tempted to describe it as unquity) melody that grows into a lively mainstream-style piece with extended improvisation for Pat's six-string guitar before turning back to the melody at 3.10. The finish is clean and involves a super coda that Pat and Jaco play in unison.

Midwestern Nights Dream starts with a double-tracked solo intro from Pat on 12-string guitar. It then moves into a melancholic theme and there are some heavy bass notes behind Pat's chord-based playing, again on 12-string. Gone is the single-note picked melody as Pat and Jaco work together to create the dream-like mood the title demands. This continues at 3.59 with a Pastorius solo dubbed over his own bass accompaniment. He plays it in the same vein that does not disturb the vibe of the piece and the music ends without the expected guitar solo; unusually, there is no return to the first theme. Thus the structure and the sound of this number show Pat clearly experimenting with entirely new ideas on jazz guitar.

Unquity Road begins by making great use of the Jaco sound as he lays down the basic theme, which is both rhythmically and harmonically challenging. From 0.35 Pat's standard jazz sound is on top as he takes on a solo over the difficult structure he has asked Jaco to play. The piece is filled with all sorts of new colour and especially interesting is the match of Pat and Jaco such that it is hard at first to realise they are different instruments. This is a most intriguing track.

Omaha Celebration is rather more conventional in most respects, though there are some extensive chord shifts throughout the piece. When Pat's solo begins at 1.02 the funky sound returns and the accompaniment seems to open out wide at 1.23 as Jaco changes from sustained to staccato notes. Pat is released to make his licks, while Moses roughs up the cymbals as much as the vibe of the album will allow. This is a lively, exciting number that does all three players proud.

The final track is the only item not composed by Pat, but by Ornette Coleman, who has always been a favourite for Pat. *Round Trip/ Broadway Blues* is a bop-style tune that Pat and Jaco take together before embarking on a standard fast mainstream improvisation. Jaco plays a hopping and skipping (as opposed to a walking) bass line. If Manfred Eicher ever held any doubts about Jaco's ability to play jazz, they were surely dispelled at this point. Pastorius is showing here that he is a truly exceptional player for this kind of sound had been heard from no other player. Jaco was about to attract much attention with his own solo album *Jaco Pastorius* (1976) and would be hired by the mighty band Weather Report soon after this. Meanwhile, Pat plays his six-string guitar with the dexterity of players much older than he, and Jaco is eventually freed up to allow them both a flourish together. A brief statement of the theme from both in unison leaves Jaco a final joint solo with Moses, Pat (rarely) quiet for once. Finally, at 4.10 the theme points the way to the door.

Thus, Pat Metheny rose with meteoric speed to the top of his profession by virtue of his musical genius and with the help of Manfred Eicher, who saw his work with Gary Burton and recognised his talents. He gave Pat his first contract, which resulted in ten albums on the label at the rate of about one per year, until Pat left ECM in 1984.

This album is remarkable for a number of reasons. For a jazz recording, there is a lot of orchestration and relatively little improvisation. The days in which tunes are pulled from the Great American Songbook, given their head and then improvised upon for 90% of the length of the recording are gone in this new Metheny blueprint. The bass provides new textures, with Jaco on this album and Eberhard Weber on the next. Pat's use (and juxtaposition) of 12-string and six-string guitars also adds much that is new to the sound. Meanwhile, compositions are given challenging chordal structures, advanced melodic constructions, difficult syncopations and changes of tempo. The result is a unique album for its time. All this is done without recourse to the use of the kind of *avant-garde* techniques that were now comparatively well established and proven to be unpopular with audiences.

Bright Size Life was to be a one-off. Both Pat and Jaco had their own ideas as to how their careers should progress and that did not include each other. Pastorius was launching his own career with his solo album, his feet placed firmly in the fusion camp as modelled by the club scene he knew so well. It was also about live performance and defining a new role for the bass within a fusion band format. He was soon to target a seat in one of the great fusion bands of the time, Weather Report.

Pat also wanted to define a new role for his own instrument but that was by no means the end of his ambition. He wanted to do this through the creation of new forms of music; the type of fusion Pastorius eschewed was much more based in rock than was Pat's and Pat had already decided he did not want that. Furthermore, the two men had supersize egos: Pastorius, brash and ebullient, Metheny, mild and considered, but totally dedicated to the advancement of music. It was a major consideration to their working successfully together. There was no animosity involved – indeed they would re-join forces in Joni Mitchell's 1979/80 band for the *Shadows and Light* tour – but first they needed to explore farther along their own paths.

Pat Metheny: *Watercolors* – 1977 (***)

Although it doesn't say so, this is the *de facto* first album by the Pat Metheny Group. For *Watercolors*, his second album as leader, Pat chose Dan Gottlieb, Eberhard Weber and Lyle Mays whom he had met in Wichita.

Lyle Mays was born on 27 November 1953 in Wausaukee, Wisconsin. As a child with somewhat unusually academic interests like chess, mathematics and architecture, it is fortunate for us that he eventually chose to take music more seriously than the others. His parents were both musical: his father played guitar and his mother church organ. Thus, Lyle was soon learning keyboard, guitar and trumpet, improvising from an early age, and fascinated by pianist Bill Evans, amongst others. After high school, Lyle studied music at the North Texas State University (now called the University of North Texas) where he met bassist Marc Johnson. Both men joined a popular big band known as the One O'clock Lab Band, for which Lyle composed and arranged numerous pieces. Remarkably, in 1975 an album recorded by the band received a Grammy nomination. On leaving University, Lyle, like Marc, played in Woody Herman's band for some eight months before joining Pat's Group.

Pat and Lyle struck up an immediate rapport and a close relationship was formed that has lasted to this day. Although the album, recorded in February 1977, contains a significant amount of material from Pat alone, there are some substantial pieces here that outline the way forward for the music and style that we now recognise as defining the Pat Metheny Group.

The title track opens the album and introduces PMG for the first time, with Weber on bass this time, later replaced by Mark Egan. It consists of a standard guitar quartet in terms of sound, although Weber's bass is not the normal acoustic sound but is electric in tone. For many listeners there will be nothing startling about this music, but the originality in the recording is the format of the composition. The first part of the piece is the main idea or theme. It consists of a slow phrase and a fast phrase, with the fast phrase repeated twice between statements of the slow phrase, which is played out of tempo (known as *rubato*). The skill here is in the musicians all following the leader and staying together for there is no beat to latch onto. The fast section does have a beat, but contains bars of unequal length, which is hard to follow. The composition of this section of the music is therefore quite complex and is rather pointless trying to describe without precise reference to the score.

After this is complete, from 1.30 the piece takes on a more familiar style with pairs of chords that follow an evolving pattern through a 32-bar cycle. This section of the piece is pretty much 'standard' mainstream playing in what is called the modal style, as developed by Miles Davis in the time of *Kind of Blue*. The players follow a fixed pattern of chords and improvise over it. Pat's guitar plays the 32 bars and then adds a further four as a bridge before repeating the whole thing again. At 4.07, the piano solo starts, which then does the same. Once this is complete the initial theme returns for once through the fast and slow section where it ends. It's a very pleasant piece of music that you can listen to without worrying about the construction.

Track two is called *Icefire* and is a solo by Pat on an instrument called harpguitar that has fifteen strings. It does not sound like jazz in the normal sense of the word and we must assume that there is an element of improvisation going on. However, it is Pat's use of these kinds of unusual sounds to invoke new responses in his listeners. Inevitably imagery comes to mind that hopefully resembles the title Pat has assigned to the music. Pat has always been interested in extending the range of the guitar in jazz and his use of unusual instruments in order to add new tones and textures to his music continues throughout his career. This instrument appears to be the forerunner of a later instrument that he uses a lot, in a similar musical context, called the Pikasso 42-string guitar.

Track three is *Oasis*, and consists of multi-tracked acoustic guitar with a synthesiser voice overlaid. Again, the guitar work is novel and evokes the sound of the harp, but it's not very close to either jazz or jazz-fusion.

Lakes returns to the normal quartet format, but once again, the structure of the composition is far from normal. First there is a 32-bar introduction that we can think of as spelling out the theme. From bar 33 onwards we enter a cycling phase, based on 24 bars, itself divided into three. The first eight are quite straightforward as a descending sequence of chords; the next two sets of eight are rather harder as the band go through a cycle of chord changes that progresses through the entire scale. It's a pretty impressive thing to do. The musicians are showing off, if you like, and they're letting us know that they can do these musical acrobatics. Both guitar and piano go around this cycle of 24 bars three times each and then it's back to the initial theme for a final time and played out in 24 bars. It ends cleanly on a little hook phrase that listeners will have remembered from the first time through. This is a splendid piece of music. Again, you don't need to worry about the structure, just sit back and enjoy it, but realise how good these guys were to be able to perform it.

Track five is *River Quay*, which is in a moderately paced common time and with the quartet. There is an eight bar introduction before guitar plays the main theme of eight bars, repeated once from 0.20. At 1.01, the third set of eight is actually increased to nine and then the cycle begins again at the first bar. It's another strange construction, but it works and sounds very pleasant because of the way Pat has built the melody into it. The guitar plays this odd cycle twice, piano once, and the guitar a last time through, the last phrase repeated to finish cleanly. This is quite a straightforward piece, except for the unusual bar pattern I described.

The next two tracks, six and seven, are listed as being a suite: the first entitled *Florida Greeting Song* and the second *Legend of the Fountain*, each just 2 minutes and 30 seconds long. In the first, Pat plays freely with drums alone and simply improvises on a theme he has in mind. It's a clever thing to do and requires excellent rapport with the drummer who needs to be on precisely the same mental wavelength to make it work. Dan Gottlieb shows how good he is and why Pat was keen to hire him for the PMG. Pat still loves doing this today in his live gigs with Antonio Sanchez. The second piece is an acoustic guitar solo. It's a good piece with some beautiful phrases within its short length.

The final track is a ten-minute piece entitled *Sea Song*. It also begins with a *rubato* section and the first half of the piece is devoted to acoustic guitar playing *ad lib* with a piano alongside and a solo synthesiser voice (which may be Weber's electric bass sound) and cymbals. This type of synthesiser voice is replaced by a human (wordless) voice in later PMG albums, but that is an evolution of the band for the future. Electric guitar takes over where acoustic left off and the free piece continues to Mays' piano accompaniment. At 4.57 the bass enters along with percussion and bells and a four-way improvisation starts up to a prescribed set of chords. Whilst the sea is constantly in local random motion, there is still pattern and regular rhythmic variation to be found in wave movements. All of this can be found inside this creative, inspiring music, more so than a similar project about water that Dave Liebman invited Pat to play on many years later.

Altogether, this album contains some very interesting music that is always most relaxing and atmospheric. There is variety and some clever writing in places. It also demonstrates some of the features of Pat's music that we will observe becoming highly refined in later albums.

Pat Metheny Group: *The Pat Metheny Group* – 1978 (*****)

In 1977, soon after *Watercolors*, Pat decided to form a new band with Lyle Mays, Mark Egan (bass) and Dan Gottlieb (drums). The decision to team up with keyboard player, Lyle, was inspired, for through this partnership Pat gained the deep intellectual support that resulted in much of the creative success we now recognise. Without doubt, the partnership with Mays has enabled him to reach the very pinnacle of jazz guitar playing and PMG to be one of the most successful jazz-fusion bands of all time.

Pat soon started to win awards and with them came cash prizes. Some of this was invested in transport and more equipment, and with these and his new band, he began to tour in May 1977. Thus began a truly remarkable period in his life during which he played an astonishing number of live gigs every year, criss-crossing the United States and Canada to play at whatever venue he was invited to. Partly because his music "is not radio music", he built up a fan base by "incessant touring – we were doing 250 dates a year for 15 years, and still do 150 or so". (Joni Mitchell wore herself out doing less than 150 gigs per year during her early career.) Being on the road "is now so normal, I don't notice it, although it wasn't so good for personal relationships".

Apart from Pat's last album, *Watercolors*, there was no record of the Group in 1977 to promote, although we have seen that some of the early songs in the band's repertoire did appear on *Watercolors*. On 31 August 1977 the band was recorded live at the Great American Music Hall, San Francisco. Years later, four tracks from the concert were released unofficially on the Jazz Door label as *Blue Asphalt* (1991). The title track of *Watercolors* appears in a very similar form on it, except that Mark Egan is now replacing Weber. *Wrong is Right* was an amazingly fast number that did not quite fit the PMG brand and does not appear elsewhere. The two other tracks were *Phase Dancer* (sic) and *San Lorenzo*, which Pat announces as being based on a different tuning for 12-string. Both of these appeared on their first eponymous album *The Pat Metheny Group* that was finally recorded in the studio in Oslo in January 1978 on the ECM label.

Because of the difficulty of distinguishing the album title from the band, Pat often refers to this album as the 'White' album. It soon sold over 150,000 copies, which was then (and still is) a very successful result for a jazz group. Today, total sales are progressing towards half a million. This alone would have been beyond the wildest dreams of many musicians, yet, besides his success with the band, Pat continued to maintain his solo career and went on to record with almost all of the best living jazz musicians – the one exception being Miles Davis. (This is itself somewhat ironic since just about everyone else did play with Miles Davis!)

Pat has said that, right from the start, the aim of the band was to push the guitar quartet format to the very edge. By the late 70s, much had been achieved in the field of jazz with this combination of instruments and it was difficult to see just how it was possible to create anything new. It is thus testament to Pat's ingenuity and creativity, greatly assisted by Lyle Mays, that they have achieved this goal with distinction over a period of almost thirty years. Pat is clear about how this was to be achieved: the music had to be "more than just a toon". (And this from one of the best "toon" writers in the business!) The ability of musicians to write wonderful tunes alone was quite enough for most.

A key observation is that great emphasis was to be placed on musical form, getting the band away from the simple forms that had largely been used in jazz-fusion up to that point. One popular form is as old as music itself: verse and chorus being repeated a set number of times, with a brief flourish to end. Of course, these descriptions were assigned to song forms in which each verse had different lyrics, whilst the chorus generally had repeated lyrics. However, the terms are now applied to the music itself, even when there are no words. This has been used throughout all genres of music from folk, to pop, rock, blues and jazz too. With recorded music being limited to the brief three-minutes of space on a vinyl record, this evolved into the pop-song form with a middle section sandwiched between two expositions of a theme, often a verse and a chorus. Latterly, the middle section (sometimes called middle eight or middle sixteen, depending upon how many bars it contained) was an opportunity to add a new flavour by means of an instrumental solo. Additionally, the use of a fade-out to end the piece relieved the composer of the chore of having to think of a new way of ending each piece. As songs began to evolve, the verses took on a slightly more complicated form. They were often divided into sections of eight bars, the first eight (called A) being repeated, a second set of eight bars called B then being played, and a final repetition of the first eight again to make a cycle of 32 bars. This takes the form AABA, one that PMG have not been afraid to use, despite their aim of creating entirely new forms. Two of the five tracks on the 'White' album have this format, *Phase Dance* and *Lone Jack*.

The 'White' album is the first Pat Metheny album to receive my jealously guarded five star rating. The record starts really well with a short motif that is also to be used for the ending. It's a kind of fanfare that says, "Wake Up! Here's a great new musical adventure about to start." The sound is fresh and new and Egan's fretless bass draws on his time spent with Pastorius: it's the sexiest bass sound on the planet at this point in time, and it still sounds good today. There's a significant section during which this theme appears three times and then we start a gentler theme that oozes one of the two main melodies. Unusually, this is followed by a spacey pause for breath and then the fanfare. Finally, some two minutes into the piece, we commence the real meat of the number, a delightful melody that is repeated four times for us to pick it up quickly. A light passage with the sound of flutes on keyboard acts as a bridge for the main theme to be repeated before the first theme is replayed, this time with a gentle Metheny solo added. When the fanfare returns it is delightfully muted because what follows is one of Lyle Mays' wonderful piano solos, as luscious as you will ever hear. Lyle builds it gradually from the softest, sweetest sounds, through a section of slight angst, but always returning to the affirmative colours that he prefers. There are some lovely blue notes in there too if you listen carefully. The solo climaxes and then the band returns to pull the piece back to familiar ground. This time a long held keyboard note plays over the early theme, toying with us, demanding our full attention. The band stops on the edge. And then the fanfare bursts out in full glory to end. It's a magical piece, indeed, and is followed by something just as special.

Phase Dance is a band favourite, even today, and appears again in a live version on the album *Travels* (1983). The main riff is a (kind of) two-note motif that constantly oscillates between major and minor keys. After twenty bars, the main theme begins, spread over a cycle of 32 bars in the AABA format. A solo from Pat follows that uses the mainstream jazz method of improvising over the sequence of chords that make up the theme. He plays this twice. Lyle then spends the same number of bars developing his own acoustic piano version of the theme. For me, it is not only the great melodies used but the luscious chord changes that produce the excitement of the piece, coupled with the creativity of both Pat and Lyle, each providing support for the other in their different ways. The piece is changing constantly and never dull. When the solos finish and the band returns for the ensemble, all would seem to be done, yet it is not. The composition enters a new phase! Here the original motif is subjected to a series of intricate modulations that just go on and on, evolving with each repetition. And finally, there is an absolutely magical section in which Lyle comes in with a bold baritone sound that trumpets the final statement of the theme and ends in sheer triumph. What a fantastic track!

To name the following track *Jaco* is interesting when we consider that Pat had played on Bley's album of the same name, itself named after a track called *Jaco*. Mr Pastorius was clearly having considerable influence on a lot of people. Though it is written in a standard common (4/4) time, the opening theme is tantalising for it follows its own rules, apparently randomly arranged, whilst a Jacoesque line ruminates beneath. Then the piece takes on a rather more solid form, though there are the usual syncopations and unexpected twists in the melody. Pat repeats it with a solo on electric guitar, before Egan is given a bass solo over it. After a repeat of the theme, the band start a coda by shifting up a gear to play that opening phrase again, but this time Pat puts his foot to the floor and we have to hold onto our seats until the very end when the brakes are slammed on hard.

Aprilwind is a solo on 12-string guitar that acts as a kind of introduction to the substantial track, *April Joy*, the opening bars of which feature another of Egan's solos and incorporates the main theme. Pat soon takes over, both to play through the theme and then to improvise over it. It's a generous tempo, happy sound with the usual palette of bright colours that makes me feel good. Suddenly, the music comes to a halt and I hear an echo of the previous track as 12-string acoustic guitar takes over. Next, at four minutes, Lyle comes in with a delicate keyboard theme over Pat's musings. The music is sweet and gentle; it doesn't need to lead anywhere else, yet, just a minute later, with a sudden flourish, a wonderful wash of luscious sound sweeps over me and every spinal nerve I have tingles in sympathy. For me, this is one of the finest moments in recorded history – a moment of superlative harmonic joy. This moment is what I yearn for when I pick up a CD. It dissolves all stress and any thoughts for anything other than the beauty enveloping me. A perfect moment perhaps, but this one is not quite over in a moment. It continues as Pat uses the vibe to build another guitar solo, unhurriedly, over some three minutes through to the end of the track in the way that he uses from time to time, as, for example, on his favourite *Are You Going With Me*.

The final track is *Lone Jack*. It starts off at a tremendous pace. The themes are straightforward and the strategy is similar to that used in *Phase Dance* whereby the theme is a 32 bar cycle in AABA format. Listen out, too, for an odd bridge section between the themes. Pat takes the theme through three times on this occasion before handing over to Mays who changes the mood by removing the pace from the theme. Clearly he is going to adopt the normal practice of building it back up once more, a well tried and tested method at which PMG excel. I never tire of the superb, unhurried way in which they go about it. First time through, May's playing of the chord changes through the B-section (around 3 min 45 sec) are quite divine. Second time through Egan joins in with a renewed vigour, but the drummer holds back for now. Mays finger-work is astonishing with superb arpeggios that hold tightly to the chords of the theme. Then drums kick in and the piece is back on full heat for the return of the guitar. The odd bridge I mentioned is used finally to form the coda, which makes a brilliant ending to what is a truly great album. It is astonishing that a band should come up with a five-star rated album as its first contribution to a long career, but that is why PMG is so very special. Almost at a stroke, Pat had discovered one magic formula for success in jazz-fusion. For him, the way up was white.

Pat Metheny: *New Chautauqua* – 1979 (***)

New Chautauqua is a solo album, though Pat plays all his own instruments and it could easily be a small group delivering the material. It's about now that we start to become aware of Pat's intrinsic musical roots that stem from his home in rural mid-western USA. As his music develops over the coming years, his home-cooked ingredients frequently give rise to the kind of music that Stump describes as "mom and apple pie" impressionism. [5] It is, of course, music that contains strong elements of all the traditional positive qualities such as love, beauty, fidelity and patriotism, but the taste of home cooking – though popular – isn't for everyone. Defenders of the Faith, such as Richard Cook, are unable to accept the "thick strain of sentimentality" when it appears in a jazz context. [6]

After all, they imply, where is the relationship between music derived from the black and Creole culture of Louisiana and that from the European white settler culture of Missouri, Kansas and Oklahoma? I could argue that there were many similarities between the two situations, since both communities – one white, the other black, were derived from immigrants surviving harsh conditions in a developing country. Pat's music happens to be quintessentially white American because that is what he is! Pat has taken his own character and background and turned it into a new musical style that he owns. It is another kind of fusion, as different from the energetic jazz-rock fusion of bands like Mahavishnu Orchestra, Return to Forever and Weather Report as apple pie is from Cajun gumbo.

The title track presents a relaxed rustic vibe that Pat loves so much. Once again, it's hard to see this music as jazz and it should not really be considered as such, except that it is instrumental music with elements of improvisation. Here is a full-blown barn dance played in the finest tradition of acoustic guitar work.

The second track continues the theme, as the title *Country Poem* admits. A sonnet, rather than an epic, the piece is thoughtful and beautiful. A longer piece follows, with two pieces stapled together as Pat likes to do. *Long Ago Child* is used to develop his interest in new string sounds and he uses the 15-string harp-guitar to produce some interesting and rather hypnotic sounds, notable for the slurring of the notes caused by the fretless design. The 6-string electric guitar is then used for an overlay. *Fallen Star* follows without a break with an acoustic backdrop supporting a melody that, though it is beautiful enough, tends to wend its way aimlessly through the rustling chords behind. *Hermitage* is a more structured piece with a bass line and an electric guitar theme over his acoustic tapestry. Slow and careful, the piece develops its theme logically and we are treated to some luscious and relaxing music.

Sueno con Mexico is an impressionistic piece without the usual structure. It opens with a sweeping panorama, a rustling wind, and some beautiful harmonics. Then new features appear that break up the landscape briefly. Our imaginations are encouraged to fly unfettered as we listen to this piece, which was chosen to represent the album on one of ECM's compilation CDs entitled *Works* (1984). The album ends with *Daybreak*, another delightful composition that opens with a colourful impression of one of those aspects of the natural world that clearly provides Pat with much of his inspiration. Then, just when you think that the album is going to end on one of those long drawn-out sections of atmospheric musings, a Metheny trio kicks in to deliver a lively and most satisfying end to what is a good album. This album will give much pleasure to listeners who enjoy beautiful melodies played on guitar.

Pat Metheny Group: *American Garage* – 1979 (****)

PMG continued to make a big impact on the jazz-fusion scene with an iconic album that seemed more than many other albums of its period to capture a popular mood of the time. The album is regarded by many as the best of the early phase of Pat's releases, though others prefer the 'White' album.

The title of *(Cross the) Heartland* conjures up appropriate images of lengthy journeys across a flat, featureless North American plateau in the band's tour bus. A complex rhythmic motif is used throughout most of the track that might represent the repetitive sound of the suspension, but the use of the sound of chimes, however, makes it seem more like a reindeer-drawn sleigh ride. Whatever, the motif is fast and pulsating and very difficult to keep alive, especially once the other even more complicated themes start and Dan Gottlieb is pushed to the limits to hold the band together for the ensemble playing. However, the quality of the melody used in the first section is superb and simply sweeps us up like a swirling snowstorm. At 2.36, there's a quiet section, contemplative and poignant, and is the more so when Egan's fretless bass starts at 3.31 to play a sad tune that sounds very much like Pastorius. The contemplation soon turns to decision. A rousing crescendo ripples out of the speakers at 4.45 as the main theme reappears once more at 4.58. The piece then enters an improvisation on electric guitar, which leads back at 5.58 to the first theme and a great climactic ending.

For us non-Americans who are unfamiliar with it, *Airstream* is the name of the type of trailer (caravan) depicted on the front of the album sleeve. It is regarded as a classic of 1950s American design and there are many enthusiast groups who take great pride in their preservation. Surprisingly, this entire album seems to have captured the warm glow that those who lived through it associate with the period when the Airstream was the King of the Road. The composers (Metheny and Mays) draw wonderful parallels in their music, presumably because their imaginations are fired by their own childhood memories. It is as if we are on vacation, driving through some of the most beautiful countryside with our own Airstream trailing behind, gleaming in the hot summer sun. We come to a crossroad and take a left turn. To our amazement, the new road is even more beautiful than the last. Metheny and Mays are able to do this with their compositions and there are many others I shall describe that have the same multiple levels of creativity.

This piece begins on piano with the first part of a beautiful melody that will form the backbone of this fantastic track. Soon taken over by Pat's guitar, it changes key and introduces new facets to its character that are captivating, notable with a short conversation between bass and guitar and this is followed by a brief glimpse of the main theme at 1.50. In the normal manner, these themes are then developed through Pat's improvisation so that when they return for a second time they are familiar and more substantiated by repetition. The whole piece returns to the start for a second run through, but this time, the main theme returns in splendour, first on its own and then as background for Pat's improvisation, and it is with this that the track closes with a fade.

The Search has an acoustic guitar backwash with a keyboard pipes sound that became a part of the PMG brand. Once again, the piece starts out in a direction that sounds good enough, a lovely full acoustic sound on 12-string guitar that ripples in the background to the delicious pipes. Then, in only a couple of beats, it turns a corner into a new direction, in this case with Mays playing a superbly lyrical piano section from 1.02. Unhurried, yet fabulously fluid, it meanders with total logic up and down the piano keyboard like nectar oozing from a honeycomb. Pat follows on at 2.48 with a wonderful entry that sounds like nothing ever heard before on a jazz album. The music just gets better and better as the piece proceeds. At 3.42, the opening instruments return and the number ends on a wonderfully inspirational high note.

The title track must be nostalgic for many. It paints a picture of kids playing their stuff in the garage. A portrait of rock 'n' roll, it's full of fun, of embryonic music making, of noise, heavy rhythm and wailing guitars. There are many passing nods to familiar phrases, styles and sounds from the world of rock 'n' roll and all are encapsulated in a wrapper of Metheny brand sounds.

With only five tracks on the album, and still trapped in the grooves of vinyl discs, PMG was clearly beginning to explore the art of longer composition in the final track, *The Epic*. As the title indicates, there are numerous themes and melodies being explored throughout this fifteen-minute piece. After a first section of theme, the tempo is doubled up at 1.50 for a really fast-moving piano improvisation at 3.00 that allows Lyle to really come to terms with his themes in the beautifully melodic and structured way he has made his style. This section will please the most ardent supporter of mainstream jazz. At 5.22 Pat takes over with his standard Gibson electric guitar sound, but new avenues are explored with some intriguing percussive ensemble playing at 7.10 before the fast tempo dissolves at 7.35 into a slower meditative section taken up by Egan and Mays' Oberheim. The piece draws to a close with an ending that is eminently suitable for an epic and ought to provoke you into some kind of physical response.

The Epic is a major, multi-faceted musical composition that happens to involve improvisation, which makes it jazz! It is a signpost to the future in which, with *The Way Up* (2005), PMG deliver pieces of increasing length and depth. As we see throughout, PMG has consistently refused to be pigeonholed and this is no exception. It is a thoroughly fascinating piece of music that bears much exploration and repetition and represented another step forward in the epic journey that PMG has made over the best part of thirty years. This is stirring stuff!

Pat's relationship with Egan and Gottlieb was not to last. Egan was first to leave the band, after *American Garage*; Gottlieb lasted longer, replaced in 1984 by Paul Wertico who would hold the drum chair until well after 2000. Egan and Gottlieb's early promise as premier league musicians failed to materialise. In 1982, they formed a long-lived band called Elements. They quickly secured the services of young saxophonist Bill Evans and keyboardist Clifford Carter, who would later work with James Taylor and Michael Franks. Sadly, although Elements produced albums periodically for many years, the band was not able to produce albums of sufficient quality to attract sizeable purchasing power in a competitive field.

By 1980, acoustic bassist Steve Rodby had replaced Egan on bass and become the third permanent member of the Pat Metheny Group. Though Pat had demonstrated that he had no real need for dedicated bass and drums around this time, the same, however, was not true about percussion. Around 1980, Pat heard the fantastic percussionist, Nana Vasconcelos, an event that was to have a big impact on the development of 'Metheny fusion'. Not only did Vasconcelos play some of the most remarkable percussion sounds in jazz at that time, but he also employed wordless vocals extensively. Pat and Lyle were very impressed and he was hired. As we shall see, much of the trademark sound of Metheny fusion is based around the feel of the natural world. Vasconcelos was able to provide this in abundance. Good examples of the advances they made with his help are *The Bat* from *Offramp* (1982) and *Farmer's Trust* from *Travels* (1983).

Joni Mitchell: *Shadows and Light* – 1980 (*****)

In the summer of 1979, as Pat and Lyle were involved with the making of *American Garage*, they were also committed to one of the most memorable tours by the great folk-jazz singer Joni Mitchell. Joni had started her career in the style of the conventional singer-songwriter, influenced by Bob Dylan, of course, as well as fellow Canadian Neil Young. She worked her way around the circuit of folk clubs singing a repertoire of songs to the accompaniment of her solo guitar. Her songs were so good that other better-known artists soon took them up. For example, Tom Rush had a hit with Joni's *Urge for Going*, whilst Judy Collins entered the charts with *Both Sides Now*. Then Joni had a big hit of her own with *Big Yellow Taxi* (1970).

A consummate artist who loved language and painting as much as music, her penetrating lyrics were soon encapsulated by music that showed strong jazz influences, a point in her development at which she parted company with the rest of her musical peer group and started out down a track that only she could follow. From this point, mostly defined by her album *Court and Spark* (1974) she chose to work almost exclusively with jazz musicians. She acquired a ready-formed band called the LA Express, led by saxophonist Tom Scott, and this decision gave her music a unique sound. She felt more at home in the rock 'n' roll category than in the mould of a folk singer, but with such strong jazz influences it was inevitable that her music would take on many of the characteristics of jazz-fusion – albeit in vocal format.

Shadows and Light became one of her best jazz-fusion albums, largely because she assembled 'the band to die for'; there are no other recordings featuring this combination of musicians. Jaco Pastorius had significantly broadened his popular appeal by playing in Joni's band for a number of years and for this project he was joined by Pat Metheny and Lyle Mays, with Michael Brecker on tenor saxophone and Don Alias, percussion. Alias established a very fine reputation over the decades since this album, largely on the back of his work with Joni.

The situation we find at the commencement of this album is one in which one of the world's best jazz-fusion bands is being asked to play some of the most original vocal-based compositions that had ever been written – a truly mouth-watering prospect. Mitchell was at the peak of her career. Her artistic flair applied to the packaging and delivery of the programme would naturally be expected to deliver an added dimension. An atmospheric introduction starts the album as Joan provides a context for the music that is to come. As the opening chords of Joni's guitar emerge from the applause at the head of *In France They Kiss on Main Street*, you can but imagine what is in store. As it is, Jaco unsurprisingly first pierces the canvas by playing a very conventional bass line that is as wonderfully rhythmic as only he could play. But don't worry; he doesn't stay like this for long! At the end of the first chorus, Pat plays a short fill and then it's back to the verse. Pat gets a whole verse solo after verse 2, by which time Pastorius is in third gear and starting to throw in his party pieces. For example, listen to the harmonic at 1.20. At 3.00 you can hear a typical Metheny chord pattern from the 'White' album.

Edith and the Kingpin is one of the few tracks that you might consider has suffered compared to the studio version, for the one that appeared on Joni's *The Hissing of Summer Lawns* (1975) was exceptional in all respects. Could it be improved? Well, in such a band, anything is possible and, as usual, it's Jaco's bass that provides the main ingredients the track might need to replace the missing Crusaders. But let's not forget the contributions from the other guys, for Lyle's gentle keyboard playing and Pat's subtle contributions are different and beautiful in a new way.

Coyote is much the same in live and studio forms because of Jaco's presence on both. Don Alias's bongos have rather more presence but there are no other drums and Jaco simply drives the backing along single-handed and Joni's playing is almost incidental. Pat is only occasionally heard above nominal background levels.

Up the this point we've not heard from Brecker, but he makes a strong appearance in *Goodbye Pork Pie Hat*, a full-blown jazz-fusion track with all the boys doing what they do best and Joan wearing her best jazz singer boots. Brecker's sound is vintage – tenor sax with as sharp an edge as you would expect in a recording of this era. The solo is hard jazz with less blues content, but that's normal for a headline jazzer like Brecker, and of course the others give him great support to keep up the highest level of jazz playing in town.

Dry Cleaner from Des Moines is very different and much jazzier than on the original. The opening lines are delivered solo with only drums for backing. Then bass and sax join in with Brecker making substantial fills, the tempo a brisk swing. It's a joy to hear Jaco and Mike working together as we also get on the *30th Birthday Concert* album, recorded later in 1981. Clearly the relationship established between the two of them on this tour was to turn into something significant with ramifications beyond the Mitchell tour. This track is essentially a vehicle for the two men to have lots of fun.

Amelia begins in unaltered form as a serious song with a strong story to tell, played on solo guitar. Pat discreetly enters the backdrop as the song progresses and this leads naturally into a freewheeling solo that draws in Lyle Mays to provide some of his beautiful chords to colour Pat's creation. Then *Hejira* begins without a break – Pastorius's familiar fanfare trumpeting its commencement. Joni converts the reference to Benny Goodman into one of "strains of Michael Brecker coming through the trees" and that's a cue for him to fill on soprano and then take an extended solo that brings the song to a close. After *Dreamland* there is a band intro and then comes *Furry Sings the Blues*, a tribute to one of the early characters from Memphis's Beale Street.

No matter how much we might think (or wish) that Joni embraced jazz-fusion into her art – and I believe with this band it was a great deal – she never relinquished her hold onto her musical roots that were planted in the narrative song. Even with a fabulous fusion band at her back, and she did give them plenty of scope to do their thing, she continued to deliver her stock in trade with songs like *Amelia* and *Furry*. *Shadows and Light* was a watershed for Mitchell. It was as if she recognised that the era of jazz-fusion was complete, the euphoria of it all subsided as the sub-genre consolidated itself into new things. This, of course, was exactly what the other jazz-fusion bands had demonstrated to be true. However, the jazz-fusion careers of Pat, Lyle, Mike and Don had only just begun. Although Jaco still had some important statements to make in jazz-fusion, sadly, his career was to be much shorter.

Pat Metheny: *80/81* – 1980 (***)

It's tempting to think that the title of this album refers to music made during the years stated. However, this is not correct, for the album was released in 1980. The curiously titled album *80/81* is in fact named after nothing more anonymous than the ECM catalogue number, one number assigned to each of the two discs. For this album Pat assembled a curious line-up of performers that, on the surface looks like a saxophone/guitar quartet with a second sax player added because the first couldn't make all of the sessions. However, I feel sure that this was not the case, for both saxophones are heard on three of the tracks. Thus, we must conclude that Pat intended it to be this way. The saxophones in question belonged to players from quite different backgrounds. The first was Dewey Redman, father of the current tenor saxophone star, Joshua. The second was Michael Brecker. Along with Charlie Haden on bass, and drummer Jack de Johnette, this was truly a great combination of talent and experience that Pat intended should form a milestone on his journey along the mainstream jazz path, rather than his PMG fusion road.

This 'double' album begins with a very original selection of material in which two 'folk songs' are joined together, the first composed by Metheny, the second by Haden. The folk roots of the material are very clear throughout, yet the setting is mainstream jazz, with Brecker providing the saxophone colourings in the first song and de Johnette's superior jazz drumming the separation between the two songs. Pat plays lots of acoustic guitar, particularly so in the second song, and the entire track is a blush of originality and beauty. It is hard to think of anything that compares with this most exceptional piece of jazz.

The title track comes second and is firmly planted in the mainstream section of jazz to make Dewey Redman feel truly at home. It begins with the usual short theme played a tempo and in unison by guitar and sax, and then launches into a long section of improvisation with Pat playing his best electric guitar sound to please the purists. Redman plays hard and does not disappoint, but there is no Technicolor here.

The Bat is the first appearance of a beautiful melody from Pat that I shall have more to say about in the discussion of *Offramp*. Though you would not know it, the sleeve notes state that both saxophonists play on this track, which is presented here as a straight-ahead jazz ballad. Pat is clearly being inspired by the natural world, although this version does not have the impressionistic elements present in the later recording.

Turn Around is a piece by one of the jazz musicians who have obviously played a role in Pat's musical development, Ornette Coleman. Much has been written about this musician, a good deal of it vitriolic, for Coleman was at the spearhead of the movement in the late 1960s to play free jazz, a style of music in which there were virtually no rules at all and which most listeners found hard to come to terms with. Some commentators even refused to admit that Coleman had any musical skills whatever. Today, his contribution to jazz is rather more appreciated and clearly Metheny (and presumably Mays too) found something in Coleman's philosophy to interest them. Pat went on to record an entire album with Coleman, *Song X* (1986), which was enhanced and reissued in 2005. Oddly, this track is not the kind of composition we might expect from Coleman on the basis of what I have just said; it's a blues played in a very traditional jazz style.

Possibly more to Coleman's approval would be the following track, *Open*, a title that gives a clue to the content and in which the five musicians play a piece that they are all credited as having 'composed'. I have to say that this is exactly the kind of music that I am entirely unable to comprehend. However, Pat, who I respect more than any other musician, clearly derives much satisfaction from it. More than fourteen minutes in length it opens with a free, though not atonal, improvisation on guitar to de Johnette's sensitive accompaniment. There is no obvious theme, melody, or even a phrase to hang your hat on, just a freewheeling sequence of hard blowing conducted at a fast tempo. At the very end, the band does seem to come together and deliver a kind of theme with echoes perhaps of the other tracks on the album. Occasionally, PMG adopts this style to present an idea in the context of some broader landscape. In such cases, it is much easier to justify its existence than it is here where the piece simply stands alone. Perhaps we should be grateful that it is not farther out than it is.

Pretty Scattered continues the mainstream presentation. After the spontaneity of the previous track, this one comes as a surprise when a reasonably logical tune breaks out from the band. It is short-lived however, as Metheny and Co progress through the usual roundelay of improvised sections, ending in a cleverly presented tune that Charlie Parker would have been proud to play.

The final two tracks make up for all of the disappointment you may have experienced listening to the middle of the album. Both were selected by ECM to appear on their limited edition release of Pat Metheny's prime music entitled *Works*. As such, this was recognition that here were two gems tucked away in a little corner of the recorded world where they might escape the applause of a wider audience. *Every Day* is a wonderful Metheny tune, played by the quartet with Brecker milking the melody in the manner for which he is renowned. After a languid opening with fluid timing of phrases, the song takes on a gentle rhythm and, if it were not for the sound of the saxophone, unusual in a Metheny context. It could easily be a PMG recording. This is a substantial track of over thirteen minutes in length and it does not disappoint. Brecker has a long solo in which he fully develops the potential of the theme and the trio plays some very sensitive accompaniment. After about eight minutes, Pat takes over and pulls the piece right down to a lullaby on solo guitar. Just as your eyelids close, the quartet returns for a final statement of the theme. It's really hard to remember that we could be listening to an album from the jazz mainstream, and, indeed, we are not, for Pat wants to show us that he does not believe in the artificial boundaries that others build around music.

The final track is one of Pat's finest – and there are so many! This duet of Pat with himself entitled *Goin' Ahead* is sublime and should be played in as many venues as possible to tell the whole world just how ridiculous it is to categorise such beautiful music under the banner of jazz. So many people are absolutely not interested in listening to anything they take to belong to that category. What is so much more important is that they would never look through racks of CDs sorted under that heading. Oh, boy! What are they missing? The stereotypical response of Allan Holdsworth's New York burger chef sums it all up. "Hey! What you guys playin'? ... Jazz? ... Zat what you call that? I HATE JAZZ!" [7] The album *80/81* is exactly what Pat must have wanted it to be: a collection of music of extraordinary quality played by some of the best musicians around. It is also a defiant denial of the commercial requirement to pigeonhole artists and their work.

Pat Metheny and Lyle Mays: *As Falls Wichita, So Falls Wichita Falls* – 1981 (****)

The opening title track is an extended piece of almost 21 minutes length that is probably a celebration of their first meeting at the Wichita Jazz Festival. It starts very quietly and builds slowly through a variety of multi-layered sounds, some of which have the multi-tonal southeast Asia flavour that we come across later in PMG albums. Pat even plays bass in places and all three players are multi-tracking their contributions. Vasconcelos demonstrates that the decision to dispense with a designated drummer was entirely logical by his masterful playing on a wide range of instruments, including drums. The piece is quite free in construction and very ambitious for the kind of thing they were doing at the time. All the stops were pulled out for this track and it must have been the most complicated of their works to date. Though digital sampling was still just on the horizon, the recording employs a number of overdubs. These involve the sounds of people – a crowd, children and individuals. Even Pat is to be heard mysteriously uttering numbers at one point. The music is spiritual and uplifting.

Ozark is named after a lake that lies in Missouri to the southeast of Pat's home. The theme on piano is immediate and majestic. Here is the wide-open space of Missouri in all its glory. These musicians are shouting about their love of their country and all it stands for. This is a glorious musical landscape filled with passion and belonging.

September Fifteenth (dedicated to Bill Evans) was the day in 1980 when the great pianist died. Whether the track was actually recorded on the day he died is not known, but it was surely close. Bill Evans was one of the great idols for all jazz lovers – not just pianists, so both Pat and Lyle would have certainly been very saddened to hear the news. Consequently, the song is one of respect for a great artist who will be sorely missed. The initial melody of Pat's solo guitar is as poignant as anything he has written. Then, typically, the music adopts an outlook that reflects an optimistic future. It goes without saying that Mays restricts his playing to the piano. There is no obvious format to the piece, which finishes in a most gentle mood.

It's For You begins with Pat developing one of his new ideas, that of using the acoustic guitar as a rhythmic device and a kind of substitute for the drums. This idea has been used many times since then on his recordings. The theme itself is played by Mays and is one of the classic PMG melodies. Here is a song that anyone can associate with. It is simple, though not in the sense that you might expect from other songs. After playing the melody, the guys develop a vibe that is cool and unhurried. Pat's strumming backs Lyle's languorous phrase, which Nana sings along with. Slowly it meanders along, seemingly going nowhere, when suddenly a bass line introduces a new theme that Pat plays brightly with his branded electric sound. The piece suddenly starts to move faster as percussion drives us up a gear. Pat solos and Lyle tinkers behind, both of them slowly building. And then it disappears. We were fooled into thinking that the big melody would return. Not this time. *Estupenda Graça* is a very beautiful song in the style of a Brazilian *Amazing Grace*, sung wordlessly by Vasconcelos to the backing of a bird chorus from the rainforest.

Pat Metheny Group: *Offramp* – 1982 (*****)

The 1982 album *Offramp* was the first PMG album to be awarded a Grammy. It finally attracted the attention of the music business to the superb quality of music that the Group had been creating for five or six years and opened the gates for a many similar awards over the coming years. *Offramp* is a roller-coaster ride of emotions. It will make you afraid, it will make you proud. It will make you shout with joy and with anger. It will render you speechless with admiration at the creative skill behind it and at its dénouement the sheer beauty will surely bring tears to your eyes.

However, before we can begin our examination of the music, it is important to say something about guitar synthesisers, which appear for the first time with this record. Although the first electronic music synthesisers, based upon the traditional piano keyboard, were manufactured in the 1960s, synthesisers that could be operated by guitarists took longer to arrive on the scene. And here, perhaps the significance of the word 'operated' rather than 'played' will become apparent.

A famous music synthesiser is the Synclavier, which began its existence based upon a piano-style keyboard, from about 1972 onwards at Dartmouth College, Hanover, New Hampshire. Developed by Sydney Alonso, Cameron Jones and Jon Appleton, the first version of the Synclavier appeared in 1975 from their company, New England Digital (NED). By 1979, the great potential of the system was realised and the company produced the Synclavier II. It had an upgraded sampling capacity and memory, as well as a velocity- and pressure-sensitive keyboard. Systems were enormously expensive at first, with typical models costing anything from $100,000 to $500,000. By 1984 the Synclavier II had become the world's leading keyboard synthesiser.

From the late 1970s, the Roland Corporation began to develop their guitar synthesiser, an electronic device that allowed a guitarist to play, whilst the sounds of plucked strings were translated electronically into entirely new sounds. Suddenly, in theory at least, guitarists could make the same kinds of sounds that keyboardists had been making since the 70s.

The 1978 GR500 system was Roland's first model. It consisted of the guitar controller (GS500), a 24-way cable and the synthesiser unit (GR500). (In this context, the word 'controller' was synonymous with 'guitar'.) The Ibanez-made controller was based on the Gibson Les Paul shape but with more controls and different pickups. Roland released a second generation of synthesiser in 1980 – the GR-100 system. This included three types of guitar controllers in many different finishes. The G-505 was a guitar made in the Fender Telecaster style with three single coils. The G-303 was a Gibson SG derivative, whilst the deluxe version was the G-202 with dual humbucker pickups, constructed in the style of a Fender Stratocaster.

There is some doubt about the precise history of Pat and the Synclavier guitar. Pat is on record recalling how he had first got his Roland synthesiser in 1980: "Basically, the people in our music store got this thing in and asked if I wanted to try it, it was that blue Roland box, the GR-300. I'd tried every other guitar synthesiser and had even bought a couple of them, the Avatar and the Patch 2000, which I messed around with for two or three nights then put in my closet, because they were just unplayable!" [8]

We should remember that this early design was an analogue, not a digital system. Pat quickly learned to love it because it translated his intentions better than anything he'd tried previously. As one report put it: "Some [synthesisers] do not allow string bending and others mistrigger if you hold a note too long or in some cases if you don't hold it long enough. This forces the guitarist to play very slowly and deliberately. Picking must be precise. Strings must be muted and in the case of held notes if you move your hand while the note is held even a bit the note will either cut off abruptly or mutate into a totally wrong note before you can correct the problem. Forget slides, harmonics, and even sloppy but spirited playing entirely. If you couldn't play every note clearly and directly you might as well turn the unit off." [9]

Whilst many guitarists, like Wayne Scott Joness, thought the Roland allowed them to play it like a real guitar, Pat's description was rather different. "Well, whether I'm playing as hard as I can as loud or whatever, I've always tried to be completely loose. That's a very important quality for me, which I don't think unfortunately many guitar players have. When guitar players play fast, they seem tighten up, and to me, it translates as stiff music. It may be great guitar playing, but I don't like to hear people trying, I want to just hear the music, which I've found is when you're real loose. You have to be quite a bit more accurate in terms of pitches; like you play the guitar you slide over a string and touch it real quick, because the guitar has no sustain quality unless you're holding down the string. If you're playing a sound on a guitar synthesiser which has got a long sustain, you only play one note but it sounds like five notes are ringing. If you accidentally touch another note, the computer registers that you want to play a harmonic there. The technology is good, but even with the Synclavier, which is the best tracking of them all, they still have a bit of work to do. To me, anybody should be able to pick up the Synclavier and not change their technique at all, but just be able to play and they just aren't there yet, but they will be." [8]

It appears that Pat and Lyle were amongst the first jazz musicians to use the Synclavier I during December 1981 for their sessions that led to *Offramp* (1982). According to the album notes, Pat was using both a "guitar synthesiser" and a "synclavier guitar", whilst Lyle was using a "synclavier". Pat's gear was probably a box of electronics that acted as an interface between a modified guitar such as the Roland G-303 and the NED Synclavier synthesiser system that was common to both players. Lyle's gear was a keyboard connected to the Synclavier electronics. However, there is no doubt that for many years Pat has played his Roland G-303 guitar. Pat's G-303 guitar (shown on the front cover of this book) is in use today and he can be seen playing it on all his DVDs and live performances. Pat: "Roland controller is a term that people now use for the guitar; it's a Roland 303, which are good guitars and I've got a bunch of those. It's the first time I've ever played a solid body guitar and at first I was a little reluctant to get into that, but I now feel really close to them. The neck has a Les Paul kind of feel with Gibson scale as opposed to a Fender. I'm used to that having played a [Gibson] 175." [8]

Another notable change occurred for *Offramp* and that was the addition to the band of bassist Steve Rodby. Steve Rodby (b1954 in Joliet, Illinois) studied bass at Northwestern University, a student of Warren Benfield of the Chicago Symphony Orchestra. While at Northwestern, Rodby established himself as regular bassist for the Jazz Showcase in Chicago. "The gig was up for grabs and the owner of the club seemed to like the way I played, and I ended up playing five nights, three sets a night with all these amazing visiting musicians like Milt Jackson, Sonny Stitt and Joe Henderson."

In the late 1970s, he began a long-standing relationship with the Simon-Bard Group and the Fred Simon ensemble. He joined PMG in 1980. Steve: "I'd met Pat at various jazz camps when we were younger, and had stayed in touch. He was looking to add acoustic bass to his band and was auditioning players. My name came up so he called me and I went to NY and auditioned. Shortly after that he offered me the job." [10]

The opening track of this groundbreaking album is *Barcarole*, which creates an immediate feeling of tension because of the heavy pulse, as of an animal hiding amongst the bushes from a predator. Pat's guitar weeps the sweat of the animal in fear for its life, whilst Mays' keyboards play an orchestral backing in support of the nervousness. Sadly, the creature's predicament remains unresolved as the music fades. Listeners are left nervous and jumpy...waiting...

This is followed by one of the great pieces of the PMG repertoire, *Are You Going With Me?* At once it soothes our nerves, beginning quietly in a gravitational groove that seems circular, leading nowhere – but what the heck? The sound is luscious and body movement is irresistible. The melody, based on just two notes, is almost inaudible, absorbed entirely into the chord pattern laid down by Lyle Mays. The two notes remain in the foreground, but gently, so gently, in the background there comes the most wonderful ballad from Lyle. It's a lullaby, it's a dream, it's ecstasy, and it's unbelievable. Then a lonely harmonica sound cries through the mist. It's Lyle on synthesiser, and the melody is beautifully fluid as he bends the notes. The level of the backing rhythm rises imperceptibly as our attention is held by Lyle's voice. Throughout ten or so minutes, the cycle builds, unnoticeably at first, but relentlessly upwards. The ballad transforms into a proclamation, increasing its decibels with a pumping delivery, until, about half way through, the now improvised guitar emerges from the wall of colour and soars ever upwards to reach Pat's screaming, ecstatic climax. Here is Pat at his best. The composition has a simple form and a unique guitar sound, coupled with the strong sense of harmony and worldliness, milking every last drop of emotion from his music. This sensational track alone would form a pinnacle of many careers, yet it is but one of dozens in the PMG catalogue, and this technique has been used a number of times on other pieces such as *End of the Game* on *The First Circle* (1984), *The Heat of the Day* on *Imaginary Day* (1997) or *Approaching the Light* on *Metheny Mehldau Quartet* (2007).

With *Au Lait* we are in an ethereal location, trapped between our three-dimensional world and a parallel universe where ghosts and spirits practice their unearthly activities. Younger listeners might be tempted to hide behind the sofa, whilst older ones content themselves to know that good always triumphs over evil (so they say). The atmospherics are mostly by courtesy of the creative genius of Nana Vasconcelos, though the band unites and invokes gravitational attraction to pull the music through the vortex of space-time. This is not a piece for soloists, but an exercise in melodic percolation. First it is Pat who doodles his lines and then comes Lyle's acoustic piano. The overall experience is otherworldly.

Eighteen plants our feet firmly on the soil once more after our excursion into multi-dimensions. It's a fast rock number delicately wrapped in tissue like a precious porcelain artefact destined for preservation in the museum. But there's nothing out-dated about this piece. It's as fresh and lively as anything of its time, but it's just too shy to break out and spew its rock and roll over the dance floor. This is great fun.

In total contrast, the track *Offramp* is notable for its display of the darker side of PMG. The band has never shied away from their determination to explore all aspects of composition and harmony, even when it results in the occasional composition that, whilst not freeform, contains a greater freedom from the rules of harmony and beauty than many listeners feel comfortable with. This music is edgy if not angry, shouting for attention. Many listeners will hate this with passion and it is hard not to agree. All I can say is that this piece has an undeniable context on the record. I could not possibly play it without the protection of its sibling tracks, but if I adopt my policy of sitting in a quiet room and playing the package from end to end, I am able to justify its existence and I do not believe that the integrity of the album as a whole has been compromised. My respect for the musicians who created it is the artistic licence its presence requires.

James is the follow-up that entirely justifies the ugliness of *Offramp*. Here is a song we can all sing and for those of you not used to jazz, once you have learned the song you should try to sing the melody over the improvisations. (It was supposedly named after one of Pat's favoured artists, James Taylor.) There's no better way of really understanding just what Pat and Lyle are doing if you're not familiar with it. Also, listen to Lyle's first few lines played in chords. They are a particular treat.

Pat's ability to create the ultimate in passionate and beautiful ballads was first demonstrated with the impressionistic composition *The Bat*, now annotated *Part II* to distinguish its progression from the *80/81* album, and featuring virtuoso percussionist Nana Vasconcelos. No words of mine can do justice to the beauty of this piece of music that describes one of nature's most wonderful creations. It always reduces me to tears when I imagine this shy, fragile creature flitting through the clear night air. This piece of music should be listened to in absolute silence in a darkened room when you will feel the gentle creatures flitting around you. Go on, treat yourself.

The Bat would have been the highpoint of any album, but is actually eclipsed by *Are You Going With Me?* a band favourite that featured in PMG gigs for many years. The album is so original, such a milestone in recorded music, that I am compelled to award it five stars.

Pat Metheny Group: *Travels* – 1983 (****)

A casual observer might take a look at the album *Travels* (1983) and think, "Ah, a live recording. It's just a collection of stuff from their studio albums." Well, mostly, I suppose it is, but this is not really like any old live album. The tracks are a collection of recordings from the tour that took place in the USA in November 1982 and the band and the music are the same as our friends from *The Late Shift* spoke disparagingly about in my introduction to this chapter. Being live, the tracks are generally longer, which is a bonus because PMG never abbreviates music so as to find a place on an album.

The first of the two discs begins with *Are You Going With Me?* The form is pretty much the same as they usually play it and this is an important point, for this is jazz. Surely in jazz, the musicians take the theme of a piece and work it differently each time? The answer of course is usually yes, but this is PMG. The whole point is that this is a total composition, with the improvisation mostly in the solos. Even in 2005, more than twenty years later, the band plays it the same way. (And another rather amusing point is that in 2005 the band has a real harmonica player to take up Mays' theme. Instead of leaving it to Grégoire Maret, the two men share alternate lines, and the contrast between the synthesised harmonica and the real one is interesting.)

The Fields, The Sky is a delightful freewheeling piece with Pat playing his heart out. It is light, thoughtful, and atmospheric. Track three is entitled *Goodbye*. Vasconcelos takes up a wordless ballad and Pat continues it with his standard electric guitar sound.

Phase Dance is taken from the 'White' album. It is always a popular number and PMG still play it today. The introductory peal of bells is designed to send a shiver down any spine, but the main feature of this number is the way in which this piece has been composed – it's one of Pat's unique templates. He takes a minimal phrase of just a few notes and repeats it to a changing sequence of chords. This is his palette; it is how he develops the rich hues and shades for his paintings. And it matters not whether Mays provides the chords to Pat's solo or Pat plays the chords for Lyle, the constantly changing spectrum of colour leaves the listener open-mouthed, wondering how such music can sound so fresh. This feature dominates the whole piece and it's what makes it so very special, today, more than thirty years after it first appeared on record. Then it's down to the soloist to find that little extra, and in these two guys you couldn't look for more. As soloists they never seem lost for something new to play. As I said about track one, the jazz is in the solos, but the rest is cast in stone. The band has created the entire recipe, not the individual musicians. Another template feature well illustrated here is their use of loud and soft passages that build into ecstatic climaxes. In fact this piece contains not one but four or five. It's like shadow boxing, trying to pick up where the next one is coming from, but you can guess there's a pretty good one to finish up with and this track does not disappoint. In some musicians' hands it could be a musical cliché, but with PMG it's just sublime.

Straight on Red is an unusual composition for PMG in a style they rarely adopt. A busy Latin rhythm contains a lot of drumming that demands body movements from us, as does most South American music. Clearly this type of sound on a live programme is popular with any audience and they are treated to a significant drum solo in the middle of the piece. A particularly interesting and almost off-putting feature is that there is a line of melody that is played ahead of the rhythm and sounds very strange to the ear. However, the band manages to finish together so I conclude they must know what they are doing!

The final track on the first of this two-disc set is *Farmer's Trust*, another wonderful melody that pays tribute to some of the creatures on God's Earth. What a fantastic lullaby this would make for our children! And if we did that, they would all grow up appreciating just how good these musicians are. Our children cannot be expected to appreciate a beautiful thing later in life if we do not expose them to it when they are young.

Disc two opens with *Extradition*, a new track with Pat outlining the theme on guitar synth and establishing his own sound which has become so familiar to his fans over his long career. Here is a sound that flows like liquid, unhindered by the mechanics of plucking and holding strings. The notes bend and weave their way across the bars like lubricated lizards. After a somewhat wooden drum solo, the sound returns, this time with a shadow from Mays' synthesiser, but this is very much Pat's piece and, in a live context, is typical of the kind of item he would include to take some of the load off his band. Pat does not normally leave the stage during gigs. He loves to play and frequently plays solo to give his musicians a break. *Goin' Ahead* is taken from *80/81* and is a typical such number. As a solo he can improvise at will and freely adapt a piece to suit his inspiration at the time. He can also use it as an extended introduction to another piece, as he does here. At about 3.30 he is joined by his colleagues who create a pastiche of atmospherics that by 4.20 bridge into *As Falls Wichita*, one of Metheny/Mays most ambitious compositions to date. As we might expect, it is triumphant.

Travels is a song for all, a gentle ballad with a beautiful melody and soft, luscious music. What more could you ask for? It is astonishing just how many of the fine melodies are buried in the multi-coloured instrumental music of these albums. This is timeless beauty, suspended in the dark vaults of the performing arts. It should be regularly taken out, dusted off and played from the rooftops. A wonderful comparison can be made between this version and an acoustic one that appears on the album *Trio 99-00* (2000). Here, Pat is mostly playing single note melody whilst his colleagues fill in the background, but for absolute skill on the guitar you should also listen to the Trio version.

Song for Bilbao is another band favourite that was being played on the 2002 *Speaking of Now* tour. (This is the final track of the DVD and is truly exhilarating, especially the bass playing of Richard Bona.) Here, some twenty years earlier, the music still demands that we get up out of our seats and move to its wonderful rhythms. Once again, it is Pat's guitar synth sound that dominates the track. Listen to the ten-second burst that occurs at 6.30. His playing is simply astonishing as he negotiates the rapidly moving chord sequence without any kind of hesitation at all. This type of virtuosity is lost in a piece of this length, and rarely appears on studio albums, but in the context of a live performance illustrates how a musician of Pat's standing plays on a higher level entirely.

San Lorenzo is a fine version of the opening track from the 'White' album for our delectation. The music is played with superb sensitivity and space considering that it is live in an auditorium. This is certainly one of the bands finest compositions and deserves its repeated exposure on this album, for it is significantly different. Those of you who are learning about jazz would do well to take these two tracks and compare their treatments. In particular, Mays delivers a lengthy improvisation from which we can hear just how he approaches his work. You will detect a number of obvious errors and hesitations, which is fairly normal in live recordings (though not so much these days) but don't be distracted by them. Just enjoy his beautiful acoustic piano playing. The ending is one of the band's best!

There is an often-quoted opinion that double albums would be greatly improved by being weeded of their filler tracks and reduced to single albums. However, this album would be much the poorer if that were to happen. It is a very good collection indeed, despite some re-recording of older material.

Pat Metheny Trio: *Rejoicing* – 1984 (***)

The album *Rejoicing* featured Pat with Charlie Haden on bass and Billy Higgins on drums. Haden is well known for his leadership of a group that introduced political protest into their music, the Liberation Music Orchestra. Pat has remained friends with Charlie over many years and, apart from Steve Rodby, Haden has been Pat's bass player of choice when he was looking for a pure, free jazz sound. Besides this one, they appear together on the albums *80/81* (1980), *Song X* (1986), *Secret Story* (1992) and *Beyond the Missouri Sky* (1997).

Pat has been much influenced by the music of Ornette Coleman and it is the links of Haden and Higgins to Coleman that are under the spotlight here. Along with Don Cherry, Charlie and Billy played on Coleman's landmark album *The Shape of Jazz to Come* (1959) and Higgins (1936-2001) had been with Coleman when the 28-year-old newcomer had made his first album a year earlier. It's hardly surprising that Pat was delighted to be able to capture these two jazz heavyweights on an album, as he does with this trio for his publishers, ECM.

Pat plays acoustic guitar for the opener, *Lonely Woman*, a beautiful ballad by pianist Horace Silver. The boys play it straight down the line with a Metheny solo sandwiched between two delightful expositions of Silver's theme. Both delicate and delicious, this music is rich in tone and touch.

At about this time, Pat was developing a professional relationship with a Canadian luthier called Linda Manzer. She made Pat the "incredible six string guitar" that he used on *Lonely Woman*. "She has also made me a twelve string and an eight string guitar which has a sitar effect. She made me two miniature guitars; a triple, which is twelve string with the strings in three groups of four, rather than six groups of two and an alto guitar, which is about half way between a regular guitar scale and this mini one." [8]

Pat has greatly helped to expose the lie about Coleman's music, for Ornette was vilified for many years, and many uninformed jazzers would express the feeling that his music was pointless and unpalatable. Pat has shown that this is far from the case. For example, when you hear a piece written by Ornette Coleman, you don't expect an old-fashioned blues, but that's just what you get with *Tears Inside*. The track appeared on the album *Tomorrow is the Question* (1959) when Coleman was just about to decimate the jazz scene with his musical protestation. Played here as a swing electric guitar trio, the music moves along perfectly: nothing startlingly new, just very good playing all round. The second Coleman tune, *Humpty Dumpty*, taken from the album *Beauty is a Rare Thing* (1960) is rather different. Another mainstream piece, it's much looser. Haden plays a crafted solo in the middle of the piece and is followed by a brief interlude from Higgins.

Charlie's *Blues for Pat* is up next. As writer, Charlie takes the first solo, whilst Pat returns at 2.36 and improvises within the blues framework that Haden had carefully laid aside for his own solo. It's interesting to hear how Billy moves into new areas of his rhythm during this tune, especially during Pat's solo from around 2.55. As the music proceeds Higgins gradually makes the track his own, elbowing his way to the front in the nicest possible way. He gets a couple of short shouts during the reprise of the blues that leads to the end.

The title track, *Rejoicing*, is another Coleman tune, once again taken from the album *Tomorrow is the Question* (1959). For the first minute, it's just Pat and Billy, and Pat's playing is both fleet and impressive. The fast but never furious guitar tale is a minimal expression of Coleman's modest theme, with Higgins playing a centrepiece solo from 1.33 to 2.40. After that it's all downhill – at full speed, of course.

The album takes a surprising turn with *Story from a Stranger*. Just as it looked like this was to be a modestly proportioned album of loose homage to Coleman,

Pat introduces an entirely new direction to the collection. Here is a slowly developed Metheny ballad in 3/4 time. Then, from two minutes, Pat's synthesiser enters with the backing of some acoustic guitar overdubs. Although the music is now moving towards some of the ambitious development that we find on other records, it appears at first to be unusually out of place here.

The movement to Coleman continues with *The Calling*, an apparently spontaneous freeform improvisation with Pat punishing his Synclavier. Higgins and Haden contribute their own ideas that drive the music relentlessly towards a thrilling climax. Perhaps the best way to summarise it is by saying that it's ten minutes of sound that most listeners will not play more than once. The more curious listeners should not, however, dispense with this music too easily: these three players have something firmly in mind when they do this. You may find out just what that is by listening to the final track, *Waiting for an Answer*. It is a Haden/Metheny duet that delves deep into the spirit of music itself, looking for music's answer to *Life, the Universe and Everything*. Whether you conclude that these musicians have found it is entirely up to you.

My own conclusion of this remarkable album is that, understandably, it will not be high among the favourites of those whom I am encouraging to listen to Pat's music. Superficially, it seems just that: unexceptional in the crystal streams that flow down from the jazz glacier. It's only obvious sparkle is from the musicianship of these excellent musicians. Having said that, it is important to realise how much storyteller Pat refuses to fit into the slots we make for him. The music here just might be probing the invisible depths of the glacier before bursting out into the light of day.

On the other hand, there will be some listeners who will rate this album very highly, for it is possible to interpret the collection of music in different ways. Some might see it as a holistic musical journey from the early days of blues, through the times of swinging mainstream, into the kind of electronic future that Pat envisaged, but had not yet fully delivered. Coleman was the inspiration, a man at the heart of a jazz revolution who at least two of the musicians knew intimately. Metheny, the stranger, was also the narrator. For Pat himself, it may have been the arrival of the Synclavier into his life that resulted in his leading Billy and Charlie towards this electronic destiny. In the absence of any further commentary, we are left to make up our own minds.

Pat Metheny Group: *First Circle* – 1984 (*****)

Pat Metheny does try *everything*, perhaps sometimes with mixed results. On PMG albums, it usually works. The opening track of *First Circle* is *Forward March*, a strange concoction that sounds like a bad junior school marching band. The mix of crude military drum and out-of-tune trumpet creates an uncomfortable feeling that unsettles the listener in the same way that some of Picasso's painted figures offend the uneducated eye by the unusual positions of the facial features. The abandonment of representation in art is well known and somehow more acceptable in an art museum than it is for the opening track of a jazz album. Jaco Pastorius employed a similar technique for the first track *Crisis* on his album *Word of Mouth* (1981). His record company nearly refused to publish the record on the grounds that the first track would put people off buying it, but Pastorius held his ground and won the battle. It could easily have been an example of Pastorius thumbing his nose at the established practice, but we cannot be sure. It was almost certainly a defiant statement of some kind, in keeping with Pastorius' tendency for the irreverent. In Pat Metheny's case, this would be the last reason for employing such a tactic. In fact, on *First Circle*, the juxtaposition of this track with the one that follows is a joy to experience.

All is forgiven immediately that the opening salvo of *Yolanda, You Learn* drives out of the speakers. The album is without doubt much better for the inclusion of the strange, first track. *Yolanda, You Learn* begins with an urgent rhythm from the newly installed drummer Paul Wertico. It just never lets up for an instant yet the band play a slow melody across it and the contrast is wonderful. On this track we start to see Pat with new tools in his box. Slide guitar, sitar and Synclavier guitar are listed on the album sleeve and it is clear that the tones are new. Naturally, the effect is stunning. Pedro Aznar's wordless vocal demands that you sing along with it and I always do.

Next up is the album's title track. Here's another new experiment, this time with a complex rhythm. Set up with handclaps, the complexity is provided first by Lyle on keyboard, then by Pat and Pedro in unison with the first melody. Percussion and keyboard comes in with yet another rhythmic overlay. You simply can't keep any rhythm in your head as you listen to it, but relax, it just sounds good. The complexity doesn't end there for next up is Pat playing an acoustic melody (with bells on!) in another completely unfathomable rhythm. Eventually, at around 2.29, the piece settles into something that at last seems ordered. Beneath a superb melody you can now count a rhythm of eleven, a six beat followed by a five beat. Everything is now clear. Start the track again and count alternate sixes and fives. Obvious isn't it? It was not the first time it had been done: John McLaughlin had already based his early career success on a series of extraordinary metres, but PMG's use of this rhythm is a real feature of the success of this track.

Once again, we find an example of a theme that moves along at a rapid lick, whilst the melody itself is slow, haunting and in a low register at first. It's impossible not to sing to it. Isn't singing and dancing what music is really all about? Aznar's voice is completely asexual and, with no words, the effect is ethereal. There's also a kind of whistle that accompanies him from May's keyboard. Pat strums vigorously in the background throughout. Then, after four minutes and forty-five seconds, the piece almost comes to a halt. All that is left is a gentle percussive shuffle from Aznar. The piece opens right out into a big empty space filled only by the fabulous sensual sound of May's piano. The tone is magical: every note seems inspired. This is how I would describe the 'inevitability' in the music that Pat sometimes talks about. It's as if the piece is running on rails: there's nowhere else for it to go, yet it is absolutely not predictable. What a total paradox! At 7.07 the piece turns a corner into entirely new territory. The mood becomes sombre with a threatening drumbeat, but, as with all the best scripts, the good overcomes the bad. Such a wonderful main theme inevitably breaks through once more; only the twisted minds of the world would have it fail. The ending is magnificent.

The composition, *If I Could*, is played on Spanish guitar. This wonderful love song is so outstanding that other artists have covered it on their albums – a rare accolade in jazz these days for music that never gets played on radio. Most notable among these was the version by saxophonist Nelson Rangell, who strangely chose not to play the melody on the saxophone, but to demonstrate his remarkable skill in whistling. The result is arguably even more beautiful than the original Metheny version. However, this is the original. With the lightest of touch, Pat caresses the melody like a new-born child and Mays delivers the most basic of accompaniments on Oberheim keyboard, executed with the maximum of legato such that only the tones can be heard. Such beauty needs no further adornment. The music is as pure and perfect as it is possible to imagine and the end is a tearjerker.

Pat was especially pleased with this track. "The ballad *If I Could* was the first time I've ever had the experience of playing something in the studio, and after finishing playing it, being glad that the tape was running because I'll never ever be able to do it again; like one of those special moments that happen, not every night, but almost every night. Usually when you see that red light go on, you know it's going to be transcribed in a guitar magazine or something, and you start thinking all the wrong things, like, what if I make a mistake? But that whole day it was just loose and we were having a blast." [8]

Tell it All begins with another impenetrable rhythm played by Lyle on an instrument called 'agogo bells'. After a lot of counting you can figure out that it's two sets of five followed by a six! Drummer Paul Wertico just keeps up a regular beat on the cymbals that smoothes out the wrinkles in space-time and Aznar sings a vocal along with it that is quite independent of any time frame at all. At 0.55 Pat comes in with an electric guitar solo that is fairly typical of the sound he is trademarking and the piece slips unnoticeably into the common-four time that Wertico has probably been playing all along. Pat puts on his serious hat and lays down some pretty rapid riffs at around 2 minutes. Then at 2.58 a middle section follows in which keys and guitar play a chordal sequence together with Pedro singing behind it. At 3.56 Lyle follows with another of his beautiful evolving piano solos. Like a bird gliding and turning on the wind, he uses the undercurrent of the rhythm to carry him up and over the bar lines, letting his wings relax with never a thought of falling out of the sky. Then at 5.55 it's a brief return to the chordal theme and at 6.31 a last statement of the first theme on asynchronous bells. This is a very powerful and complex composition, executed like no other band in the world.

End of the Game is awesome. The first theme is comprised of seven notes in one group of three and one of four, the first fast, the second slow; the first five notes are the same. It is spelled out on legato chords to a backwash that rises and falls, and all the time, the notes of that theme are changing like the colour of some chameleon fish. It's a gentle, musical tide that ebbs and flows, the waves swashing around your feet as you listen, and there are no less than thirty-seven waves in each cycle of the tide. OK, so who composes a theme consisting of thirty-seven bars? Well PMG do! Then comes Pat with his guitar synth. It has become another of his trademark sounds and he will use this many more times on coming albums. It first appeared on *Are You Going with Me?* The thirty-seven bar tide floods again, Metheny the fish, floating free. Nothing can touch him. He's in his natural element. He doesn't need to count thirty-seven. It just happens around him. It's inevitable. On the second of his adventures towards the shoreline, the tide seems to retreat fully, leaving him stranded on the sand. Is this the end of the piece? Absolutely not! The seabirds are hovering, looking for a meal. The tide returns for another thirty-seven, but the fish is gone. The seagull got him.

Mas Alla (Beyond) starts with Lyle on piano. It's a tale of sorrow, and Pedro takes it up in full song. There are lyrics this time, and for the first time the vocalising is in front of the song instead of integral to it, but it is always a Metheny melody. This is the only point on the album at which I could accuse Pat of pandering to a formula. It's as if he is saying, OK, we've had one fast number, two slow numbers, one novelty number – we need a vocal here... Indeed, I was about to write that this is something he absolutely does not do. PMG albums are not created in such a way and that is one reason why they are so special. I guess for once he broke his own rule at this point.

The final track *Praise* is exactly where it should be. It's a celebration of a first class album and we should all jump up and shout "Hallelujah!" In 1984, the Grammy Panel agreed and voted this truly remarkable album *Best Jazz Fusion Performance, Vocal or Instrumental*.

Pat Metheny Group: *The Falcon and the Snowman* – 1985 (***)

In their first major film score project, Pat and Lyle worked together on music for *The Falcon and the Snowman*, a spy drama directed by John Schlesinger and starring Timothy Hutton and Sean Penn. A true story of the close friendship of two church choirboys, Christopher Boyce and Daulton Lee, we see them grow up together, get involved, first in drugs and then espionage, whereby they sell American secrets to the Soviets.

Pat and Lyle wrote all the music that was played by their Group with Rodby, Wertico, Aznar and Vasconcelos. The music is entirely typical of the Group's output at this point in their existence. The depth of development that we might normally expect from PMG music is absent here, as we might expect, but the themes are so well blended together that the album is entirely coherent and never disappoints. The main song is *This Is Not America*, co-written by Pat and Lyle with David Bowie. A single was produced from it that became a popular hit and reached no. 14 in the UK and no. 32 in the USA. The remainder of the music is extremely fit-for-purpose and is comprised of a number of thematic threads that are woven together across the tracks exactly as storylines are in the film. Lyle leads much of the music on synthesisers, supported by percussion, with Pat taking more of a back seat, although in two places he does play one of his beautiful but brief melodies in the style of *If I Could*.

The main characters appear in the early tracks, *Daulton Lee* and *Chris*, represented by melodic lines that can be recognised from time to time throughout, or else repeated outright as in *Capture*. The dramatic tension of the movie is covered by some electronic imagery that ranges from the disturbing emotional feel of *Extent of the Lie* to the freeform improvisation of *Level of Deception*, two pieces that would make difficult listening outside the context of the movie. Nevertheless, the album as a whole is extremely well sequenced, encased in two versions of *Psalm 121* and ending with a variation of Vasconcelos' wonderful bat effects that create a breathtaking ending to this fine album.

Pat Metheny and Ornette Coleman: *Song X* – 1986 and 2005 (*)

Just before the recording of Song X, Pat Metheny executed a commercial coup. He formed his own production company that licensed all his recorded material to record companies for a limited time. At the time, the licensee was the Geffen label, owned by David Geffen who also held Joni Mitchell's contract. Pat had realised that licensing material afforded him the artistic freedoms that otherwise may have been curbed by a label. When the license expired he was able to regain all rights to the recordings. Consequently, since 1984, he has been able to do everything he wanted to do, exactly the way he wanted to do it and his company will continue to make money from the music as long as it remains in copyright.

In 2005, Pat used this freedom to revisit the master tapes of sessions recorded with free jazz exponent, Ornette Coleman. Geffen had given them only two days to record and little longer to mix and master the tapes, so Pat had always harboured the feeling that he could have produced a better album of the occasion. In addition, the CD format (rather than the original vinyl disc) now allowed him to include an additional eighteen minutes of music, so he prepared a further six tracks to add to the original eight.

There is not much I can say about this album except that, to me, it sounds absolutely terrible. I fear that an unsuspecting customer in a record shop will pick up this album and never buy another Pat Metheny record again, which would be tragic, of course. I have written some comments below under the heading of "The Dark Side" that I hope will explain my position. I will simply assign this album to Pat's parallel career and keep the album on the shelf where it belongs.

Pat Metheny Group: *Still Life (Talking)* – 1987 (*****)

During the 1980s, Pat Metheny, then in his thirties, was prolific in his output, not just with PMG but also with many other top jazz musicians. For PMG, a steady stream of album releases ensued. *Still Life (Talking)* contains some very fine compositions that appear in the band sheets at gigs today. *Minuano (Six Eight)* is one example that combines a wonderful melody with a throbbing six-eight rhythm and a typical PMG climax that leaves you shouting for more. This PMG favourite is the encore number for the DVD of *Imaginary Day* and is unmissable. On the audio CD, the track begins with a wordless vocal over an undulating piano and guitar accompaniment. As we listen to this piece it is worth bearing in mind that minuano is the name given to a cold southwesterly wind of southern Brazil, occurring during the Southern Hemisphere winter (June to September). At first, the melody is calming and beautiful and takes the first two and a half minutes to generate a lovely environment in which the piece will be developed. As we relax into the mood of the piece, we pass through some minor climaxes indicated by cymbal skims. We need to remind ourselves that countless popular music recordings would end at this point, but not here. The first section is but an introduction to the main feast.

At 2.45 the main melody breaks out on Pat's guitar and it's one that we can all sing along with. It's light, joyful and played with vitality. Pat enjoys his improvisation and after a brief replay of the melody another section begins in which the character of the piece changes completely. The melody here is more complex and the rhythm even more so as we are caught up in a strong dance rhythm. The wind is swirling through dusky courtyards, picking up leaves and other detritus, gusting between buildings and across bridges. The music is percussive and syncopated and seems to develop through ever more complexity until eventually the main theme breaks out in joy once more, this time sung vociferously by the team of musicians now employed to provide the enhanced vocals. The backing builds in intensity over the now familiar and delightful melody. A coda section succeeds in reaching a thrilling climax and we are left breathless at the sheer quality of what we have just heard, another of PMGs many great pieces.

So May it Secretly Begin is a fine melody played with a tinge of melancholy or apprehension. You simply must learn to sing these tunes for they are wonderful.

They stay with you long after the music is gone and lift the spirits in unexpected moments. This melody is fine and there is a good contrast between the languorous melody and the accompaniment, which again takes on a South American hue. After a first exposition, Mays comes in for a pass through, improvising exquisitely on acoustic piano. Then Pat comes in with a small flourish and a lifting of the key that raises the music to a new level. The clean ending on a minor chord retains the mood of uncertainty that is the main theme of the piece.

The third track *Last Train Home* is a truly nerve-tingling composition that has become another PMG favourite. This track has influenced many people and has been covered by musicians such as the fine British saxophonist, John Harle. This is an unashamed representation of a train journey of the kind that many of us have made at some time or another. Imagine being away on business for several weeks. Christmas is approaching and it's time to return home to your family. The excitement is palpable as the train urgently wends its way across the continental plateau, the endless dusty horizons coming and going past the window. The tired, homesick traveller pictures his wife and little children eagerly waiting to greet him. He smiles and settles down into his seat as the trusty old locomotive works hard to get him home. It is without doubt one of Pat's most beautiful compositions. Shed a tear, and be proud to do so.

(Its Just) Talk is an example of the facility with which PMG slide so comfortably into other types of dance rhythm, in this case, the great South American cha-cha. The jazz uses guitar, piano and voice, superimposed with the slickness of true professionals and this piece would sit beautifully in the dark recesses of a smoky Chicago nightclub. As a bonus we are treated to the occasional extra percussive ornaments from Paul Wertico, demonstrating how PMG is never content merely to use a standard style without additionally developing it. Here we find the "cha-cha extraordinaire", and surely it is impossible not to dance to it? The track is filled with so much fun and beautiful music. Lyle treats us to yet another lovely improvisation of this eminently singable tune. This entire album is just crammed with things to sing. If you learn to sing this one you are doing well because amongst the wonderful tunes there are some pretty nifty chord sequences buried beneath to throw you off balance.

The track *Third Wind* is fast and driving, and sets an entirely different musical feel to the track that preceded it. Here Pat shows us just how well he can play guitar, the sound adopted being a normal electric sound with added reverb that places him in the premier league of guitarists. Then, unexpectedly at 3.10, a new section begins which embraces the best percussive combinations you could imagine. The overlaid voices contribute to this piece being suddenly African in style. Towards the end at 4.50 a remarkable syncopation occurs, and then a further new linking section starts at 5.35 where Mays turns on his skills. The last section from 6.00 is a constantly twisting and turning tune that is hard to analyse. And then Pat plays us out with his own guitar synth in overdrive, sliding around every part of the scale. Finally, just when you think the fade-out is inevitable, comes a great resolution that is a far more satisfying conclusion. This track, like the wind direction, is constantly changing and is an unpublicised masterpiece of composition.

Africa seems to be carried into the next track entitled *Distance*, for it seems that we are back in the jungle with snakes and other hidden dangers. However, there are many interpretations here and this piece is a fine musical sculpture that acts as a smooth link into the final track. *In Her Family* sets the scene for the typical Metheny composition that he has used on his recordings outside of PMG. A beautiful, tearful ballad it forms the model for some of the compositions on his orchestral *Secret Story* album. This pairing of tracks demonstrates how PMG was to develop the idea still further on the 2005 album *The Way Up* in which there is only one continuous piece of music.

Still Life (Talking) is a brilliant album that continued the unbroken sequence of Grammy awards to PMG albums. The band had now been expanded to seven musicians and was the one in which wordless vocals were formally accepted as a full part of the musical orchestration. There are always a lot of songs for us to sing on PMG albums and it seems there are more than usual on this one. (The album might also be remembered as the one with the irritable parentheses.)

Michael Brecker: Michael Brecker – 1987 (***)

For his first album as leader, Michael chose his friend Don Grolnick, not to play piano, as he usually did, but to produce. Thus, with Don in the box instead of at the keyboard, Mike hired pianist Kenny Kirkland, along with Pat Metheny, Charlie Haden and Jack de Johnette. Brecker is recorded as saying that he "wanted to make a record with some mystery, one that bears more than one listening." [11] Brecker's style of contemporary jazz relies heavily on the more academic style of modal jazz, a tool used by purist jazzers to elevate themselves into exclusivity from the long grass of popularity and commercialism. It's a decision that firmly places him in the company of premier league jazz musicians attracting the hallowed respect of the fraternity of jazz purists. Forget any idea you might have formed from listening to the Brecker Brothers' albums or Steps Ahead fusion that Michael was to be forever incarcerated on popular terrain. Here, the name of the game that Brecker now led is called *contemporary jazz*. This design is a mostly blank canvas on which the artist can experiment with a wide range of styles and techniques. In a sense, this is his own personal brand of free jazz, and thanks to his high profile in the world of jazz it was to prove as influential as anything else he did in his career. We could have guessed the angle of the new musical direction by simply looking at the musicians he chose to play alongside him. Metheny, Haden, de Johnette and Kirkland were all partial to a freer brand of jazz than might be expected in what is generally referred to as the *mainstream*. In so doing, Brecker was adopting the Miles Davis musical philosophy by being true to himself and not capitulating to any particular genre, style or convention.

Pat Metheny Group: *Letter From Home* – 1989 (****)

At just over an hour, the 1989 album *Letter From Home* is long when compared to the previous album (42 minutes) and reflects the newfound freedom that musicians experienced when allowed to record for CD, rather than vinyl. This collection of compositions succeeds in creating the idea of a theme, in which (we presume) Pat is in the middle of a long world tour and homesick.

The album opens beautifully with the very rhythmically complex *Have You Heard*, which demonstrates just how lovely a piece with such a difficult structure can sound. All the typical PMG trademarks are here, the clean guitar arpeggios flowing effortlessly from Pat as they weave so naturally through the shifting keys and chord changes. A brief linking section from Mays' grand piano takes us back to the complex wordless song of Mark Ledford and David Blamires. Then the piece wends its way out of sight, appearing to lead into a fade, but instead reaching a decelerating series of chords and final dark flourish on piano and cymbal.

Every Summer Night is a musical portrait that cannot fail to create wonderful images in your mind. After a marching main theme, a slick and beautiful waltz is adopted that just demands you sing along with it. Pat's improvisation is similarly smooth and entirely in its place within this great atmospheric piece, followed by Mays in waltz time sounding like Mantovani. This doesn't last long before the jazz flavour flows out of his fingers and across the bars. New sounds appear in percussion and synth, and then the original theme returns for a final full statement to remind you how wonderful summer nights really are in cold climates, and there is even a final icy blast in the last chord of the piece. Then, just when you are wondering how such lovely sounds can be bettered, without a break, we transform at once into *Better Days Ahead*, an incredibly lyrical modulating melody from Pat's top drawer. His improvisation is stunning, as usual, with no electronic whistles and bells – just clean lines of jazz guitar played impeccably. Short (by modern standards) and extremely sweet, this number is great, and you should listen for a delightfully unexpected ending.

Spring Ain't Here is a subdued, broody statement with a simple theme and the usual short fill that makes you sit up with its odd rhythmic pulses. Then it's back to the main theme once more, clean and sharp, gentle and considered. Pat comes out carefully into his improvisation, ensuring there is no break in the feel of the piece. The harmonic development is perfect, with just a hint of a crescendo, before returning us sympathetically to the main theme. The ending is a logical development of the previously used filler bars and perfectly closes up this number.

The next track *45/8* presumably refers to the complexity of its structure. A quick-fire acoustic guitar piece, it lasts slightly less than one minute and, besides being a delightful experiment in unusual musical form, also serves as a 'palette cleanser' before the lengthier, more considered piece with a similar structural title, *5-5-7*. Here are echoes of many other Metheny compositions brought together into a vehicle for Pat's slick guitar improvisations. After a good number of bars for guitar, the piece turns a corner and adopts a pulsing rhythm with a wholly sweeter melody in voice and whistle, with Lyle's synthesised orchestra below. Modulating upwards, and entirely naturally is another trick frequently employed by PMG as it moves towards its closing statement. This too is somewhat unexpected, demands our attention and satisfies.

Beat 70 shakes us firmly awake after the more subdued rhythms that preceded it. Here we are subjected to a Caribbean type of sound that uses more whistling and wordless singing for its main theme. Its unpretentious melody is fun and extremely tuneful. Then Mays' lyrical piano is an introduction to Pat's stance centre stage. The improvisation picks its way nimbly through the difficult changes as if it were a mere nursery rhyme. A second statement of the theme leads us quickly into the next track, an altogether more serious piece, *Dream of the Return*, which offers us an uplifting spiritual, hymn-like character that cries out for a section of classic Metheny guitar synth. This is delivered briefly, before the voice returns with its hymn. Unusually, this piece tends to lose its way and never quite lives up to the expectation it creates. Its success is in the way it prepares us for the musical experience that is to follow.

The track *Are We There Yet?* adopts an altogether different mood. Its theme is troubled and moody, played out in sharp tones. Percussion is used to great effect as it leads us into the darkness of the second section. Here Mays excels, creating the unnerving atmospherics he specialises in. Imperceptibly we are led into the next track, *Vidala*, a track unusually using lyrics and composed by the vocalist, Pedro Aznar.

Slip Away is a foot tapping melodic song from Aznar's wordless voice. Each chord change seems to be unexpected, in the wrong place or even both, yet the piece works extraordinarily well. A transition to a quiet section on piano comes as a welcome change before Pat returns with his guitar. A pleasant number it does not, however, reach the higher planes we have come to expect from PMG, but rather meanders its way into the final, title track of the album, a sad expression of homesickness after a long time away.

Pat Metheny Trio: *Question and Answer* – 1990 (***)

Pat writes on the sleeve notes to his album how he had reached the end of a long year recording and touring with PMG with the music from *Letter From Home*. He says how he wanted to try out something simpler and had always wanted to work with Roy Haynes. He asked Dave Holland to join them for a day at the Power Station studio in New York.

Pat arrived at the studio with just his Ibanez guitar and almost nothing else. The three men played together for eight hours with no plans to make a record. They began by trying a Miles Davis piece called *Solar*. Recorded just once on 3 April 1954 at the Rudy Van Gelder studio in Hackensack NJ, it was one of the first of Davis's pieces in his new career with Prestige and appeared on several albums, *Walkin'* being the most significant. On this occasion *Solar* was recorded after just 15 minutes of starting and Pat was stunned at the intensity between the three men, one of the highest levels of listening he had experienced up to that time. Pat rates Haynes as the father of drumming in the generation before Jack de Johnette and Tony Williams, two drummers who have both drawn upon Higgins' influence. Roy's experience was some of the broadest available at the time, having played with Bird and Pres, Trane and Miles, as well as just about every major star in the jazz sky. That's a very impressive CV, and Pat, who comes from an even younger generation, likes to get close to these great musicians through working with their closest associates if not the guys themselves. Pat reminds us that Dave Holland was the original candidate to play on *Bright Size Life*, but Jaco of course did the gig. Pat was glad about that, in view of Jaco's later history, and says he wasn't ready to play with Dave at that point.

Question and Answer is a memorable Metheny original tune in 3/4 time. It has a fairly standard format with a faded ending. Meanwhile, Pat's *H&H* was presumably written for this session with Haynes and Holland. It's a straight-ahead up-tempo piece with just 30 seconds of theme that gets into an immediate improvisation vibe. It sounds like it's modal, but by 1.30 appears to be twelve-bar-blues-based after all. By 2.30 it's very clear that's what this is. Holland takes a solo, followed by Roy who takes alternate 12s. A final repetition of the theme ends the piece. Then comes *Never Too Far Away*, another Metheny piece that is an undemanding ballad played sensitively.

A change of groove takes place for *Law Years*, a song by Ornette Coleman, one of Pat's heroes. In fact, this time it's Holland who unusually takes it away, adding a fresh dimension to the structure. The final playing of the theme is a very good example of Dave and Pat playing perfectly together, well backed of course by Roy. *Change of Heart* is an over-used title that is soon forgotten here in favour of another lovely new ballad in waltz time from Pat. Play this a few times and you will have it in your head for days and as a favourite for life. The track is so good that it won a Grammy for the best instrumental composition for 1990.

The presence of a standard like Kern and Hammerstein's *All the Things You Are* is inevitable on an album such as this. It's always a good idea to have an icebreaker when players turn up for a session with no prior rehearsal. This is probably the most common such icebreaker for serious mainstream jazzers, yet just listen to how this is played. I'm sure even Roy and Dave must have felt challenged when Pat first suggested playing it at 310 beats per minute. It's just as well these guys all know it well. The section from 5.30 digresses significantly from the theme but leads into Roy's solo that is amazing for a 65-year-old – better than most players half his age. I'm sure Pat wasn't thinking of Roy when he chose *Old Folks*, another slightly less well-known standard from 1938 by Hill and Robison. Pat's playing is beautifully laid-back whilst delivering the beauty and respect the song deserves.

The flightiest track on the album is *Three Flights Up*, played at 326 bpm. Another Metheny piece, it's testament to the professionalism of Roy and Dave that they were able to generate such credible music in such a short space of time with pieces they had not seen before. There is some overdubbing of synthesiser here that makes the piece almost like a Metheny Group number and is almost like Pat is finally giving in to the 'it's just a trio' syndrome. Pat acknowledges that it's very difficult for a jazz guitarist to play trios like this because "you don't have the dynamic range", which is his way of saying that there isn't the variety of possibilities that you have when there are other lead instruments to play against. For me, that's not enough colour, by far. That's one reason why I didn't buy this album for many years, but now that I have it, I'm glad I do. These are three great masters playing great jazz.

Gary Burton: *Reunion* – 1990 (****)

When Pat left the Gary Burton band in 1977, there was no musical contact between the musicians for eleven years. Then, in 1988 Gary was invited to play a couple of tunes with Pat at the Montreal Jazz Festival. Gary accepted the invitation and, during the course of the five tunes they played together, was very surprised to discover just how much Pat had developed. A new collaboration was inevitable and *Reunion* (1990) was the result.

Once they got together in the studio, there was a certain amount of role reversal: the master had, to some extent, become the pupil. Burton: "It was a treat to watch him work, how he used the recording techniques, how he paced the music, his rapport with the musicians – I learned a ton of stuff from him." [12] As Neil Tesser noted, "For many people, such a realisation would occasion self-doubt or jealousy; for Burton, it represented the occasion to admire, to learn, and to grow." [13]

The musicians they chose for the recording were from the premier league. Mitchel Forman (b1956) was a brilliant musician who had become the keyboardist of choice for many of the best jazzers. He had played on the Mahavishnu Orchestra's comeback album *Mahavishnu* (1984) alongside John McLaughlin and Bill Evans, and on Bill's brilliant *The Alternative Man* (1985); also on *Adventures in Radioland* (1986). After that, he appeared with Mike

Mainieri and Mike Brecker in the band Steps Ahead on their great jazz-fusion album *Magnetic* (1986). In the late 1980s he played with Wayne Shorter, Mike Stern and Mark Egan. Bassist Will Lee (b1952) was also a top fusion musician, making his reputation with the Brecker Brothers and David Sanborn, but moving into the wider arena with the likes of Gloria Estefan, Carly Simon and Mariah Carey. Unusually, he also entered the stratosphere by playing with artists like Barbra Streisand and Frank Sinatra. Finally, drummer Peter Erskine (b1954), another artist at the centre of jazz-fusion, had established himself with Weather Report and Steps Ahead. He was also a member of Jaco Pastorius' Word of Mouth band.

The opening track is *Autumn*, written by a young composer who Gary had discovered called Polo Orti. It has all the characteristics of a PMG number – melody, orchestration, sound and rhythmic feel are all from the same mould, and it is therefore a great start to the album. During the ensemble work, it even seems as if Gary has been seamlessly added to the Group too, although he does play a typically slick vibraphone solo that adds greatly to the joy of this *hors d'oeuvre*. Led by Erskine's unobtrusive but irresistible clockwork, this is an elegant display of melody-making from both Pat and Gary.

It seems as if this is full-on easy listening and the tone is set for the whole album as the second track, a piece written by Forman called *Reunion*, continues the PMG atmosphere. Lee's regular bass pattern provides the foundation this time as Pat takes the melody in his standard electric guitar sound. It's a piece of regular high quality jazz-fusion, with the solos taken at one minute intervals by Pat (1.20), Gary (2.20) and Mitch (3.20) who plays through a particularly neat side-step and into a majestic solo that sounds as if Lyle Mays is sat at the piano stool.

Origin is also by Forman, and with Pat now playing his rich-toned acoustic guitar, this is a wonderfully smooth ballad played with a gentle Latin rhythm. Burton's playing here raises hairs on chilled skin as his mallets slide so fluidly over the notes and find every subtle harmonic variation to perfection. Meanwhile, Pat's playing is similarly masterful. It doesn't really sound like him because he plays like a Spanish maestro with many restrained, delicate touches. For him, it's yet another way to play that is as fresh and pure as anything he has yet played.

Will You Say You Will is a play on words that puts the focus on Lee, whose slap bass is lively and lifts this otherwise smooth and intricate melody up above the pastel backgrounds. Composer Vince Mendoza has found some subtle chord sequences that offer the band some great opportunities for colourful creativity and they deliver handsomely. The piece is melodic and rhythmically varied, picking up through the second half after a gentler start. The perfectly matched guitar and vibes sounds are especially notable.

Imagine one of those typical New England houses, big, old and rambling, constructed of timber frame with wooden slats nailed to the outside. Its many dark, curtained windows look out over a neat garden behind a white picket fence. There's an air of mystery that emanates from it as you walk past each morning on your way to work. You never see the occupants and your imagination conjures up images of an old sea dog living alone amidst his strange artefacts collected over years of travel to remote corners of the Earth. Pat's tune, *House on the Hill*, evokes some wonderful thoughts and feelings as Gary and Pat share its delivery.

In complete contrast, Paul Meyers' tune *Panama* is, lively and a lot of fun, but doesn't create Panamanian images, for me, at least. Pat's use of the Synclavier creates a fantastic brassy sound as he plays the main theme, supported by Mitch, and Gary's marimba solo from 1.30 positively dances over the keys of his instrument. Later, during his solo, Pat changes the sound of his synth, at which point it becomes another PMG-type piece. From 3.55, the piano takes the lead in this bright 6/8 piece and Will Lee is always there, perfectly in touch with the angular melody.

Chairs and Children is another of Vince Mendoza's unusual compositions. His strange melodic structures are very much like entangled wooden chairs, but I don't see children here – just adults with a wicked twinkle in their eyes! Smooth but rough, loose but tight, straight but bent, this piece is like some Chinese puzzle from a Christmas cracker that needs to be pulled apart without forcing the metal components. And Erskine's insistent beat sets a time limit on the operation.

Pat's tune *Wasn't Always Easy* is the antidote to Easy Listening. Slower and with a more child-like melody than its predecessor, it has a deeper, more mysterious mood that demands concentration. Gary's improvisation is in total control of these non-intuitive changes, and he leads the piece forward like a man with a torch on a dark, moonless night. If I have led you to believe that this album is an easy listen, Pat tells us it most certainly is not, especially with a set of imperative chords at the end – the negatives to all those other positives.

The negative is, however, immediately swept aside with Pat's composition, *The Chief*, another PMG tune that isn't. Pat's playing of his own stuff is entirely natural, but we need to remind ourselves just how unique is his sound. But the real freshness is Gary's beautiful entry at 0.42 that blows all stale air from the house like a breeze through an open window. The final fade on suspended chords is an excellent innovation from a writer not especially noted for clever endings.

Tiempos Felice (Happy Times) is another piece by Polo Orti. Again, it is very easy listening, yet there is not a single moment of the lowbrow to be found in this presentation. The final track, also by Orti, is *Quick and Running*, a piece that is like dry sand running through your fingers as you try to close your fist on it. The crystal-sharp theme lasts precisely 23 seconds and is repeated at the start before the band embark on a long orchestrated sequence that includes all the familiar elements of lead solo, bridge sections and theme repeats. Gary plays marimba through this nimble and sporty music that also includes an intriguing thirty-second 'broken glass' linking section. From the start to the crafted coda, this piece is completely beguiling and total entertainment. This track, and most of those that go before it, is joyous and uplifting.

Reunion perfectly portrays the sound that, for the GRP record label of the late 1980s and 1990s, attracted the descriptor 'Smooth Jazz', a rude variant of 'Easy Listening'. It represented a new form of popular music that was rooted in jazz and came out of jazz-fusion. It therefore became the kind of sound that the jazz purists hated. Easy Listening music was dumbed-down, contemptible crap played by artists who had sold their souls to the devil of commercialism. Yet, as we listen carefully to this album and analyse its contents, it is quite clear that nothing could be farther from the truth. The quality of every aspect of it is at the highest level. The album is beautifully recorded, with the highest clarity and presence that provides excellent opportunities to hear everything the musicians do. So often on albums the bass disappears into the background on recordings; not here. You can enjoy the superb playing of Will Lee on every track. Erskine's drumming is perfect for the occasion, whilst Forman shows just why he was in such demand with other top jazzers.

A particularly notable aspect of the sound of the album is how perfectly the sounds of Pat's guitars and Gary's vibes complement each other. This is something of a contrast to the 1970s albums in which it seemed that Pat was trying not to sound like Gary, his electric 12-string taking regions of the tonal spectrum that were different from Gary's. On tunes like *Will You Say You Will*, or *Quick and Running*, for example, Pat and Gary play the complicated but memorable melody in unison, and you need to listen carefully to discern either one. But, when they are not playing unison lines, it's the matching of tonal quality of their instruments that is especially satisfying.

This is a very fine band with a tight togetherness, yet plenty of scope for individuals to shine. Burton called this the most satisfying record he had made in years. [12] That's praise indeed from this jazz master. There is simply no adverse criticism to make about this album. If you like PMG records, you should buy this too. It should be played with generous volume so that its beautiful, fresh tones penetrate deeply – right through to your squishy bits.

De Johnette, Hancock, Holland, Metheny Live in Concert – 1990 (***)

In March 1990, Pat appeared on an album led by drummer Jack de Johnette, along with Herbie Hancock. The Jack de Johnette Trio had played at Woodstock in December 1988 and an album entitled *Parallel Realities* (1989) resulted. The following year, now a quartet supplemented with Dave Holland, they played two concerts at the Philadelphia Academy of Music on 23 June 1990 as part of a world tour during which they promoted Jack's album. A second album, *Parallel Realities Live* (1990) was also released, containing music from the Philadelphia gig.

Excerpts from the Philadelphia gigs were also recorded on a video, now available on an excellent DVD. [14] The video opens with a drum solo introduction from de Johnette. Holland comes on stage first, and the two men create a vamp start to allow the sequential entries of Hancock and Pat for the delivery of the 15-minute piece by Holland entitled *Shadow Dance*. As the title implies, this is a piece with a complex rhythm that is difficult to interpret. The vamp is a kind of medium rock tempo and that leads into a brief exposition of the bop-type theme played by the band and led by Pat on guitar synthesiser. He is soon into a long improvisation on Synclavier. This guitar has become part of Pat's well-known sound for, as he plays it, the output is very dominating at an octave above the pitch of the usual guitar tuning. Hancock joins him on this journey by playing his electronic keyboards and the band develops a very significant tension. Pat repeats the theme to indicate he is done, by which time Herbie is ready on grand piano for his own solo, delivered at double time in a fiercely swinging rhythm. After a long modal solo, Pat returns and the band revisit the theme for a final time before finishing as tightly as any band could.

The second track is *Indigo Dreamscapes*, a composition by Jack with a Latin rhythm that demands that Holland takes up the electric bass – unusually. Pat uses his maple Ibanez. The music is a very pleasant, non-complicated piece of Latin jazz typical of the rich melodic period at the end of the 80s, and the band makes light work of it, whilst playing with verve and polish. Hancock's work on Steinway grand is especially slick, while Holland plays efficiently on his second instrument. Jack is, of course, never stretched on this one.

Nine Over Reggae is just what it says: a reggae rhythm with a 9/8 basic time signature. Written jointly by Jack and Pat this is, of course, a contradiction in terms because reggae is strictly formulaic. This is a far more challenging piece that is delightfully fresh in rhythm and easy listening to boot.

Solar was fresh in the heads of Pat and Dave from the album *Question and Answer* (1990) so it was not hard for Herbie and Jack to run with it too, and that's just what they do, delivering a fast (250 bpm) modal mainstream form. Dave Holland and Jack both get a chance to show their skills on this one with significant solo breaks that really fly.

Silver Hollow is another number by Jack. This beautiful gentle ballad starts with an unaccompanied intro on amplified acoustic guitar. Pat switches from full finger-picking to using a pick quickly taken from his teeth as the band comes in behind him. After Pat's solo, Herbie plays a solo on his Yamaha DX7.

The Good Life is by Ornette Coleman, a number that Pat and Jack worked together on for their album with Ornette, *Song X* (1986). Herbie leads the band in with a couple of notes from his tin pans synth sound. This is a tune with a strong Caribbean flavour and is quite melodic and not like what we might expect of Coleman. With Pat on Synclavier, Herbie opens with an acoustic piano solo that bounces along joyfully until Pat takes a turn. Jack gets a solo at the end before a final delivery of the theme with Herbie straddling piano and synthetic pans.

Blue is a slower, more serious piece by Jack with a traditional jazz quartet sound and Pat playing his Ibanez. Though not a 12-bar blues, it is strongly in the blues tradition. This is followed by Hancock's *Hurricane*, which does have a 12-bar structure and is delivered at a characteristic high wind speed of 290 bpm that puts everyone into a sequence of rapid solos, first Herbie, then Pat and Dave. Few bassists could cope with the speed of this piece for an improvisation and Holland is quite superb, literally blowing everybody away! De Johnette completes the solo sections with a series of 12s where he alternates with the band, Herbie and Pat each alternating, on each repetition of the 12-bar theme. He never loses his timing in these conditions, as is often the case when drummers do long solos. Finally Herbie straps on his own guitar-slung yellow keyboard and comes in with a synth trumpet sound, yet just once before returning to the piano for the ending. Jack performs a final cadenza on his Sonor kit at the end of this piece, which must have made him sweat.

The Bat is the penultimate number played on Ibanez. It's an old Metheny favourite in a beautiful new arrangement for quartet delivered as a slow straight-ahead jazz piece. Herbie takes a very thoughtful solo on piano and the band delivers a superb piece of quartet jazz. Pat's clever use of a foot pedal adds a lovely effect in the final re-run of the theme.

The final track is Herbie's *Cantaloupe Island* with Pat taking the theme on synth and Herbie starting out on piano. Herbie gets first solo, then Pat. By the time the final theme returns Herbie is playing his funky synthesiser. It's a grand finale finish to a grand concert. As the postcards are supposed to say, I wish I was there.

Pat Metheny Group: The Road to You – 1991 (****)

In 1991, Pat and the band went on a summer tour of Europe and the United States; it had already become a common event and there would be many more. The last PMG recording was now two years old, and Pat had been busy with his "other stuff", so the time was good for a *Letter from Home* Tour, splashed with some tracks from *Still Life (Talking)* and a few new tunes. The album entitled *The Road to You* was the result.

The band consisted of Pat, Lyle and Steve, with Paul Wertico, Pedro Aznar and Armando Marçal. All of the gigs were recorded in July 1991 during the European phase of the tour and the best material selected to produce a coherent package from the band's dates in Bari, Pescara and Jesi in Italy, and Marseilles, Paris and Besançon, France. The recording quality is excellent and the editing is so homogeneous that the splicing is almost unnoticeable.

Have You Heard is the opening track on *Letter From Home*. It has become one of a number of band 'anthems' – pieces that are strongly associated with the PMG by many listeners. As an opener for this album too, it is perfect, Lively, lyrical and uplifting, it never fails to please, and the recording quality does great justice to the band's top quality performance of it. Then comes *First Circle*, one of the Group's truly magnificent achievements, with immense scope and intense musical drama. It was the piece that won Pat his first Grammy and it is as fresh and beautiful today as when it was written. For a live recording, this is a remarkable version that loses nothing whatsoever from its studio version. Indeed, many listeners may feel that, with the benefit of ten years of life, the piece has taken on an even greater standing with this version. Pedro's vocals are impeccable and the skill with which Lyle controls such an array of keyboards to produce the massive sound is amazing.

The Road To You is a very gentle ballad in which Pat plays his luscious Spanish acoustic guitar to Lyle's gentle accompaniment with some deft brushwork from Paul. The title describes exactly the kind of idea being expressed by the music. Then comes a piece of grand vision. *Half Life of Absolution* is a darker composition that explores some of music's more extreme tonalities. Whilst not entirely stepping off the harmonic stairway, the music is challenging and needs close consideration as it develops its inky imagery. After a period of contemplative group improvisation sustained by atmospheric percussion, Pat outlines the case for his defence from 2.50, a plaintiff cry for help that receives short shrift from 4.00. He repeats his arguments more vociferously from around 5.20, trying to justify his actions with ever more philosophical arguments, but who is listening? Lyle then takes up the challenge with all the energy he can muster until Pat screams to be heard one more time. The drama of outpouring from Pat's Synclavier is utterly breathtaking and that audience realises that it has been witness to a special event.

Last Train Home from *Still Life (Talking)* was a very popular piece by this time and, played quite straight with Pat's 'sitar guitar' sound, the fans clearly enjoyed this one very much. It would feature in many more gigs to come.

Better Days Ahead is another of the truly joyful PMG pieces that brings smiles to faces and a twinkle to the eye. It's played quite straight here, although Pat and Lyle play some variations that are most welcome. It's a challenging tune to sing, but worth every second of the effort.

Naked Moon is another of Pat's ballads, this time played with electric guitar. Starting out more or less solo, the music develops along usual Methenyesque lines and acquires a *soupçon* of energy from his colleagues before lapsing to a quiet ending once more.

Beat 70 is played with some interesting variations that freshen it significantly, not least of which is Lyle using a steel drum sound as well as his harmonica clone. The opportunity to play some fresh licks in the solo sections is also not wasted and the result is a really good energetic track that is significantly different from its older brother.

The beautiful title track, *Letter From Home*, is played with great feeling and delicacy. The audience is clearly in total symbiosis with the band for, as the piece grows ever quieter at the end, the fans are so quiet that you could hear a pensioner's pacemaker.

Third Wind is also taken from *Still Life (Talking)*, another up-tempo piece that has formed the backbone of the PMG brand. Pat uses the same clever fast chromatic run to introduce his solo and then develops it vigorously. The fast and highly syncopated mid-section that begins at 3.12 is a joy whenever it is played and we need to be reminded just how innovative and skilful this long section is. This moves into an even deeper section at 5.12 as Lyle takes us into the final theme. Pat begins with it in skeleton form at 6.01 and then it just grows and grows into ecstatic climax. Normally this could have been the grand finale to a great gig.

At the end of the European tour, the band returned to the USA where, in Boston on 29 July – 2 Aug, a video was made that was given the title *More Travels*. Although still obtainable, it is now very scarce. A solo piece that Pat recorded in Boston was added as the final track to *The Road to You*.

Pat Metheny: *Secret Story* – 1992 (*****)

Secret Story is not a PMG album, but it might as well be. This is a truly remarkable project in which Pat joins up with a cohort of his favourite musicians, such as Lyle and Steve, Charlie Haden, Nana Vasconcelos, Armando Marçal and many others. There is also the London Orchestra under the direction of Jeremy Lubbock. With such a grand scale of working, Pat now begins to work closely with keyboardist Gil Goldstein, who has a great capacity for production, large-scale arrangements and the generation of sheet music. Gil will become an important member of the Metheny Group Productions team over the coming years, and a lot of work will be with Michael Brecker's future projects.

Pat Metheny has said that this album is a themed or 'suite' album, but the precise nature of the story being told seems to be, as they say, secret. It's not too hard to build your own interpretation, though, and most involve love affairs with unhappy endings. You can get the gist of them for yourself by surveying the track titles. Whether they relate to Pat himself we don't know, but we might presume that they do. We have discovered that Pat is master of impressionist jazz and we can expect to find plenty of hints about the ideas behind the music from the (mostly) helpful track titles. We know Pat has spent a lot of time in the Far East and perhaps it was here that he finally became torn between the rigours of constant touring and the love of a woman. It might even be that he has to decide from a choice of two. There is plenty of scope for speculation...

Whatever the reality, the theme of the album has given rise to some of the finest music and some of the sweetest Metheny melodies. Before you listen to this album I sincerely suggest that you save it for a quiet 75 minutes or so at dusk when you know you will not be disturbed. Turn off the phone. Relax and close your eyes. As the darkness falls, you will experience the most superb atmosphere as the real beauty of this music envelops you.

Above the Treetops sets the scene for this album in the most wonderful way possible. Using voices from a Cambodian choir, the exquisite Western melody is perfectly blended with the sounds of the East. The voices sound like children, and the image of Cambodian children singing so beautifully, especially given the terrible history of their country, gives the piece added poignancy. The backing is orchestral – conductor Jeremy Lubbock has been employed throughout to conduct the musicians – and Pat's acoustic guitar melody is, as always, quite special.

Facing West is another premier league Metheny song that will have you singing along with it in no time. At first, it feels as if we are back out on the prairies of cowboy country. Perhaps we are, but Pat's use of a sitar sound tends to indicate that we are still out east. Later, Pat plays some good solid electric guitar improvisations and Lyle accompanies him on acoustic piano, although the music is essentially orchestral. Whatever, it's a Big Country sound, reminiscent of great Hollywood movies with happy endings. At this point early in the album, the mood is optimistic and the music is uplifting and very beautiful.

Cathedral in a Suitcase is an enigmatic title for a most interesting track. The music seems to be a superposition of two themes, one a faster rhythmic clockwork sound in the background, the other a slow melody played on what sounds like harmonica but is a synthesiser. First one dominates, then the other, and the piece is a constant competition between the two. A kind of urgency or tension is created as the piece proceeds that is unsettling. In the seconds from 2.30 to 3.15, there are echoes of voices and other sounds that imply that all is not well. At 3.15, a new phase begins in which the orchestra comes in for a calming flourish, but the tick-tocking background continues throughout and has the final say as the track fades. This is an indicator of a similar effect of tension building used much later in PMG's *The Way Up*, although by then it has become even more sophisticated.

Finding and Believing continues the Eastern theme once more as Pat picks up what the sleeve notes describe as 'electric sitars', presumably one at a time. This is an extremely clever piece that once again combines a number of parallel effects. The rhythm is generally a complex seven beat backing, set up with some excellent Eastern percussion and voices. Starting with just one or two instruments, more and more are added slowly, almost like the extra vocal parts come in during the singing of 'rounds' like the kids' song *Frère Jacques*. By the time that the frantic array of mixed contributions has been established, the song is ready for something else. This occurs in the form of a high-pitched vocal melody, again delivered in the style of a Cambodian or Vietnamese street musician, otherwise known as Mark Ledford who joined PMG for several albums at this point. The overall effect is a fantastic oriental groove, probably the first on record. At 2.14 a short break occurs in the proceedings only to return almost immediately to the groove, which is actually most welcome. Another break occurs at 3.33 and this time we are left alone and uneasy, as if we have fallen through an open manhole into the dark underground sewer system beneath the streets. The orchestra searches for light through the maze of tunnels as we hear echoes of the percussion band above somewhere. We fight our way through the rat-infested maze looking for the ray of light that will lead us to the exit and back to our friends. As we turn a corner, the effect is pretty much instant at 6.45. We come right out into the light of the summer's day and soon rejoin our street band. The singers are glad to see us again and sing a new song of welcome. Pat picks up his electric guitar and celebrates with a burst of clean, delightful improvisation that leads the rest, Pied Piper-like, away into the distance.

The interpretation of *The Longest Summer* is that we have the central love song of the entire album, the main statement for the love affair that dominates the theme. It is, therefore, a very beautiful melody played by Pat on acoustic piano, of all instruments. Steve Rodby and Paul Wertico join too for the early phase of the song. At 1.27, Pat adopts the familiar practice of changing to his guitar synth to create one of his classic improvisations that unhurriedly builds a climax. However, on this occasion, there seems to be trouble ahead for by 3.20 all is not well. The optimism of the music is replaced by a melancholic theme that works hard to dispel the doubts and slowly rebuilds the confidence we all want to see in the relationship. By 5.10, he seems to have achieved it, for back he comes with his beautiful screaming guitar, proclaiming his love as never before.

With love now well and truly in the air, it is natural to have some cameo tracks depicting the ups and downs of the relationship. *Sunlight* is a song of people deeply in love. It's happiness that only lovers know about. It's walks in the country and picnics under trees on hot summer days. This track would put a smile on the face of a Scotsman! Just sit back and absorb this wonderful music.

Rain River is monsoon, hot, humid rain forest. The air is filled with mosquitoes and the smell of dank atmosphere. Everything is hard in these conditions. Even the simplest journeys become energy-sapping as each step through the treacly mud underfoot becomes a trial of strength. Westerners take time to acclimatise to this. The music is brilliant in conveying the imagery. And even amidst such taxing terrain, Pat still finds plenty of room for good melody.

It's hard to imagine how music can get any better after some tracks I've described, but it does in *Always and Forever*. The title gives an indication of the depth of sincerity that Pat wants to convey at this point. Wow! Does he succeed! The track is an acoustic guitar anthem to love with one of the finest of all melodies in the style of *If I Could* from *First Circle*. With Steve Rodby and Paul Wertico completing the trio, Pat has the full orchestra at his back and then another wonderful masterstroke is pulled out from his bag when Toots Thielmans comes in to give one of his delicious harmonica solos midway through. This is a very, very fine piece of music.

In the track *See the World* it seems as if enforced separation is now in play whilst some business trips are made. The sound is certainly part of the classic PMG brand with an up-tempo bright outlook that encompasses expansive terrain. Pat now employs some extensive brass sounds as well as the orchestra and the budget is rising fast, but who cares? This music is worth every penny.

The track *As a Flower Blossoms (I am Running to You)* seems clearly to be describing the woman's side of the story, lovesick and lonely. A very rare touch is Pat's use of a female vocalist Akiko Yano to express the emotions. A short track, it is beautiful and sentimental. It is also the first obvious appearance of Pat's remarkable 42-string Pikasso guitar.

Antonia invites us for the first time to attach a name to the female image, but the contradiction is that from the preceding song we have been given the impression of a beautiful oriental lady. The imagery here is breaking down... *Antonia* is another love song, presented with completely different tones and colour. An accordion is the instrument of choice, played of course on a synthesiser. Perhaps we are being presented with a third party, a complication in the relationship? There's a lot going on inside this song – a lot of different parts, and a lot of themes. You can therefore have a lot of fun unravelling them.

The depression begins with this song. *The Truth Will Always Be* implies inevitability, a sense of the passage of time and the hopelessness that is sometimes associated with the ticking of the clock when you know that bad times lie ahead. The music is nerve-tingling. We sense the intensity of the beauty before us, but we now know that whatever was longed for in the early tracks is now impossible. The lines are awash with pain, but presented in unashamed beauty and passion. The desolation is felt all the more as the drum crash presents us with the final decision. The orchestra is becoming ever dominant and it is only a matter of time before Pat comes on stage to tell us just how shattered he is by what he now knows to be true. His screaming guitar is gut-wrenching. We just want to weep in sympathy for him.

By the time we get to *Tell Her You Saw Me* we know that it is all over. Here is the sheer anguish, the pain in the deepest recesses of your chest that makes you want to shout aloud. She's so real in your head, but you'll never see her again. Yet, how can you blame her? How can you feel hatred? Your memory plays tricks. First you see her clearly, then you don't. Why can't you picture the colour of her eyes? Why can't you remember the feel of her hair? My God, she is so, so beautiful!

The compassionate thing would have been to end the album here, but Pat now puts us through yet more anguish. *Not to be Forgotten (Our Final Hour)* is the memorial track. The pain is at last beginning to dissipate and the sky is starting to turn from grey to blue. A small crescendo reminds us of the love there once was, but now we must face the challenges ahead.

It is impossible not to award this album five stars. There are several tracks that could merit the ultimate accolade so I am going to just lay down my judge's clipboard and submit unconditionally to the achievements of Pat Metheny at this point. It seems a million miles away from the Miles Davis fusion of *Bitches Brew* – and it is. It's as if the Davis music was the stuff of the Universe at its birth, formless and ugly, but the primeval ingredients and precursor to the life on Earth that is Pat's music. Pat encapsulates everything that makes that life so wonderful.

What exactly is the achievement on this album? Well, Pat conceived the entire project and all of the music, which included a large amount of fabulous melody. He conceived the original arrangements, which includes the choice of instrumentation, a lot of which is original. If there are echoes of PMG music here, well he's entitled to do that since he originated that too. The fusion of eastern and western musical styles is beautifully executed. We could argue about how original it is. Oh, and he also played some pretty good guitar improvisations. Although he did not physically write out the charts for the musicians and he did not actually arrange the orchestral parts, he did direct the process, which was according to his own musical ideas. And finally, he produced the album. The result is a recording that is not everyone's idea of a jazz record, or perhaps of a fusion record. There's no obvious swing or blues, but there is plenty of wonderful rhythm, colour and texture, as well as improvised electronically generated music. Whether we like it or not, *Secret Story* is jazz and it is fusion. Stan Getz recorded wonderful melodies with orchestral backing, so did Charlie Parker. John Coltrane recorded ballads and metaphorically claimed ownership of popular songs like *My Favourite Things*. The parallels with Miles Davis's album *Miles Ahead* are clear and Pat's overall achievement here is greater than was Davis's. It is important to develop a clear idea of the relative contributions of the two musicians when discussions of greatness are in the air. It is far too easy to repeat the mantra that "Miles Davis is the greatest..." for nobody argues with you, but we don't need to wait until Pat is dead to appreciate his greatness in the field of jazz; we can go to his gigs now and appreciate the wonderful music he makes for exactly what it is – very, very special.

You might wonder where else there is to go from here. It is 1992 and Pat has succeeded in producing one of the most beautiful albums ever recorded. Relax, for there is more to come – a lot more!

Gary Thomas: Till We Have Faces – 1992 (***)

Gary Thomas (b1961) came to prominence playing with drummer Jack de Johnette's Special Edition in 1984. Through that gig, he was invited to play with Miles Davis, and he made numerous appearances at gigs, but did not appear on record with Davis. Forced to choose between the two leaders when there was a clash of dates, Thomas chose de Johnette and remained with him for nine years in total. As a leader himself, he has not recorded prolifically. He is perhaps best known for a short spell in John McLaughlin's band, The Heart of Things in 1997-8. Today, Thomas has opted for the life of an academic as a professor of jazz studies at the Peabody Institute – part of the Johns Hopkins University in his hometown of Baltimore, Maryland. It's a case of quality, not quantity where Thomas is concerned. His appearances frequently inspire listeners to remember his name as a saxophone player of special abilities. On this, one of his rare projects as leader, the album delivers an unusual musical experience.

Pat Metheny plays on all but one of the eight tracks of this album, recorded in May 1992. The band is small and tight, with the excellent Terri Lyne Carrington (drums), Tim Murphy (piano) and acoustic bass alternating between Anthony Cox and Ed Howard. The sounds could hardly be farther in style and feel from the kind we have found on *Secret Story*. This is music for storm troopers, not store keepers. The selections are all fairly well known jazz standards, but, although there may be a few familiar sounds, don't play this at a cocktail party. This album should be sold with a licence, as it's for suitable only for those authorised to carry light-sabres. It is therefore in considerable contrast, for example, to Pat's album with Joshua Redman on *Wish* (1993), music that is far more appropriately matched with couth cocktails.

Thomas's approach seems to have been to take a selection of fairly well-known but not overplayed standards and to push them to the very edge of the known galaxy where, in harmonies and textures distorted by gravity, they take on entirely new characteristics. There's the possibility of a clash between acoustic piano and electric guitar when trying this sort of approach with this combination of instruments, but Pat takes care not to let this happen, and in any case, the group of players gathered here is not interested in gin and tonic music.

Pat's electric sounds on this album are more Hendrix than Hall and, despite the fact that the band is classifiable as acoustic, they all do their best to lurch towards some kind of anarchy at most available opportunities. Hence, Pat restricts himself to a blistering solo on track 1 *Angel Eyes*, while Tim Murphy's piano remains free to explore space-time unhindered. Thomas sets out his stall perfectly and makes us sit up at once with his hard-hitting lines.

The pianist sits out on track 2, Irving Berlin's *The Best Thing For You*, allowing Pat to play all through. Again, this is Berlin like you've rarely heard him before. Track 3 is the beautiful song *Lush Life*, a duet between Pat's acoustic guitar and Thomas playing what sounds very much like alto instead of the listed tenor instrument. It's a rare chance to relax from the fray that starts again on track 4, the familiar *Bye Bye Baby*. Clash is again avoided where Pat takes only the solo and some very gentle accompaniment towards the end.

J J Johnson's *Lament* is about as honest a description as the New Orleans funeral scene in the James Bond film *Live and Let Die*. This very energetic piece has Pat once again replacing Tim on piano. Terri Lyne Carrington flails impressively to this one, whilst Thomas's soprano sax sounds far too nice for the bad-boy sounds Pat induces from the rest of the band.

Thomas plays flute for Horace Silver's *Peace*, opening up with an *ad lib* with Anthony Cox, then lapsing into a 6/8 Latin tempo, this time with piano and Pat playing together whilst carefully avoiding stepping on each others' toes. Apart from *Lush Life*, this is the only track that remains calm.

Pat sits out for track 7, the impressively frantic *It's You or No One*, played as a trio. Ed Howard kicks off with a very spunky bass solo to Carrington's driving accompaniment. Then Thomas comes in for some three-way banter, sparring with drums and bass in a bout that's as combative as a fight scene from *House of Flying Daggers*.

The last track is *You Don't Know What Love Is*, played as a five-piece with Pat adding decoration with another acidic electric sound on his guitar synthesiser. Pat's playing on this and throughout the album is mostly hard and gutsy, with new guitar sounds that once again introduce an entirely new characteristic to his repertoire. With the exception of the superbly resonant duet that makes up Billy Strayhorn's *Lush Life* at track three, this is almost an experimental run-out for Pat as he tests some of the sounds he uses less often. The novel juxtaposition of Pat's coarse chain-saw sounds against the smooth acoustic bark is risqué, but works for me. However you feel about the balance of sounds, it is remarkable just how frequently Pat is able to conjure up new ways of playing the guitar that never arouse that disappointing feeling of *déjà vu*. Miles Davis would surely have been proud of Pat's performance on this album, but it will not be every listener's choice of drink.

All of the musicians are exciting on this album, but perhaps the most impressive performance is from Terri Lyne Carrington who instantly dispels any prejudices storm troopers might have towards female drummers. Her contributions are testy, creative and always appropriate, and if you were told it was Dennis Chambers you were listening to you would not be disappointed.

In this project, the polite, compliant jazz quintet playing standards at a cocktail party at Caesar's Palace has packed away its instruments. Instead it has a short residency in the Empire lounge of *Star Wars'* Death Star. Though I myself could not get a ticket, I feel that they must have brought the house down, and I would not be surprised to know that Darth Vader picked up a copy of the CD at the merchandising booth on his way out to destroy the Earth. Or did he join the queue for a new face? Pat's presence had a lot to do with that. He's got much to answer for!

Joshua Redman: Wish – 1993 (***)

If you are looking for an album with that dark-smokey-jazz-club feel – something that's middle-of-the-road easy listening jazz – then this is it. Indeed, the last two tracks are actually recorded in the Village Vanguard, its atmosphere, no doubt, (at the time) extremely smokey! Charlie Haden and Billy Higgins join Joshua and Pat to play through a collection of pieces that is mostly ordinary, although there are some good moments. This was Redman's second album as a leader, the other being *Joshua Redman* (1993). Redman (b1969) had won the Thelonius Monk International Jazz Saxophone competition in 1991 and had clearly already made a name for himself as a top-flight player. This album contains pieces ranging across a wide spectrum from Ornette Coleman's *Turnaround*, to Stevie Wonder's *Make Sure You're Sure* and a delightful version of Eric Clapton's *Tears in Heaven* played as a duet with Pat on acoustic guitar. Charlie Parker is also represented with *Moose the Mooche*, a tune that Pat sits out from. Bearing in mind the extreme difficulty of playing classic bop pieces like this, Joshua knocks it off as if he is still warming up. The remainder of the selections are tunes contributed by members of the band. Redman composed *Soul Dance*, *The Deserving Many*, and *Wish*, whilst Pat contributed *We Had a Sister* and *Whittlin'*. The album ends with a spirited version of Charlie's *Blues for Pat*.

There is no doubt that Joshua is a superb player. The listener is left with the immediate impression that he is completely in control of his instrument and the sprinkling of embellishments he throws into the mix ranges from the comic to the amazing. Playing the melody in harmonics, as he does towards the end of *Wish*, is extraordinarily difficult, whilst I laughed out loud at the brilliant little motif he played at 2 minutes on *Whittlin'*. His tone throughout is warm and huggy, in the style of Stan Getz, and, to complement him, Pat adopts a similar sound throughout on his Ibanez.

Redman is still only about 24 years old at this point in time and although his sound and technique is clearly exceptional, his vision of the way ahead for his career is still only at the level of an average player. (This will be rectified at the end of the 1990s when he begins to take on some very serious challenges and is involved with some exciting innovations.)

Joshua Redman Quartet: Blues for Pat – 1995 (*)

An album in which Pat plays live with the brilliant saxophonist Joshua Redman is quite irresistible to collectors like me. The trouble is that this is almost certainly what is known as a bootleg – an unauthorised recording. Members of the audience often make bootlegs using a single, poorly positioned microphone. They are usually characterised by irregular and varied sound quality that ranges from good to inaudible and this is no exception. Discs may also vary from one copy to another of the same album because of poor quality control during manufacture. The final characteristic is inaccurate or non-existent sleeve notes and on this album the second piece is incorrectly labelled *Sketches*. (It is actually *Question and Answer*.) Bootlegging is, of course, an illegal practice and an infringement of copyright. It is presumably because of this kind of practice, along with the simple illegal copying of genuinely issued albums, that Pat's record company has, in recent years, gone to considerable trouble to use new kinds of packaging for Pat's albums.

All this is a great pity, for Pat's presence in this quartet is of great interest to us and the band was performing superbly for this gig, recorded in San Francisco in 1994 when Pat was 40 years old. Published by Jazz Door, an outfit that has many other jazz titles, this is a very poor recording, with most of Christian McBride's bass solos almost inaudible. The microphone was probably situated closest to drummer Billy Higgins, for his sound is close and rarely affected. The performances of Pat and Joshua, the two main characters, are remarkable nonetheless, despite variable quality. Joshua, son of Dewey, who Pat also played alongside on his album *80/81* (1980),

The real highlight of many on the album is the soloing during the classic Sonny Rollins number *St. Thomas*. In a stunning solo introduction to the piece, Redman plays his own bass line accompaniment whilst improvising West Indian calypso in the upper registers and varying the key signature throughout. This amazing feat of playing succeeds in inspiring Pat to play out of his skin for his own solo, which he does with a strong rock guitar sound that is unusual in his repertoire. Unfortunately, like the other tracks, this great track is marred by serious sound deficiencies in places, but gems like these are the reasons why fans like me must buy these unofficial discs.

Bruce Hornsby

In 1993, Pat took part in some recordings made at Bruce Hornsby's home and which eventually appeared on Bruce's album *Harbor Lights* (1994). Hornsby had recently installed the recording facilities in his house and was enjoying the fun of using them. Principally involved were John Molo, the drummer from his own band and Jimmy Haslip, the brilliant electric bassist of the band Yellowjackets. Jimmy, however, was also fascinated by the processes of making music and was involved with the entire process of making this record. In the notes, Hornsby wrote about how he and Pat had talked for so long about doing something together and how they had finally achieved it on this record. Pat's role was limited to playing in the background on four tracks: *Harbor Lights*, *Talk of the Town*, *Chinatown* and *The Tide Will Rise*, although he did play some significant solos. Later, in 1995, the episode was repeated and Pat recorded more material for Hornsby's album *Hot House* (1996), which apart from Molo and Haslip once again, this time included Béla Fleck and Chaka Khan. Pat's appearances were on five tracks this time, *White Wheeled Limousine*, *Walk in the Sun*, *The Changes*, *Country Doctor* and *The Longest Night*.

John Scofield, Pat Metheny: I Can See Your House from Here – 1994 (****)

John Scofield (b1951) is, of course, best known for his membership of Miles Davis's band from 1982-86 during the second part of Davis's jazz-fusion career. He appeared on *Star People* (1983), *Decoy* (1983) and *You're Under Arrest* (1985). Besides being a graduate of the Berklee Music College in Boston, John had first played with Chet Baker and Gerry Mulligan, but made his first mark in jazz-fusion with the Billy Cobham/ George Duke band. He became a member of Gary Burton's band just after Pat left. Naturally, John got to know Steve Swallow during this time and formed a trio with him and Adam Nussbaum (drums) in 1979. Bill Stewart replaced Nussbaum in that trio and the three men established a strong reputation with albums like *Shinola* (1981) and *Electric Outlet* (1984). It was this trio that joined up with Pat Metheny for a great album that is insufficiently recognised.

The opening track, *I Can See Your House From Here*, is a very remarkable piece that is difficult to describe. One of the obvious features is in Steve Swallow's electric bass that is continually rising – seemingly at random – through chromatic sequences of variable length and starting note. Like many of the top guitarists, John's sound that, at first, make you wonder if his equipment is working properly – if there is a loose wire somewhere or a dodgy transistor perhaps? On top of that, his phrasing and punctuation is often fractured in a kind of musical stutter, and the combination of distortion in both his human and electronic delivery gives him a sound that is instantly recognisable. So, in the first track, we at once hear both of these characteristics, the melody superficially appearing to be conventional and catchy but never quite settling into anything solid, whilst Steve Swallow is doing his best to drive the music around in random circles with his peculiar constructions. Pat, meanwhile, is also doing his best to provide a totally matching sound to John's and the result is really quite spooky.

The second track is the first appearance of the excellent piece called *The Red One*, which appears some fifteen years later on *Day Trip* (2008). It's an energetic jazz-rock piece with a straightforward structure, played here with two delightfully complementary rock guitar sounds.

No Matter What is a composition by Sco that, for once, is conventionally harmonic, in waltz time and is a real pleasure to listen to. Steve Swallow's well-recorded electric bass now comes properly to the fore and his playing is constantly inventive and sprightly as he takes on a solo that starts in the upper register and gradually finds its way down to the sonorous reaches of the basement. Bill Stewart's brushes make a playful accompaniment alongside. Sco's playing, as usual is characterised by the random way in which his notes emerge with distortion attached.

Everybody's Party is a very simple piece that is primarily a monochordal vamp. The theme is blues-rock in style and played over a jazz rhythm and the drone constrains Steve to a very narrow range of repeated notes as John and Pat let go. There's a cute little middle eight that breaks the monotony and listen out for some unusual guitar giggles at the end.

Message to My Friend is by Pat, a piece that he says was written with Charlie Haden in mind. It makes an appearance on Charlie and Pat's album *Beyond the Missouri Sky* (1997) that was recorded a few later. This version is great for it presents Sco in way that is quite unusual. The quartet is acoustic, with Steve playing an acoustic bass guitar and Sco on steel-stringed acoustic; Pat plays a nylon-stringed acoustic guitar. The luxurious, sound and rich melodies are a real treat.

Track six is *No Way Jose*, another of John's full-on modal assaults. There's some clever interplay between the two guitars during the theme.

Say the Brother's Name is a beautiful piece that has a gentler melody with a kind of Latin rhythm that could be described as a shuffle. Again, Sco plays his acoustic guitar, which now makes a nice contrast with Pat's standard Jim Hall sound, whilst Steve Swallow plays acoustic bass guitar. This is the first appearance of one of Pat's fine pieces that appears much later on *Metheny Mehldau* (2006). By the time we reach the grand ending, it is beginning to feel as if Pat is totally dominating the proceedings. It seems unfair to even think it, because Sco is a very fine guitarist, but so far on this album at least he has chosen a number of modal pieces with harmonies that are generally foreign to the human soul, whilst Pat is delivering things that are more heart-friendly.

In the next piece, however, now it is Pat's turn to supply a modal piece in John's compositional style, and somehow I am left with the impression that he is turning on the style in a way that leaves Sco trailing in his wake. S.C.O. is a truly crazy piece that is clearly nodding at Sco in its very title, and even when Metheny brings in a tune in Scofield's style, he is still the dominant figure. The structure is quite startling for there is a churning of harmony here that leaves the listener breathless. It is quite incredible how musicians can solo over something so fluid.

After losing our puff, we are let down very gently for *Quiet Rising*, another of Pat's pensive slow numbers. It's not really accurate to call it a ballad as this is hardly a song presented by one lover to another. Again it is presented with a series of evolving chords from the electric quartet. Pat allows himself a few excursions into PMG territory as he explores its deeper recesses. And then, just as we think the song is at its end, from about 4.35, there is a quite exquisite ensemble effect that is over far too quickly.

With *One Way to Be*, Sco is back on track with another of his modal pieces in a fast swing time, yet once again it is Pat who demonstrates a total mastery of the musical environment. His sheer versatility, both in sound and style, as well as the ability to conjure novel improvisations at a time when he is playing compositions written by other musicians is surely unparalleled.

The final track is *You Speak My Language*, which is a 'bent' blues from Scofield. The characteristic of the melody is that, having chosen a starting scale, it simply keeps sliding around from one to another like a penguin on an ice flow. Then it's off into the solos, with Pat first. In such a popular but well-worn musical setting, he could so easily slip into strings of clichés, but no. Pat's solo is novel and closely related to Scofield's wrinkled melodic structure. He does throw in a couple of his own quotations, however, with a quick nod to *Bright Size Life* at 1.55 and an occasional PMG echo, but in such a classic scenario, it is remarkable how Pat refuses to take the standard approach. Sco, on the other hand, does exactly what is expected, albeit with panache, and develops a strong blues sound that by 3.30 is close to rock. Steve Swallow wallows in the luxury of playing lines he grew up playing and takes a bass solo alongside Bill Stewart that is superbly rhythmic. Then it's back two the two guitars, jousting playfully in fours with a final frolic that blues always invokes amongst jazzers having fun.

This is a very good album that contains music so varied that the seventy minutes of content is quickly over as you eagerly anticipate what's next. I believe it provides firm evidence of just how good Pat Metheny is as a jazz musician. Normally, there is a lot of clear water between the styles and sounds of these two guitarists. Scofield uses a sound that is quite some distance from the mainstream of electric guitar with a heavy reliance on distortion and a hesitant delivery. Throughout this album, it is Pat who continuously builds bridges across to John, both in guitar sound and also in style of play. It's a clear sign of the way that Pat listens so much to his playing partner of the moment and responds to what is going on. I have always been a fan of John Scofield, and greatly respect his abilities as a musician and composer. However, on this album, Pat is so dominant in all respects that Sco is made to look like a second league player. He is not. It's just that Pat is so very, very good.

The Dark Side

Try to imagine the horror that Luke Skywalker must have felt when he discovered that Darth Vader was his father. Well, that's just about the same way I felt when I discovered Pat Metheny's dark side. All the finest ambitions I have for music are realised in Pat's music and in these pages I have been trying to explain why. According to my theory, the antithesis is to be found in two albums that Pat recorded in the mid 1990s. The first is called *Zero Tolerance for Silence* (1994). This is a solo album with five tracks under the heading of Parts 1 to 5 that have been described as "semi-organised noise". Listening to it, I would question whether there was any organisation at all, but I must respect the opinion of someone who has the patience to analyse this material. I don't. The album is unashamedly included in Pat's official discography, though it gets virtually no public attention. The second album is even stranger. *The Sign of 4* (1996) is a quartet recording with British *avant-garde* guitarist Derek Bailey and percussionists Gregg Bendian and Paul Wertico. There are three CDs to this pornographic release, with titles in order: *The Science of Deduction*, *The Balance of Probability* and *In Quest of a Solution*. The first and last discs are live recordings, whist the second is a studio recording.

It is not difficult to find Internet reviews of these discs, written by enthusiastic listeners. Conclusions about the music are of the kind, "For those who appreciate adventurous, exploratory and experimental music, *The Sign of 4* is an amazing journey into the realms of pure sound" and "In terms of sailing uncharted waters, this album is a complete success."

In writing this book I have tried to adopt a logical approach to music analysis. I believe it is unarguable that music is a complex spectrum of experience covering such factors as melody, harmony, rhythm, form, texture, timbre and pitch. It's like the set of slider controls on a graphic equalizer that range from zero to max and cover all the frequencies from bass to treble. Jazz-fusion has a combination of settings that are high on most of the sliders, but in music such as this, the sliders for melody, harmony, rhythm and form are set very close to zero. Zero form would indicate totally random playing, which this seemingly is not because tell-tale phrases from the reviews talk of "evidence of interaction between the players" and "you can actually hear the players bouncing ideas off each other." Another reviewer said that in one place on one disc there was "a hint of melody" so the melody slider is probably set to 0.1 rather than exactly zero. As for texture, well, given that the guitarists perform their craft by "odd harmonics, pulling and snapping strings and playing behind the bridge of the guitar", whilst the percussionists employ household objects such as "bedposts, egg beaters, plastic packing material, measuring tape", we must presume that the texture sliders, at least, are set close to max.

I should not have been surprised to find this material, for there are plenty of indications in Pat's other albums that it existed, but I cannot help feeling like the teenager that finally realises his parents actually do have sex. Pat has never disguised his views about music and the other albums I have described here contain a number of individual tracks that fall into the category of 'noise'. Even the PMG recording *Quartet* is pretty close to noise in parts.

Scientific analysis helps us to write about music and, more importantly to explain it to others. However, if you subscribe to the idea that music is something that interacts with your soul, it is unsettling, to say the least, that there are people walking the planet who derive pleasure from things that are the exact opposite of beautiful. The slider that is missing so far in this type of analysis is the one for value. It is missing, of course, because it is the one that is not scientific. However, I am quite certain that music such as this has the slider for value set to zero. It is obvious from even the most cursory glance at history that it is art made by the most skilled artisans based upon the principles of beauty and love that has contributed most to the culture of any civilisation. There is no doubt that this rule will continue to apply into the future of mankind and that art with the value slider set at zero is destined for the dustbin of history.

Beauty and love are fundamental parameters in the structure of the Universe, but so are ugliness and hate. Beauty and love created humankind; ugliness and hate are the seeds of its destruction. I will never understand why people prefer to submit themselves to the forces of darkness, but the fact is that some do. Perhaps it is because they do so from the position of security that is available only to those living in a sophisticated society. The surprising point about *The Sign of 4* is that, at the end of the second disc of the live recordings, the audience cheers enthusiastically. As an artist, Pat has every right to explore this part of the musical spectrum, but it is equally surprising that he did not conclude many years ago that this type of effort is valueless. Pat would be the first to know that when you set all the sliders of the graphic equalizer on an amplifier to zero, silence is what comes out. Therefore, he's right in one respect: there should be zero tolerance of silence. Valueless art that is so easy to create is dissipated like confetti in the wind.

Pat Metheny Group: *We Live Here* – 1995 (*****)

The album *We Live Here* is a beautiful example of the PMG getting it together perfectly and I am delighted to give it my five-star award. Every track on the album is a masterpiece of craftsmanship, which, taken together results in a holistic musical experience of the first order. Though it is especially hard to define any clear stages in the development of PMG, it seems to me that this album does represent the beginning of a second era of the band when it took on a new level of sophistication. It may be that the 2005 album *The Way Up*, described below, has marked a new, third phase for the Group, but only time will tell.

The first track *Here to Stay* is an excellent opener that, in common with all of the tracks, has a memorable, singable melody. Writing a great melody is tantalisingly difficult, for it seems to be an unwritten law of musical composition that when a great melody is analysed, it appears to be extremely simple. Let's look at some of the elements that make PMG melodies so great.

A melody is, first of all, a sequential combination of notes. In this case, the introduction is comprised of two phrases of just three notes played on piano. These two phrases form an accompaniment to Pat's guitar melody at first. Later, the three note phrases become the melody that is sung by David Blamires and Mark Ledford. In music, an interval is the size of the musical step between notes, and it is generally the case that small intervals are preferable for good melodies. (This is, as we have seen, the exact opposite of a bebop melody that was frequently built on large intervals.) If you think of any of the truly great melodies, you will find this is true. For example, Bing Crosby's *White Christmas* is one of the world's biggest selling songs. Its melody is composed of notes that move simply, in gentle steps up and down the scale. Another is *Mull of Kintyre* by Paul McCartney. Whether you like these songs or not, the melodies are undeniably attractive, made more so by having memorable lyrics. Indeed, McCartney is unquestionably one of the world's greatest writers of melodies such as *Yesterday* or *Eleanor Rigby*. I was struck by the matter-of-fact way that McCartney reports his writing of some of the world's greatest melodies. [15] To him, it was the simplest thing in the world! I contend that PMG melodies are also some of the best ever recorded. Of course, the only reason why they are not as popular as *White Christmas* or *Mull of Kintyre* is that they have no words. How sad! Why are we so fixated on songs with words? You do not require words to be able to sing a good tune, and most people don't actually know the words to the tunes they sing anyway. It's true that lyrics without music can become wonderful poetry, but that is not true of *White Christmas* or *Mull of Kintyre*. This characteristic of creating not only wonderful music, but great lyrics too is typical of Joni Mitchell and Steely Dan, of course, but is very uncommon in the music business. But the wonderful melodies created by jazz-fusion artists remain largely unknown to the world's population because of their ridiculous fixation on having songs with words. Note that once you add David Bowie singing lyrics to the Metheny/Mays composition *This Is Not America* you have a major hit record that is remembered as a David Bowie record. The same is true with Bill Withers singing *Just the Two of Us* for Grover Washington.

Anyway, I digress. In *Here to Stay* these two phrases could hardly be simpler to sing. However, the musical context in which they are used is more complex. With PMG, one of the secrets to their success with melody is in the voicing of the chords they employ, that is, the way other notes are added to the phrase. Thus the two very simple phrases on piano that begin the track are made of intervals with modest spacing, and transformed into something that is melodically magnetic by the way Mays incorporates the three simple notes of each phrase into chords. The latter element is part of what constitutes the 'colour' of the music and it is in jazz that we find a much greater range of colour than we do in other kinds of music. This is what attracts people like me to jazz, for the colours I hear press my buttons in special ways. The final element is the timing with which the phrases are played, and this is a combination of two things: the number of beats in the bars, and the positioning of the phrase over the beats. It is the way this is done that constitutes part of the genre of fusion music. These two elements are essential ingredients to the style of playing in the genre of jazz-fusion, as also are the textures from the instruments used to create them.

When Pat joins in, the guitar begins another melody that adds superbly well to the accompaniment that Mays has established. It's almost as if two melodies are being played simultaneously. You hear not just one melody but two different ones blended together. You can focus on either, or both, and this helps to provide the variety to the music so that you can play the songs over and over and never get tired of them.

The next detail of the art of constructing a great PMG melody is in the use of different voicings over the same phrase. A simple explanation is required here. Let's take the note G on the piano. This note is the root (the fundamental, or basic, note) of the chord of G major, itself made up of the three notes G, B and D. On the piano keyboard, that has, say, eight octaves, there are eight G-keys, eight B-keys and eight D keys, so there is a lot of choice for playing the chord of G: you can choose any combination of G, B and D keys. Each permutation is a different voice for the chord of G. Of course, there are similar permutations available on the guitar fingerboard, but fewer octaves – usually only three or four, depending on the guitar. And there are restrictions on what the fingers can actually reach.

Now suppose we have a melody that consists of the three notes EFG played consecutively, just as in the first three notes of this song, *Here to Stay*. Suppose G is the last note of the melody. When we play the melody, we could finish on the chord of G major because that is the note we are going to play at that point. However, the note of G is also part of the chord of C major: this chord contains the notes, C, E and G, with C now the root note. In a pop song, or a folk song, or a rock song, it is almost always the case that our three-note melody would be played the same way each time it occurs. Thus it will always finish on the chord of G. It is part of the brand of PMG music to take a phrase or melody and play it in different ways each time. So, PMG might chose to play the melody ending on the chord of G the first time, but ending on the chord of C the second time. I greatly simplify, of course, but I hope you get the gist.

The two phrases are used for the first forty seconds on piano, repeated four times. Then comes a new line based on the phrases but slightly changed, and this is followed by a return to the original phrases. The singers take up the three-note phrases at 1.20, singing them twice. At 1.41 they take the phrase and shift it up slightly. It's a modulation and sounds so natural and fresh. A short fill follows this on Pat's solo guitar that leads into his improvisation. Listen to the way he improvises over the chords that were used to cover those two phrases. The whole piece flows beautifully. The phrases are still there, though somewhat subdued so as not to distract from Pat's playing. This number is a feature for Pat's soloing so it runs through much of the number, repeating over the top of the chord pattern that was established in the first minutes. At 4.20, the song might end, but does not. Another characteristic of PMG compositions that is well demonstrated by *Here to Stay* is that there are always additional sections that are quite different to the rest of the piece. This is rather like having two or more songs in the same piece, all seamlessly stitched together to provide a smooth-flowing piece of rich music. At 4.20 the song enters an entirely new phase in which Lyle, backed up by fantastic rich orchestral sounds, creates a beautiful atmospheric setting. There's a small climax and then we return to the original phrases. We recognise it at once, but this time, the music is somehow enhanced to a new level. It's like the first time was just a practice run; now they're going to do it properly! Now the phrases are used as the main melody and we can sing along to it. The modulation is there as before, but this time, it modulates back down again so that we can cycle through the full melody. Now Pat takes a back seat with his improvisations while we continue to sing the melody over the top. Pat is never afraid of the fade-out ending, but neither is he enslaved to it and he uses it to good effect on this track.

This is of course, only a very simple example. The whole colouring of jazz music involves the use of voicings that we don't find in other genres, but the PMG principle of changing the voicings throughout the course of a piece adds a fabulous layer of complexity. They have great depth because the compositions are not forced to finish after three minutes because it's too boring to play them any longer. If music is really good, you don't want it to finish – that's also the principle of groove writing. Fagen and Becker of Steely Dan are masters of that art. Thus PMG compositions are rarely short. The music bears repetition and is simply so good it never gets boring. It is therefore long-lasting and the earliest albums are as pleasurable to listen to today after thirty years as they were when first released.

The second track *And Then I Knew* is a composition that combines terrific melody with wonderfully rhythmic accompaniment. This tune is a real foot-tapper. The basic harmonic scheme is laid out from the beginning and involves a neat combination of percussive and sustained chords, presented in a tricky little syncopated package. This becomes the backing for Pat's soloing, but as with track one, it later becomes the focus of the whole piece. At 1.12, Lyle enters with a solo on synth that presents a middle section and then the original theme returns. At 2.16, a new section begins that consists of just guitar and synth. It presents a beautiful pastiche of colours before being joined by the rhythm section. It then moves through a long sequence of chord changes that simply evolve in wholly unpredictable directions that leave you breathless. At 4.00 there's a tiny climax. Then, just listen to the descending sequence of chords that begin at 4.10 so as to return us to the original theme. Pat never once stops playing. His fingers flawlessly pick out an amazing string of notes that perfectly match the chords of the descent such that, at 4.18, he returns to the main theme with total precision, ready to carry straight on improvising over the theme. This playing is quite stunning. It continues through to 4.48 when the voices take on the middle section that comes to a good 'big band' crescendo. Then guitar joins in for a final pass through the theme. At 5.55 an entirely new section begins that is brilliant in its rhythmic construction. It darts from bar to bar, changing rhythmic emphasis and key with each change of direction. The final section of the song involves the guitar playing the theme with the voices improvising over the top – a role reversal from before. This is a truly wonderful track, reaching a faded ending after 7.50.

Track three, *The Girls Next Door*, uses a simple muted two-note brassy accompaniment to its straight-ahead jazz melody on Pat's standard-sounding jazz guitar. Laid back, almost to the horizontal, this tune is actually a blues, disguised by a quirky two bar fill at the end of each verse. In true PMG style, the number develops new aspects as the piece proceeds. The quirky fill at 3.49 leads into a frictionless trumpet solo that weaves cleverly around the original chord sequence and slides distorted between the normal pitch points of the scale. The overall sound of this piece is like a musical cartoon in which a replica has its characteristics stretched and squashed such that it remains recognisable but is weird nonetheless. It almost pretends to be a Big Band image distorted through some kind of wormhole in space-time. It's like we are listening to Count Basie from another dimension. Pat's guitar is real, however, and he plays a solid improvisation over a sequence of chords he should be quite comfortable with.

To the End of the World is a highlight on an album already filled with superlatives. It begins with a Steve Rodby bass figure that introduces a subdued Metheny sound and gives you no idea of the aural experience the band has in store for you. Here is a wonderful example of the way the band takes a simple, muted phrase and builds it imperceptibly over many bars so that it grows, like a great movie drama, towards a tense, driving climax that has you on the edge of your seat if not out of it. As the number builds, so does the pitch of the guitar, set to deliver the trademarked Metheny sound. A brief lull in tension occurs at 3.08 with Mays' luscious concert grand piano solo that builds for over three minutes, first imperceptibly and then remorselessly towards a climax in which the voices join in. At 6.35 the guitar re-enters for the final build. Modulating through the typical PMG maze of keys, the screaming guitar drives on and up, leading us directly towards the abyss. Then, at 9.05, a shuddering clap of thunder introduces an ending synonymous with the end of the world, rather than just a piece of music. Just as a storm passes overhead, the original Rodby motif brings you back from the edge where you saw things that no human should. Chastened, you walk into the sunset. Altogether, this is a twelve-minute piece of heaven at the edge of the Earth.

The fifth track is the title track of the album. It is presented as a hymn for the people of the planet, rather along the lines of Joni Mitchell's *The Jungle Line* from *The Hissing of Summer Lawns* (1975). The accompaniment is straight out of the African jungle, over which Pat plays outside the rhythm of the backdrop. Here we see another example of the band's mastery of complex rhythmic patterns and sounds. Overall, the beautiful sweet melody suitable for any occasion is woven into a thick tapestry of rhythms and chords. This is music with the smell of the rain forest, full to the brim with imagery and emotion. There are many possible interpretations of the music. The album cover artwork has images of the musicians in their childhood and of the places where they grew up. Yet the use of the title *We Live Here* is clearly attached to Africa. Perhaps the idea is to link the kids from the Midwest of the USA with the peoples of Africa: the deluxe, sophisticated sound of Pat's guitar blended with the primitive African drums. As other musicians like Joe Zawinul and Herbie Hancock proclaim, nationality is irrelevant, as also is the amount of money in our pockets or the property we possess. We're all children of the planet. Another subtlety, if you look carefully at the cover art, is the inclusion of a short list, presumably of the musicians' favourite musical inspirations. We know that Miles Davis's *Four and More* is at the head of Pat's list (he told Courtney Pine [16]). These guys live in music, after all.

Episode d'Azur is a rare solo Mays composition. It has complex chordal sequences that don't represent the kind that we can usually associate with. This is much more like the kind of work Chick Corea or Herbie Hancock would present. The fast-swing opening theme develops into a short singable motif, but the main theme is essentially full-on mainstream jazz. It receives only brief exposure before Mays slows the whole thing down on grand piano, playing to chart. Then Pat returns with his improvised verses over the complex chords sequence. His supreme dexterity on guitar is amply demonstrated with a burst of machine-gun fired notes. A deceleration follows to allow Mays an improvisation at his preferred pace. Longer than his first appearance, the section sees Mays expand the themes under total control. The entry of the voices indicates a transition to a brief percussive section and a final expression of the main theme. This time, however, there is no exit by default, for a final run-through with voices at 7.20 leads into a full Coda. The synchronised and imaginatively syncopated chords lead to the end in a final blaze of colour. It's a great track, but it's more for the purists than the fusioneers.

The Ballad, *Something to Remind You* is a slow, beautiful melody on matching guitar and piano that starts innocently. Imagine a poor diamond prospector digging in the beautiful South African landscape. Diamonds are rare and he knows he will be lucky to find anything larger than a speck. He'd like more, if only to feed his family better. Nevertheless, he is happy in his work, content to spend his time amidst such beautiful scenery. Listen to the superb melody of the early part of this song, set amidst the lush green grass of the svelte. Listen for the sound of the glockenspiel, for it leads to a spine-tingling mini crescendo at 1.56 and then at 2.00 into the first statement of a special melody that runs up to 2.20. Suddenly there is that glint in the soil that the prospector knows so well. Is there something special here? What is this that is different from the soil? A short eight-bar chord sequence emerges from the basic theme of the piece, briefly displays its charms and then disappears into the rich dark soil once more. It seems that it was just a pleasant link between verses. The miner smiles; he has just discovered a tiny sparkler that will keep him happy for a while. Pat digs with his guitar, improvising on his original theme. From 4.00 to 4.23 we hear that crescendo - bigger this time - that tightens the tension and raises our expectations. Then it happens. The diamond shows itself once more, but it is larger than the miner first thought. He stoops, picks up the earth-covered lump and dusts it off to uncover a magnificent gem. Here, before the tune eventually fades away, is a priceless gem with ten brilliantly shining facets, each of eight bars. The miner turns the diamond between his fingers, and as the diamond turns, new features are revealed. At first they all look the same, but somehow they are subtly different. In the light of the setting sun, the colours that burst out of each facet are stupefying, different from every angle. This unique section of music takes a line of melody and attaches the most subtle colour changes in the form of accidentals, but the effect is small compared to the rich hues of the underlying chord sequence. Twisting and turning through a number of modulations, like the rotating diamond, the piece returns to its original orientation.

PMG music frequently employs the idea of a simple melodic thread underpinned by chordal sequences that change in complex and unexpected ways to create a beautiful woven fabric. *Something to Remind You* is an example of the ultimate in master craft. Both the melody and the underlying changes are complex, and a startling impact is achieved. The jewel of the piece is the cycling final third in which modulation is used in such a way as to be a highlight. So cleverly is it achieved, and so easily does it pass from major to minor that the educated ear is in awe of the sheer imagination involved.

So, in *Something to Remind You* we have a composition of two parts. The first part could have ended at around four minutes and still been special. However, the final three minutes consist of a great melody that was glimpsed but briefly in the first four minutes. The melody is simply constructed with intervals of small steps, but with some of the finest voicings and chord sequencing that have ever been composed. You can listen to this three minutes of music over and over and never get tired of it. The sheer number of ways the same melody has been converted into chords is simply stunning. I therefore give this piece a five star award for musical composition and I shall go so far as to say that I believe this is one of the great musical compositions in any modern genre.

After such a success, track eight *Red Sky* could be a serious anti-climax, but it is not. The atmospheric title is apt and the acoustic guitar melody flies over the moving landscape below in a six-eight rhythm that breaks periodically into common time. Mays' synthesised concert sound of strings and flutes is used for the main chorus, the voices challenging you to sing along with them and Paul Wertico's drums in rock mode. Then back we go into six-eight, led by Mays' gentle synthesised chords. The piece soon develops into a reminiscence of *Are You Going With Me?* in which the simple guitar motif is gradually wound up in pitch and tension until, after a final chorus of brass and loud, full accompaniment, it screams out to the faded ending. Pat clearly loves this way of playing; after all, he's used it already on *To the End of the World*. This track is definitely no anti-climax.

Even the final track maintains the high quality of the entire album, with Pat playing the guitar stunningly. *Stranger in Town* has a two-part verse with a rapid-fire first melody and a slow second motif. An improvised guitar section is unusually free of backing except for the ticking cymbals. This is always very difficult to do, because the soloist does not have the comfort support of the backing chords. He has to retain them in his head whilst generating fast, smooth lines that match the invisible chord structure. Mays and Rodby join Pat for a second improvised section. The easy path out is never taken in PMG, for at 3.55 comes a new section led by Mays on keyboard and synthesiser, its melody sounding like church music, with a fast pulsating background that at 4.37 breaks back to the main verse once more but without the slow motif. All the main instruments echo the rapid melody line before there is a final improvised verse leading to the fade-out.

Taken as a whole, this album is a PMG classic with all the features of style, sound, composition and form that the band is famous for. The musicianship of both Lyle and Pat is even better than it has been previously. The quality of the entire album is of the highest and there are some quite extraordinary tracks. I award it my highest accolade of five stars. Oh, and by the way, it won the 1995 Grammy for *Best Contemporary Jazz Performance*!

Pat Metheny Group: *Quartet* – 1996 (**)

One album of the PMG series, *Quartet* was an experiment with spontaneous composition. The sleeve notes report that the band had spent so much time on the road together that Pat felt they were playing more as a single unit than ever before. Pat wanted to discover what would ensue if the band tried the more freeform style. For most fans, the result was an album that is almost never played. The collection of music in which the composed element is at a minimum is for most ears, deeply unsatisfying, especially when compared to the heights of emotion experienced on listening to the other albums. Clearly, despite Pat's contention that the band was as good as at any time in its history, there is something missing when such a loose direction is taken with the material. This was the biggest flaw across the whole spectrum of Miles Davis's many bands: the total lack of considered musical direction from Davis continues to leave many jazz listeners wondering what his music was all about. There are some purists who will always prefer their jazz this way, but they are a minority. Pat has always wanted to retain his links with the pure jazz fraternity, but it is hard to explain how work such as this fits in with his beliefs about communication that were reported above. At moments such as this, we always return to the age-old arguments about abstract versus representational art. Let's not get into that again now, but simply agree that this is not a good album for the jazz-fusion listener. Needless to say, it is the only one of the last eight PMG albums that was not awarded a Grammy.

Michael Brecker: Tales From the Hudson – 1996 (****)

Pat's longstanding close friendship with Michael Brecker was revitalised when Pat joined Mike once more for a solid straight-ahead album populated with Jack de Johnette, Dave Holland and Joey Calderazzo. (McCoy Tyner substituted for Calderazzo on tracks 3 and 5, which also have Don Alias on percussion.) The first track is *Slings and Arrows*, a mainstream piece with a fast swing tempo and conventional harmony. The theme is complex, the melody tight and it's a good start to the album. *Midnight Voyage* is a Calderazzo number that is slower, mainstream and has a slick bluesy 8-bar theme. If ever an example was required of the use of syncopation in jazz, this could be it, for the delightful way in which the music departs from the standard 4/4 metre is a true delight on this track. It's beautiful playing in the cracks and as a cool jazz for late night enjoyment and Michael's solo is a stunner. The third piece is Pat's *Song for Bilbao*, played similarly to the way he does on his own album. Metheny and Brecker play the melody in unison, a unique sound as Pat uses his characteristic guitar synth, a departure from his normal 'Wes Montgomery' sound on this album. The construction of the melody is complex and provides a challenging environment for the soloists. Track four is a Brecker-composed jazz ballad called *Beau Rivage*. There are unusual harmonies and constructions here that have become almost a trademark sound for Brecker and you will hear pieces on other albums that have the same characteristics. *African Skies* is a terrific Brecker piece used to great effect also on the Brecker Brothers' five-star album *Out of the Loop* (1994). It has a memorable, if quirky, melody and Tyner's playing is quite exceptional, ably assisted by the rhythm section. This piece is a highlight, with Brecker demonstrating beyond doubt that he is a master saxophonist in all respects.

The second half of the album begins with a longer piece called *Naked Soul*, which has a short improvised intro. The early part of the theme deceives with a waltz feel, although the normal 8s are comprised of a combination of 3+5 beats. After the twists and turns, the piece settles down to a regular four-beat rhythm and the piece is cool, melodic and doleful. Brecker's style is intense and philosophical taking us to highs and lows, but it's not joyous or beautiful in the sense that many would recognise. However, if you can make a connection with this you're likely to fall in love with it for ever. Brecker is never afraid to include pieces by other musicians, especially Don Grolnick with whom he had a great affinity. (Unfortunately, this was to be the year of Don's untimely death.) The eighth track, *Willie T*, is one such piece. It's a cool swing piece based on a typical Grolnick tune that is entirely sympathetic to Brecker's own style. In the simple modal style of Miles Davis's *So What* it has a standard sequence of solos. The final track is *Cabin Fever*, a hard-hitting blast of modal jazz with little in the way of theme – a freewheeling freak-out to blow away the cobwebs, just in case any jazz critics should think Brecker was going soft!

Tony Williams: *Wilderness* – 1996 (****)

Many jazz musicians have flirted with orchestras at one time or another in their careers. The closest Miles got to it was the *Aura* (1989) project with Palle Mikkelborg, though that was really a big band work. Chick Corea is probably the most accomplished jazz musician to work in the orchestral field having composed many pieces in the classical style; Herbie Hancock has frequently been involved with orchestras, notably performing a piano duet of Gershwin's *Rhapsody in Blue* with Chinese wonder pianist Lang Lang at the 2008 Grammy ceremony. John McLaughlin worked with a classical orchestra for *Visions of the Emerald Beyond* (1975), but later went so far as to write *Mediterranean Concerto for Guitar and Orchestra* (1990). Performing with an orchestra is one thing. Few jazzers try to write for one!

Probably the last person you might expect to work with – even write for – an orchestra is Tony Williams. As Tony himself says, people don't expect drummers to write, not even for small groups, let alone orchestras, but Tony regarded himself as "a musician who plays drums". [17] In the 1990s, Tony embarked on a formal programme of study in composition and *Wilderness* (1996) is the result. It's a sophisticated and unusual work. The project would have been a good deal less successful without his ability to attract the likes of Herbie Hancock, Pat Metheny, Mike Brecker and Stanley Clarke to support him, but that might give the false impression that the project would not have been worthwhile without them. This is a themed album, with loose links between the tracks, some obvious, others less so. There are also some very acceptable distractions within, but nevertheless, the whole work is coherent and very rewarding to the jazz enthusiast listener. Tony wanted it to reflect the times of the early American settlers as they found themselves in the midst of a vast new land. [18] He has achieved his aim. The opening track is *Wilderness Rising,* a simple yet very effective orchestral piece scored by Williams himself. It sets the scene perfectly. Punctuated at intervals through the rest of the album are other shorter orchestral pieces: *Infant Wilderness* (track 3), *Wilderness Voyager* (track 7), *Wilderness Island* (track 10), *Sea of Wilderness* (track 11), and *Cape Wilderness* (track 13), all written by Williams with some help from John Van Tongeren, who orchestrated 3, 7 and 11.

China is one strand of the theme with three related tracks, *China Town*, *China Road* and *China Moon*. The first, *China Town* at 2 is a complete contrast to the opener and is an excellent jazz-fusion piece that pushes the envelope surprisingly hard, even though Williams admitted that fusion had not been on his mind during this project. There's a lot of funky rhythm superimposed with some interesting sustained chords. Michael Brecker plays some of his best licks, that vary from the breathtakingly fast to the curious phrases that occupy space at the top and bottom of his range. Pat Metheny is there, adding to the chordal backwash with his guitar synth that is as much at home here as anywhere else. After this very strong user-friendly quintet piece, which has about as much colour as any other track I know, the other two pieces are variations, with *China Moon* at 9 a kind of farther-out version of track 5, *China Road*.

Track 4, Stanley Clarke's *Harlem Mist '55*, is one of the real highlights of the album, another piece with a strong orchestral content, but this time written and scored by Stan, a musical academic. The piece starts out as an orchestral soundscape and then moves into an accompanied trio, with Herbie leading on acoustic piano, backed up by Stanley and Tony. It would be churlish to compare it with Tony's work since Tony is very much a beginner at orchestral composition, yet Tony's work stands up well. *China Road* works well as an impressionistic piece with the boys all working together to generate a wonderful cacophony of ideas.

Pat's *The Night You Were Born* is track 6. It's seems to be a distraction, not really part of the Wilderness theme, but the music is a sophisticated, gentle, slow ballad that is entirely welcome in its context. Michael Brecker shows just how emotionally he can play without needing to break the sound barrier for speed. This is an excellent example of how jazz is about so much more than just the notes, as Michael squeezes and bends his notes, moulding them into so much more than is written on paper. Extra poignancy to the piece comes from Pat's dedication of it to Anna Marie Shorter who, seven months after it was recorded, was killed when the airliner in which she was travelling to Paris was destroyed in mid-air over Long Island.

After *Wilderness Voyager*, a curious contribution is track 8, *Machu Picchu*, not because of its musical content, which fits well, but because it is written and part-performed by guest musician, Lyle Workman. Lyle, little known at the time, was an original member of the 80s band Bourgeois Tagg and today is more famous for his theme to the film *Superbad* (2007). Supported by Herbie, Stanley and Tony, this is an atmospheric track that sits well with its siblings. Stanley makes the most of a good opportunity to play some beautiful acoustic double bass, whilst Herbie's synthesiser work greatly adds to the atmosphere.

China Moon follows, in which the China theme is developed into something even more abstract than before by a kind of fragmentation and reconstruction process that almost makes me laugh out loud. Again, the band is well placed to take the music into new ground as they explore some of the ideas of free jazz that Tony has always eschewed, whilst not overindulging themselves.

Wilderness Island is a short three-minute band piece that consists of a loose written framework into which Tony has freedom to present some of his drum work, again in the context of his theme. Coupled to a second three-minute piece, *Sea of Wilderness* – this time orchestral – the album continues to hold our attention as we wonder what is left to come. Well, the penultimate track is another Williams composition, *Gambia*, played by the band. It is a lively straight-ahead, mostly acoustic jazz piece that combines the feel of 6/8 rhythms with fours. The main themes are interesting and mature in that they stand up well to multiple plays.

Finally comes track 13, *Cape Wilderness*, a variation of the opening overture now rendered for a jazz finale that could easily have come from a Pat Metheny Group album. Played by the band it is an excellent résumé of a substantial musical project. It draws together the essence of the past hour of music and ends on a beautiful calm vibe that leaves me feeling entirely content.

Overall, I found this album a big surprise after the disappointing material from early in Tony's career. I have played this album more than many other albums in my collection because each time I do so I find new sounds and ideas. Whether he intended to or not, Tony has succeeded very well in creating a fusion of jazz with classical music – the so-called 'third stream'. In contrast to those early albums in which Tony's style was very dominating, here he seems to have found his place sitting perfectly amongst a group of expert musicians with each being allowed an appropriate amount of time and space. Tony, never dominates, but is always contributing sympathetically and creatively. The collection of substantive tracks is very well planned and these are considerately bridged with the shorter *Wilderness* pieces. The album has great variety, enormous amounts of colour, is coherent in its compilation, has many different melodies and phrases that listeners can associate with and is brilliantly executed. What more could you ask?

Pat Metheny: *Passaggio Per Il Paradiso* – 1996 (***)

Also known as *Passage to Paradise* and *Gentle into the Night*, *Passaggio per il Paradiso* is the story of Martha, an American woman, divorced and living in Tuscany, and Renato, an Italian twenty five years her junior. The film stars Julie Harris as Martha McGraw and Tcheky Karyo as Renato. Pat wrote and performed all the music, most of which is played on synthesisers, although there is some guitar music.

I'm sure there is a danger of film music becoming very formulaic. If I thought I was going to write a film score, I'd sit down and write pieces of hero music, villain music, nice music, creepy music, love music, family music, going away music, coming back together music etc... and then ask what the story was! You can pretty well guess the film's plot from looking at the track titles and all of this does not take a lot of description. There are thirteen tracks, some just short cameos, like *Private Eye* or *Wolf Story* – just sixty seconds of menacing music. On the other hand, there are plenty of well-developed pieces that contribute to making this an album that is coherent and satisfying. There are a couple of strong melodic themes that percolate through this album, which is not too long at around 45 minutes. As a result, listening to this CD is a pleasant way to relax. Compared to the depth and impact of *Secret Story* (1992) this is lightweight, but this one should not disappoint fans of that work.

From Pat's point of view, perhaps he uses such opportunities as a sketchpad for development of firmer ideas he can use later. I was interested therefore to find the use of a resonating synthesiser background on *The Roads of Marche*, which is very similar to a sound used on *The Way Up* (2005) that I call the Matrix. Anyway, the film score went down well with some folks because Pat won the 1996 President's award at the Fort Lauderdale Film Festival.

Kenny Garrett Quartet: *Pursuance: The Music of John Coltrane* – 1996 (****)

When an album title advertises a relationship to John Coltrane's music, it could easily be a licence for the musicians to lose themselves in hardcore blowing.

The scope of Coltrane's approach to jazz expanded exponentially after he left Miles Davis's band in 1961 and took jazz into entirely uncharted waters from where he became a legend in his short lifetime.

For a quartet comprised of Kenny Garrett, Pat Metheny, Brian Blade and Rodney Whitaker to take on Coltrane's music is slightly unusual, if only for the fact that Garrett is an alto player, whereas Coltrane played tenor and soprano saxophones. Himself a graduate of Miles Davis's last jazz-fusion band, Garrett is a very seriously gifted saxophonist who sees no reason at all to compromise his work for commercial gain. Consequently, like Michael Brecker, his solo albums have generally been directed at advancing the art of playing his instrument. Unlike Michael Brecker, Garrett has so far refrained from taking part in the wider, more commercial world of instrumental music. And then there's the choice of Metheny, a guitarist not until now associated with this style of jazz, who might be expected to fulfil the part played by Coltrane's long-time pianist, McCoy Tyner. Brian Blade (b1970) was one of the best young drummers of his peer group when he was hired by Joshua Redman in the early 1990s. Wayne Shorter would soon hire him for his perspicacious interpretations of complex designs. Rodney Whitaker is today a professor of double bass at the Michigan State University where he is also director of jazz studies in the Music College. Clearly, here was a team well capable of taking up the challenge of Coltrane's music.

So, does this foursome seek to exercise the full scope of their licence? Well, mostly they don't. Hardcore blowing is exactly the kind of fare served up in *Countdown*, a busy Garrett/Blade joust that makes the listener wait until the last few seconds to hear the original theme. The album's final track is *Latifa*, in which the band plays a very loose group improvisation in the style if not the letter of some of JC's later work. The title track *Pursuance* is the third part of Coltrane's epic suite *A Love Supreme* and you'd expect this to be a very serious effort. So it is – fast, probing and pertinent. Similarly the eyes of everyone who picks up this disc would be expected to focus on the most famous track, *Giant Steps*, a piece that is supposedly used for compulsory exercises in harmony in every jazz course in the world. How would this professorial band deal with it? Well, brilliantly, of course. In fact, it's a Garrett master class and Pat does not solo on this piece of exhibition playing.

There is plenty of gentler, straight-ahead music too. *Equinox* is a piece of laid-back swing with cool front-to-back action. Coltrane recorded *Liberia* a couple of days after *Equinox* on 26 October 1960 and both tracks appeared on his album *Coltrane's Sound* (1960). Both songs, being from this period, are traditionally mainstream. *Liberia* is more like leather than latex and has a firmer core with a slick exterior. *Dear Lord* is a soft, gentle jazz hymn that Garrett's band play very straight and sweet. *Lonnie's Lament* is a straight enough tune that for once is given a more modern treatment, especially as Pat overlays his favourite guitar synthesiser sound onto Garrett's plaintiff cries. *After the Rain* is for the most part a touching interpretation that develops into a section of group improvisation that conveys a strong sense of grief and anguish. *Like Sonny* is in pleasant contrast. It's a straightforward lively swing number from the 1959 *Giant Steps* pages of Coltrane's book. Listen out for some extraordinary saxophone playing and a lyrical bass solo to match. *Alabama* is from 1963 when inter-racial tensions were running high in the USA and portrays a strong sense of the time in which it was written.

So, overall, the album is an uncompromising, honest attempt to portray Coltrane's music in a 1990s context, but in a style that is remains contemporary with Coltrane's at the time he wrote it. Brian Blade doesn't really get to show just how good he can be, although his contributions on *Countdown* and *Pursuance* are outstanding. Pat's playing is rather more low-key than usual as he keeps within the constraints of the project. Nevertheless, his role is impressive as he demonstrates yet another facet of his abilities. The album contents are a well-chosen selection of songs from across the broad spectrum of work from the most significant jazz musician in history and lovers of good jazz will find this album extremely satisfying.

Charlie Haden and Pat Metheny: *Beyond the Missouri Skies* – 1997 (****)

In 1996, Pat recorded an album with his close friend Charlie Haden called *Beyond the Missouri Skies*. This was Charlie's project and Pat was the invited guest, so it seems a little disrespectful to spend too much time describing Pat's contributions to the album, which are significant to the extent that Pat does tend to dominate. Charlie's reputation is strongly associated with the *avant-garde* and with Pat never afraid to take on any type of material this album could have been a bag of barks and burps. It's not really a surprise, however, that when musicians draw their own families and backgrounds into their music, they usually revert to more traditional sounds and harmonies. Indeed, this is an album full of love and beauty and deep respect for their heritage. It's also an album for all those who love pure sounds and the wonderful tones of the acoustic guitar at the highest level of performance.

Charlie collected together a solid set of tunes from a wide range of sources for this recording, only two of which were Pat's. Charlie, naturally, had his wife in the forefront of his mind for three selections: the new *Waltz for Ruth*, and the old numbers *Our Spanish Love Song* and *First Song*, also dedicated to his wife. The first is a pure duet and sets the scene for the rest of the album. In the second an overdub is easy to miss as Pat uses his own accompaniment to support his lead, but it's very unobtrusive yet adds body to the music as well. *First Song* (track five) is a slow ballad whose plaintive refrain is exquisitely phrased and developed by both men. It was also the piece David Sanborn chose when he briefly fell out of love with jazz-fusion for *Another Hand* (1991).

Track three is *Message to a Friend* which, according to Pat, was something he wrote with Charlie in mind. This slow, sometimes mournful, ballad is a pure duet played impeccably on Pat's steel string acoustic. Next is *Two for the Road*, a slow, romantic piece with a Latin rhythm that Pat plays straight through with Charlie solidly behind.

A subtle shift of emphasis then takes place as more orchestration and instrumentation is added to the pieces from track six, sometimes successfully, sometimes less so. After a superb introduction with his steel-string acoustic, Pat starts to use a synthesiser for the piece by Jim Webb called *The Moon is a Harsh Witness*. The piece then moves into a PMG-ish mode and it pays off, although I found myself asking why it was necessary. Charlie admitted that it had always been his plan to use more electronic instruments. [19]

Two pieces from Charlie's family background are derived from the American folk music heritage. *The Precious Jewel* is a well-known Roy Acuff melody that Charlie chooses to sing with his beautiful bass as Pat strums behind. As the song develops, more instrumentation is added until the sound is like a full Appalachian string band and then evolves further into an electric guitar-led PMG-type sound. It's both imaginative and a delight to the ear. Next is another old folk song *He's Gone Away*, by far the most poignant on the album as (without words) it tells the story of the pain of separation. Building from a perfect duet sound, it has some of the most sensitive guitar work you will hear.

At times, the music moves too far from the luscious guitar and bass tones that form the bulk of this album. However, the two bass lines, for example, on Johnny Mandel's previously unrecorded tune *The Moon Song* are a delight and Charlie's fabulous deep resonances on the *Main Theme* from the film *Cinema Paradiso* set nerve-ends tingling. The *Love Theme* from the same film is well-known and runs back-to-back. Sadly, Pat's acidic sound on *Tears of Rain* would burn many cheeks and, though it might have been well placed on another album, it rather disturbs the delicate equilibrium of this one. At the other extreme of the sweetness scale is *Spiritual*, written by Charlie's son. The sugar is crystallising from this disappointing concoction of syrup even as it plays; it's too much even for this old sentimentalist.

Of course, the deeply personal statements offered by this music towards Charlie and Pat's families and their common Missouri childhoods are not necessarily translated in the same way for all listeners. However, what surely comes across is the strong sense of respect for their roots (only 100 miles or so apart) and for the stable, loving relationships to which they both belong. Overall, this is a very good record with many highlights. However, it's easy to see where some of the more critical descriptions of Pat's work being "over-sentimental" [6] or "all mom and apple pie" [5] derive from. The broad spectrum of jazz fans will taste very different flavours in this music.

David Liebman: *The Elements: Water* – 1997 (**)

At the start of 1997, Pat joined Dave Liebman, Cecil McBee and Billy Hart for a project of Dave's that was a study of water, one of the four elements of ancient times. (The way Dave talked about it I wondered if he didn't realise that these days we actually have 114 modern ones!) Apparently the other three – air, earth and fire – were to be realised on record at some point in the future, although that aim seems not to have been achieved. Dave seemed to be having some kind of mid-life crisis and had decided to focus his work on ideas inspired by the natural world, something that Pat, of course, had been doing since the start of his career. Pat had even done his own project on this subject, *Watercolors* (1976).

Liebman had already worked with Hart and McBee on a project entitled *The Seasons* (1992) and he knew these two musicians very well. Both he described as "unpredictable" and "able to play free", by which he meant that they were creative improvisers who could play without the constraints of rigid time. He had played with Billy Hart for some ten years as part of David's band called Quest, and although he had known Pat for many years too, they had not recorded together until now. David knew Pat to be a melodic player as well as someone who could explore the depths of the music Dave would present him with. As a second solo voice in this small group, Dave knew that Pat was able to provide a wide range of guitar sounds and Liebman felt he was the ideal choice for this project.

A highly intelligent man with a University degree in American History, Liebman was born in Brooklyn in 1946. He started to learn piano at nine years of age and saxophone when aged 12. Inspired by seeing John Coltrane play live in New York, he focussed on jazz throughout his high school years and his time at University where he began to play around the club scene. As an inveterate networker, he was a leading light amongst the New York community of musicians known as the 'loft' jazz scene, at the time the Brecker Brothers were beginning their rise to fame. His high profile meant that he was soon to receive the call to join Miles Davis's band, and he worked extensively with Miles from 1970-74. It was enough to set him on the path to musical freedom for the rest of his career. He has enjoyed a prolific recording and performing career during which time he has come to be regarded as one of the foremost saxophone players.

Hart (b1940) has long been a stalwart of the jazz scene, spending substantial parts of the 1960s and 70s playing with Herbie Hancock, McCoy Tyner and Stan Getz. In later years he has used his great skills and experience to become a jazz educator. Likewise, the highly rated Cecil McBee (b1935) has moved in similar jazz circles, playing with many of the jazz stars such as Miles Davis, Sam Rivers, Jackie McLean and Wayne Shorter.

At the end of the CD of *Water*, David is to be heard in conversation with producer Bob Karcy explaining his latest work. He says that he gets images in his head when he hears the music and expects listeners to feel likewise – although they may not necessarily get the *same* images, of course. He explains that the first track is an exposition of the main theme – *Water, Giver of Life*. Each of the remaining tracks is a development of a part of this main theme, and each is played in such a way as to make quite different sounds and musical textures. Naturally, he was exactly right in choosing Pat to join him, for Pat is his usual self, contributing very different sounds to each track. For example, he plays synthesiser sounds on *White Caps* and *Ebb and Flow*, standard electric guitar sounds on *Heaven's Gift* and *Storm Surge*, acoustic nylon-string guitar on *Water, Giver of Life*, and acoustic steel string guitar on *Guitar Interlude* and *Baptismal Font*. He dusts off his Pikasso guitar for a particularly impressionistic version of *Reflecting Pool*.

The album is quite clearly the work of a musician who has put much thought into the composition and production. Personally, I found much difficulty in recognising the difficult themes of which he spoke and the music was far more abstract than impressionist. Those listeners who enjoy music that ranges more freely across the lakes of time and harmony will enjoy this disc, but it is focussed on a point far removed from the PMG meridian that unites most fans of Pat's music.

Pat Metheny Group: *Imaginary Day* – 1997 (*****)

Imaginary Day (1997) is another of the themed or suite albums where the titles give appropriate clues to the settings of the tracks. Once again, the album gets my highest award of five stars. But beware! This is not an album for the faint-hearted and a secure seat belt is essential for this magic carpet ride across the wide-open spaces of the world to the very Ends of the Earth.

Pat pitches us right in at the deep end. The title track at once paints a scene somewhere in Asia where PMG have spent a lot of time on tour and where their popularity is exceptional. PMG have a particular strength in making the sounds of the East accessible to the western ear and this track is the best example. The opening is dour. We're due to be presented at the court of some oriental emperor and our heads rest uneasily on our shoulders. One wrong word and we face immediate execution. We timidly approach the great timber doors at the entrance to the Forbidden City. At 0.45 they swing open and suddenly we know with certainty that there are both wonders and terrors to behold inside...

At 1.05 as the bass starts up a gorgeous resonant rhythm a guide takes us on a long walk through the corridors of fear. As we follow closely behind, the emperor's courtiers look at us quizzically as we strange Westerners dare to present ourselves to their world. At 1.20 the short main theme begins and lasts to 1.50. There's a bridge and we expect the theme to start again at 2.09, but no! Listen to this exquisite rhythmic section as the bridge is extended to 2.40 when the theme actually does begin again. At 3.11 we turn the corner to a fanfare and find ourselves facing a great open space alongside the palace. It's filled with the hustle and bustle of palace activities. Men, women and children dart here and there, their loose-fitting garments flapping about their lean bodies. Animals, jugglers, traders, porters – the place is buzzing with a hundred and one different activities. Strange exotic birds in cages, lizards, snakes, leaves swirling around in the wind...

At 5.12 our guide frowns and orders us back inside. We have no right to go there! At 5.35 he leads us down a new corridor filled with tapestries, paintings and strange oriental *objets d'art*. The piece moves into a heavy rock arena, little used by Pat. The effect is mesmerising as he blends the traditional rock guitar sound with the fretless effect that retains the eastern freedom from western diatonic scales. Pat's long improvisation builds in his usual masterful way and at 6.55, 7.42 and 8.14 there are some great modulations that keep us guessing. Finally at 8.38 we come back to the main theme that is now different: after all, we're older and wiser than when we started this awesome journey. The end of the piece arrives at 9.10 in a tense flourish. Our guide suddenly disappears leaving us in front of the doors to what must be the golden throne room. Are we finally about to meet the emperor? Our hearts beat rapidly. Our heads are bowed. Then, suddenly, just as we are about to come face to face with the omnipotent one, our magic carpet swoops down to take us off to another destination.

Whew! That was a close shave! We need some light relief. *Follow Me* begins with the kind of sound that might accompany a 21st century John Wayne movie. This is a real Big Country feel with superb acoustic rhythm guitars and a delightful melody played in guitar harmonics. Beginning at 0.18, the theme is a collection of three note motifs rising and falling in line with the Texan backdrop. The middle eight bars start at 0.55, a phrase wearing a ten-gallon hat if ever I saw one! This short line lasts to 1.12 and is followed by the theme again. At 1.53 a new section begins and at 2.11 one of our cowboys even starts to sing along until 2.28 when the theme is played again.

Then at 3.05, just when the edge of the town should be coming into view, a dust storm blows over the horizon and makes the ride into town rather more eventful. Neckerchiefs are tightly bound around our faces to keep the dust from our eyes and mouths. Who knows the way? I do. Okay, follow me. At four minutes we spur on our trusty horses and soon we are galloping faster than the wind itself. At 4.42 we ride out of the storm and see the ranch in the distance. I can even smell the coffee!

Into the Dream showcases Pat's acquisition of the 42-string Pikasso guitar, giving him the opportunity to display his virtuosity on a unique acoustic instrument with an amazing sound. The effect is of the remote mountainous, forested Japan, secret waterfalls amidst dense populations of trees. Somehow the liquid crystal water is alive, telling us of the wonders of ancient Japan over which the life-giving water has flowed since the beginning of time. The greens around us are luminous as the bright sun cuts through the branches above our heads. The snow-capped mountains rise above everything, sharp as smooth Samurai steel. Then, suddenly, the mountain mist swirls down and before we know it we find ourselves in the heart of Tokyo where east meets west. It is night and the city is vibrant and vital. *A Story Within the Story* could be set in the dark recesses of a downtown jazz club. The people are all smiling as we descend the stairs into the basement. There's a cool jazz quartet playing on a tiny stage. Is that Miles Davis over there? Wow! Take a seat, ladies and gentlemen. What can I get you to drink? By 3.12 everything seems hazy. Hey! Was my drink spiked? What's that guitarist playing? Well I never heard no guitarist play like that before. Is this a dream or what? Why do I keep hearing Miles Davis? He's dead.

Suddenly I'm sober and wide-awake. *The Heat of the Day* is fiercely Spanish; it tells of the central highland regions where for centuries the land was harsh and the people poor. Winters froze and summers baked. Yet they are rich in vitality and culture as this piece shows with all its cleverly mixed folk rhythms. Here the highs and lows of the native peoples are both celebrated and protested.

The piece begins with a vigorous handclap rhythm to which guitar and piano add tense, almost frantic phrases. They are free to drift up and down across the lines of the score, yet somehow there is a constraint. Just like the poor people carry on their business around their country, everything they do is hard in such a barren landscape. The tension becomes ever tauter. Surely, something must give... This melodic conflict continues to 1.48 when for the first time a phrase cuts the tension. This could be our signpost through this complex piece. We hear it twice, in different keys. It offers brief respite, but by 2.12 it has failed. Is there no hope for these people?

At 2.50 Lyle begins an extended solo as he tries to find a new route across the dustbowl. As the sun rises towards its zenith the temperature starts to soar. The piece is in an urgent 6/8 and, starting gently, he probes here and there, seeking the best way forward. Imperceptibly his questions become more penetrating and he makes progress. At 4.03, he begins a new interrogative phase and moves into an alternate sequence of six and eight beat bars, probably shown as a 14/8 rhythm on the score. This is a very unusual timing and the edge it creates is totally consistent with the tension of the piece. It's uncomfortable, as it must be if he is to make progress over such difficult terrain. Gradually, his probing pays off and by five minutes a way through appears. At 5.18 it becomes wide open, but the vista in front is not the one he had hoped for. Wearily, he steps aside. Pat describes the scene with his synth, continuing with the 14/8 that brought Lyle success. The landscape is bone dry and dust is everywhere. It's a forbidding view of Spain that seems never-ending. But Pat is our hero. He'll find a way through. At 7.42 he finally discovers the signpost. The brief joy of celebration breaks out into a full-blown dance. We've grown used to Pat's successes, but this time it is not to be. The air of foreboding rises once more and the final notes portray dreams of liberation dissolving in the despair of reality. There's nothing here but dust, after all.

The ethereal *Across the Sky* paints a wonderful calming atmosphere. These imaginary adventures are highly charged with excitement, but without a break from the dangers, how can you face the difficulties ahead? Somehow we know that the terror that is to follow is inescapable. Here's a place to rest for the night. The fiery sun sets on a cloudless sky, and as the stars take charge, you lie down and gaze upwards in awe of the power and majesty of the universe. Relax and soak up the beautiful thoughts of home, for tomorrow will provide you with the biggest challenge you will ever face...

In the Grammy-winning track *The Roots of Coincidence* we have a soundscape that would perfectly portray the story of climber Joe Simpson fighting for his life high up in the Andes. With his friend he had already achieved the first ascent of the mountain, but on the freezing wind-blown slopes of the upper reaches he breaks his leg. His friend lowers him in agony down the vertical face of the forbidding mountain, but he falls into space and is left hanging in frozen air. He can not be saved from such a desperate predicament and, finally, in despair for his own life, his terrified partner cuts the rope. Joe's final fall into the bottomless black hole of the crevasse beneath him is truly terrifying, but he lands on a ledge. Then, surrounded by the Stygian black bottomless depths of the glacier he miraculously sees the rays of sunlight that are to save him. Stand by for a white-knuckle ride. You should note also that it is compulsory to play this track at high volume. To hell with the neighbours! This track has been a band favourite for some years now and the live version is a truly wonderful experience. The sight of all (yes, I do mean, all!) band members thrashing electric guitars would be comic if the effect of their playing were not so overpowering. To fully enjoy this astonishing track, you should buy the DVD version of *Imaginary Day* or *Speaking of Now* and play the track at high volume using the hi-fi sound of your home cinema equipment.

Too Soon Tomorrow is a wonderful ballad in finest Metheny fashion. With reminiscences of *If I Could* and so many of his other love songs, Pat is drawing together all that is good in the world like a gravitational pull. He knows that the forces of Nature have both positive and negative forms and most of this record has brought the negative into sharp focus. Electromagnetic interactions have opposite phases in their mathematical descriptions, but gravity, like time, works in only one direction. Gravity is the force that created the Universe and life on Earth. Gravity is the scientific explanation for Love. In music such as this, everything in the Universe is embraced and presented to us. It is in our power to absorb it or deny it.

The Awakening seems to paint a scene in Scotland, Ireland or, perhaps, Nova Scotia, where the monotonous drone of the bagpipes is overlaid with a tapestry of pipe sounds and pastel colours. Finally, in keeping with the theme of the album, the sounds fade away ever so gently. Your magic carpet ride is finally over and you lie exhausted on the luscious grass.

Pat Metheny Group: *Across the Sky* – 1998 (***)

The stunning impact of *Imaginary Day*, and especially the two consecutive tracks, *Across the Sky* and the *Roots of Coincidence*, clearly affected many people. Once the true significance of this music had been fully appreciated, an extended 'single' CD was released called *Across the Sky* (1998). It contained the two tracks from *Imaginary Day*, plus two new versions that had been 'remixed' by leading figures of late 90s popular culture – Goldie and Mr. Spring. Goldie, otherwise known as Clifford Price and Rufige Kru, is an English electronic musician specialising in the genres known as drum and bass, and jungle. His track *Terminator* (1992), released under the title of Metalheads was a big hit, which helped him create his own record label called Metalheadz. His first album, *Timeless* (1995) was a hit in the drum and bass genre.

I'm not sure that 'remix' is the write word for these two new tracks. It's as if someone has cut up the Mona Lisa into small pieces, thrown away the pieces that contain the picture of the lady herself, and then taken the remaining pieces depicting only the background and glued them back together in a random way. Young people think this music is great, even though it contains a small fraction of the ideas in the originals. Curiously, the process of 'dumbing down' music that is going on here was the source of a reaction by Pat and Lyle in 2005 that resulted in the *magnum opus* called *The Way Up*. However, if this (now rare) disc succeeded in attracting new ears to Pat's music then it was a good thing.

Burton Corea Metheny Haynes Holland: *Like Minds* – 1998 (****)

In June 1997 Pat sent an e-mail to Gary Burton suggesting that it was time the two of them made a record with Chick Corea. [20] Chick and Gary had started their musical relationship at about the same time that Gary and Pat had first met. In the years that had elapsed since then, Burton and Corea had made quite a name for themselves amongst the jazz community by playing several series of stunning concerts of duets. These gigs had resulted in the best-selling albums *Crystal Silence* (1972), *Duet* (1979), *In Concert, Zurich, October 28, 1979* (1979) and *Native Sense – The New Duets* (1997). Even in 2008 – thirty-six years after they started – the relationship was re-ignited with *The New Crystal*

Silence. Over the years, Gary had been cautious about letting any other musicians inside their bubble for fear of losing the rapport of an intimate musical relationship between two 'like minds'. Nevertheless, he knew Pat well enough to be excited about his proposal and, when they spoke on the telephone, Chick Corea instantly agreed to the project. Surprisingly for two people described by Gary as "musical vagabonds", it was to be his Chick's first project with Pat.

The selection of Roy Haynes for drums was an obvious choice. Roy was at the very top of the tree of jazz drummers with experience of all of the major jazz figures such as Charlie Parker, John Coltrane, Miles Davis, Lester Young and Stan Getz. Gary had played with Roy when Gary first played in Getz's quartet in the early 1960s, "one of my first sideman gigs". [20] Chick and Roy had played together on Chick's second solo album *Now He Sings, Now He Sobs* (1968). Pat suggested Dave Holland with whom he had worked alongside Roy Haynes on the *Question and Answer* (1990) album. Chick, of course, already knew Dave from his days with Miles Davis. So many of the links necessary for a cohesive, inspirational, yet still loose band already existed and Gary considered it his 'dream team'. Thus, on the three days from 15th to 17th December 2007, the team assembled at the Avatar studios in New York for a new album that was released with the title, *Like Minds* (1998).

Gary knew that both Chick and Pat were prolific composers and suggested that they each come along with some of their best tunes and one new number written especially for the occasion. Gary regards himself as a performer first and a composer second, so he naturally expected not to be called upon in this regard. However, both Pat and Chick got back to him and chided him to do the same as he expected of them. As a result, whilst Chick and Gary were touring Japan that November with their *New Duets* album, Gary wrote his contribution, *Like Minds* and Chick wrote *Futures*.

From the very start of the sessions, Gary was knocked out by the tightness that the band developed and the way they all seemed to anticipate each other's playing. His feelings were proved correct when six of the tracks were first takes and two were second takes. Pat's *Question and Answer* was the first take of the first piece they tried, so it's clearly a bit special. The main theme is most appealing and, as with many Metheny compositions, eminently singable. Of course, that's just the start and although the chord sequence seems simple enough, there's a short four-second bridge between each statement of the theme (for example, at 0.58 to 1.02) that involves a tricky downward spiral. These boys take it in their stride. When we get to the solos, Pat lets Chick and Gary check out the piece before giving his own take on it, and the playing of both Gary and Chick is fresh and inspirational. Chick tries to break through the bars of the 6/8 time constraints like a caged cat, whilst Gary's pacey arpeggios are as fluid and creative as only he can play. At once, the beautiful tone of the vibraphone on this recording is a real highlight. Anyone who doubts the musical abilities of jazz musicians (classicists take note), should remember that this is the first time these guys have played this piece of music together as a five-piece band, and the first time Chick and Gary have ever played it! The performance is exquisite, eloquent and energetic.

Elucidation was Pat's new piece written for the album. In contrast to the opener, there's nothing to sing in this flighty piece, based on an evolving set of chords in the manner of Coltrane's *Giant Steps*. Nevertheless, the music is fast and friendly with Burton's perfectly lubricated lines spilling out in streams from his white-hot mallets. To maintain the quality of a new piece with a challenging chord structure, all played at such a pace is remarkable enough, but for a 72-year-old like Haynes, it's little short of amazing.

Windows is Chick's piece. Delivered in a lively waltz time, Pat's playing stands out on this track, his gentle Wes Montgomery tones sounding assured and entirely in sympathy with Corea's melodic tune. The same description cannot, however, be applied to *Futures*, a long and somewhat harmonically remote piece that sounds as if the avoidance of musical cliché has driven Chick to select chords at random. This gloomy piece could easily reflect the uncertain times that lie ahead of us all, even if it was written before we all became disheartened by the prospects of climate change.

Gary's piece, *Like Minds* is based on a rhythmic motif of five beats, played repeatedly with different notes. A fast tempo piece, it wriggles through some equally rapid, tight chord sequences like lubricant through a loose gasket. However, the music is sufficiently tight structurally that the piece arrives at its clean ending like a well-oiled machine with every cog perfectly warmed up and delivering peak performance.

When musicians get together and ask each other what they are going to play, ninety-nine times out of a hundred they will agree on a 'blues'. Of course, jazz musicians are weaned busking to twelve-bar blues tunes, so these pieces are a great way of breaking the ice when a new band gets together for the first time. It's hardly surprising when, even at this extreme level of musicianship, a blues surfaces in the running order. In this case, Gary had been asked to bring to the party the title track from his album *Country Roads* (1968). The theme immediately stands out as being in Gary's familiar late 60s style with a very fragmented melody line – the musical equivalent of running up stairs four at a time. This tune, along with the chord sequence is strikingly similar to his other piece *Leroy the Magician* from *Good Vibes* (1971). After the tune has been played, the piece lapses into a 24-bar blues, i.e. a double-length 12-bar with enough variations to render it more interesting than usual.

Pat's third piece, *Tears of Rain* is an aptly titled piece with a gloomy, grey mood and playing in which the musicians successfully convey the words of the title,

Chick's solo in particular is well crafted to present an impression of raindrops. Lightening the mood, is a jaunty version of Gershwin's *Soon*, the kind of piece that musicians select when they've already picked the compulsory twelve-bar blues and need another slot in the running order filled. Even Bob Dylan has covered this song, which is the kind of tune that most people recognise when they hear it, even if the title doesn't inspire instant recall. For this band of pros it's a tune they all do before breakfast each day and they assuredly knock it off with aplomb getting everyone's feet tapping in the process. Traditional jazz in every respect, including a section of 'fours' (actually, it's eights!) with bass and drums, everyone gets a solo in this swinger.

Pat's last selection is *For a Thousand Years*, a light jazz waltz with some tricky chord changes that cover an equally unpredictable yet somehow nicely melodic tune. Dave Holland must surely have sweated over these changes in creating his solo, yet he gives not the slightest indication of hesitancy. Chick's final piece is *Straight Up and Down*, a fast modal piece that gives everyone the chance to have a 'blow'. No impressions of emotions or meteorology here – just tight, straight ahead modern jazz and an outpouring of chops that leaves mere mortals like us amazed at how they do it.

At the time it was released, this album was at the very top of in its class as a demonstration of the latest type of modern mainstream jazz. Here was a collection of tunes played by some of the top musicians in the world, as spontaneously and tightly captured as any studio-recorded jazz group could be. With over two hundred years of deep experience shared amongst them, this is a showpiece display of mainstream jazz, and it is no surprise therefore that, at the 1999 Grammy Awards Ceremony, the boys were awarded the top prize of "Best Jazz Instrumental Performance, Individual Or Group."

Marc Johnson: *The Sound of Summer Running* – 1998 (***)

Marc Johnson (b1953) is a close friend of Lyle Mays. Marc and Lyle were born within a month of each other and both attended the North Texas State University where they formed two thirds of the rhythm section of the One O'Clock Lab Band. On graduation from University, they both took up places in Woody Herman's band for about a year. Lyle left to join Pat's Group, whilst Marc was hired by pianist Bill Evans until his death in 1980. Later, Lyle invited Marc to join him on his own albums, *Lyle Mays* (1986) and *Fictionary* (1993). Marc also worked with Bill Frisell, John Scofield and Peter Erskine on an album *Bass Desires* (1985) that would prove to be a forerunner of a similar project some fifteen years later. It was in 1998 that Pat joined Marc Johnson (bass), Bill Frisell (guitar) and Joey Baron (drums) at the Avatar Studios with Pat's favourite engineer Joe Ferla for a recording project of Marc's entitled *The Sound of Summer Running* (1998).

Bill Frisell (b1951) is a well-known guitarist from Baltimore Maryland who has worked hard to create his own signature sound by means of numerous electronic effects. A Berklee graduate, he studied guitar with Jim Hall. Frisell's big opportunity arose when Pat was unable to make a recording session for a Paul Motian project with ECM entitled *Psalm* (1982). It is reported that Pat recommended Bill to Paul. As a result of his participation, Bill Frisell became the in-house guitar player for ECM, and worked on several albums, most notably *Paths, Prints* (1981) by Jan Garbarek. Frisell's first album as leader was *In Line* (1983), a collection of solos and duets with bassist Arild Andersen.

Joey Baron (b1955) from Richmond Virginia is described as an *avant-garde* jazz drummer, largely on the basis of significant contributions to the work of the controversial John Zorn. However, he has also played in the wider world of jazz with such artists as Stan Getz, Tony Bennett, Carmen McRae, Al Jarreau, Dizzy Gillespie and Art Pepper. Both Bill and Joey were well-known to each other, having both played with Zorn, and Bill having hired Joey for his own trio later.

Marc called upon the help of producer Lee Townsend who had also produced Pat's album with John Scofield, *I Can See Your House From Here* (1994) and Scofield's *Hand Jive* (1994).

This very good album of mostly laid-back original tunes has a noticeable western twang, to the extent that it could easily be described as a country-jazz-fusion. This clearly fits with Frisell's reputation for, although he is definitely an eclectic stylist, his favoured style seems to be based on American folk culture. Although, in the round, they are very different guitarists, Pat and Bill are both unafraid to associate their sound with their American settler roots, and once again we find Pat adopting a style that has a sharp focus and is especially suited to the nature of the project at hand.

The disc opens with *Faith in You*, an optimistic piece that sets up a feeling of warmth and friendliness, largely due to the style of the composition that is not afraid of conventional melody and harmony. It's rich in melodic colour and there's a straightforward, singable tune that floats gently in the breeze like a silk streamer. The two guitar sounds are just as conventional and entirely compatible. It's a good start.

Ghost Town is one of two pieces by Frisell and it surely conjures exactly the kinds of images we all have of ramshackled buildings and deserted, dust-blown tumbleweed covered streets. This is a bare, empty, but friendly old town that has seen better days. There are occasional flashbacks to the times when there was life behind the torn moth-eaten curtains.

The album's cover art is focussed on children playing underneath blue skies, and the track *Summer Running* is action-packed as Pat provides his underlying fast strumming technique over which the two guitars gently portray happy, bright feelings. A well-designed phrase from Marc's pen perfectly captures the scenes portrayed on the cover art. Though the two guitar sounds are similar with their western roots showing, Pat's soloing is on a higher plane than Bill's, which remains at ground level.

At last, the bass comes properly to the fore in *With My Boots On*. Here is another track that puts a smile on many faces with its relaxed devil-may-care vibe. Marc's confident strutting is complemented by Joey's firm brushwork and as they step along to the sound of the two guitars – now acoustic – it's the perfect stroll down Main Street.

Union Pacific is a piece of western blues fun played in the style of a 16-bar Texan foxtrot. Similarly *Porch Swing* portrays the gentle, calm mood at the end of a long but pleasant day. With suitable words, this waltz-time composition might have been an early number by the Eagles. As with that band's music, there are plenty of familiar changes, but it never becomes a mere country cliché.

So far the album is notable for the fact that there is much careful orchestration and no desire to make great impacts by changing the guitar sounds. The guitar sounds do change, however, for *Dingy-Dong Day*, a piece that is surely intended to be humorous as its almost childish melody begins to slide across key centres like cartoon characters walking on banana skins.

It seems as if the complexion of the album is, likewise, beginning to slip, until we examine the scar caused by Frisell's composition entitled *The Adventures of Max and Ben*, a piece that changes the album's visage completely. The rhythm is provided by a tight, irregularly hit snare drum and the melodic construction is as warm and fluid as an Icelandic stalactite. The music reminds me of some of the peculiar content that appeared on David Sanborn's poor album, *Another Hand* (1991) on which Frisell and Baron also played. The presence of this track on the album is redeemed somewhat by track nine, a beautiful composition by Marc and his wife Eliane Elias called *In a Quiet Place*. Pat comes to the fore on this one with his best lyrical acoustic playing and Bill tags along too.

The final track is Pat's *For a Thousand Years*, and even this is tending towards the 'too serious' description. Even though Pat's suave jazz waltz cuts a fine groove, and Marc plays a fine solo, it is just too far from the original path set by the first seven tracks. It's a great pity that Marc could not have simply restricted the project to the boundaries set by his own music, by which criteria it would have been judged a great success.

Pat Metheny: *A Map of the World* – 1999 (**)

A popular presence in many shopping malls these days is the Christmas store. As soon as you pass through the door, you enter a magical world designed to fill you with warm feelings of nostalgia and time spent at home with our loved ones at everyone's favourite time of year. The array of goodies on show is second-to-none, abundantly colourful and all immaculately displayed. It may be that you come away from the store with one or two items, but the rest quickly disappear from your thoughts. Even the few that took your fancy enough for you to buy them are taken home and quickly put in the back of the cupboard to be brought out just once a year.

Listening to Pat's album, *A Map of the World*, is very much like a visit to the Christmas Store. There are no fewer than 28 tracks on a single CD, the majority of which are ridiculously short and quite pointless. At the sharp end is *Pictures*, a 'track' that lasts for just 20 seconds and is but one repeated phrase of four bars. However, even some of the more substantive tracks are insignificant and make little impact upon me, at least.

Of course, it must be pointed out that this recording is a soundtrack to the acclaimed movie starring Sigourney Weaver and the music surely takes on a new mantle once you have seen the film (or perhaps, read the book). Perhaps, then, I should not dismiss the album quite so cursorily.

A follow-up project to his 1996 film score *Passaggio per il Paradiso*, Pat has now moved on from playing all the music himself on a synthesiser to using a full-scale orchestra. Thanks to Gil Goldstein's lush orchestrations, Rob Eaton's skilful recordings and Pat's typically perfect guitar craft, there is some beautiful music here. All is immaculately packaged inside glossy cover-art that's better than a Wisconsin tourist brochure. Thus, if ever Pat's music fitted Paul Stump's derisory description of it as being all 'mom and apple pie', this is it.

The title track opens the album and is up to Pat's typically high standards of melodic composition. But the anticipation is rather short-lived as we then embark upon a tiring journey through a long series of dull, homogeneous pastiches and short musical fragments that simply do not stand up as original or even complete musical compositions. There is just one gem entitled *Sunday* that contains a wholly new idea that Pat should have developed into a more adult form, and – if you can last that long – the final ten to twelve minutes build to a pleasant finale. As a soundtrack album this is not in the same league as *The Falcon and the Snowman*. So given the choice of listening to this CD or going shopping, I believe I would prefer to visit the Christmas store because at least I will probably come home with some bright shiny Christmas decorations and take them out of storage once a year.

Jim Hall, Pat Metheny – 1999 (***)

As a young guitarist in the 1960s, Pat Metheny was familiar with all of the players of what could be called, the standard jazz guitar. He studied the music, the sound and the style of Wes Montgomery, Barney Kessell, Tal Farlow (1921-1998). Pat is a passionate supporter of jazz and its traditions and, even whilst pushing back the boundaries of jazz guitar as far as he was able, he still preserved and cherished the standard style of jazz electric guitar. Thus, in 1999,

Pat realised an ambition when he was able to spend time working with the last surviving member of this classic style of jazz guitarist – Jim Hall.

It is with this album that we begin to appreciate what Pat has achieved in this style of jazz guitar playing. It begins with an inspection of the cover art, which lists Jim's instruments as "electric guitar", and Pat's as "electric guitar, acoustic guitars, fretless classical guitar, 42-string guitar". Jim Hall, as what I call a first-generation jazz guitarist, plays one guitar, and has mostly one sound, although he varies the textures and tones in the way his hands, especially the right hand, attack the strings. Pat, however, as a second-generation guitarist, makes use of different instruments to greatly broaden his sounds, and his use of very different styles of play adds to that enormously. The difference is summed up in one word – versatility. These arguments seem to imply that Hall is an inferior guitarist to Pat; that is not necessarily the case, for Hall's playing is entirely masterful in its own way. It's just that the world has moved on. It's like comparing a 2008 BMW M5 with a 1929 Rolls Royce Silver Spirit; that's an unfair comparison of course, because there are probably ten generations in the development of cars between the examples, but it serves my purpose: the Rolls was the best product of its time, and there are some who would prefer it today over a BMW M5.

The difference also becomes apparent in the very first track, *Lookin' Up*, a Hall composition. This is a light, happy piece of classic jazz that takes on a familiar form and is constructed from a sequence of entirely logical and very acceptable chord changes. Played in a lively 3/4 tempo, the two, matched guitar sounds dance about like a couple of sprites in the early morning sun. When we compare Pat's tune *Ballad Z*, we find that there is no similar logic on display, that is, there is very often no obvious relationship between each chord and the next. The chords might as well have been chosen at random. The lack of a sensible name endorses my lack of interest, and, although I can hear familiar constructions in Pat's improvised melodies, the piece is not obviously exciting and makes little attempt to cross the airwaves into my brain, let alone my soul. In total contrast, however, is their version of *Farmer's Trust*, in which unquestionable logic permeates the changes, and the music from 3.58 (especially Pat's playing) is as perfect as it comes. The result is that my soul is shafted with a bolt of love from outside once again.

A final yardstick of the gulf between these two generations of musicians is, I believe, in the tracks titled *Improvisation 1, 2, 3, 4* and *5*. Of course, we know that jazz is fundamentally about improvisation, but I do not believe that the execution of these exercises was Jim's idea. We know how Pat is keen to explore as widely as possible across the spectrum of musical invention, and there is no evidence of a similar desire in Jim's work. The presence of these tracks does not add to the musical experience of many listeners. *Improvisation 1* seems filled with uncertainty and to be no more than a flaky statement of intent that achieves nothing.

Interestingly, *Farmer's Trust* is coupled to Jim's composition, *Cold Spring*, which is an impressionistic sound painting of the start of a day in icy Illinois or c-c-c-cold Kansas. It is far more of an orchestrated movie than an improvisation, the second of which comes next. I force myself to imagine it as a kind of intro to the next piece, *Into the Dream*, in which case I can write my own narrative for it, but that may be too much to hope for. It has no credibility in the stand-alone mode. Then comes Pat's exquisite song *Don't Forget*, which is one of the highlights of his film score for *Passaggio per il Paradiso* (1996). It is what most people would describe as a beautiful ballad with sensitive, loving music from both men.

The third *Improvisation* is a little more successful, but is surely just equivalent to a doodle – an early sketch of an idea that might, with craft, be developed into a wonderful composition. Why not do it? It is followed by Jim's *Waiting to Dance*, a gentle waltz that shimmys and twirls and has lots of fancy footwork. After two more entirely forgettable *Improvisations*, I am left wondering what is so special about these, compared to those that might have been recorded the day before or the day after?

The album finishes with *All Across the City*, a somewhat rambling and undistinguished piece that does at least demonstrate some forethought and musical dynamics.

In an album such as this, intended to celebrate great musicianship from two clearly disparate generations, it is perfectly normal to harvest the subject material from the widest range possible. Thus, we have some pieces that are not just standards, but standards amongst the standards. Jerome Kern's *All the Things You Are* is one, and it is really difficult to imagine how, faced with the many thousands of previous recordings, Pat and Jim decide to play it in a way that makes the recording different and therefore worthwhile. Despite that, they do try. The effort is far more obvious in the Gershwins' *Summertime*, which Pat arranged and which he plays brilliantly as a rapidly strummed acoustic version. His effect is achieved, I believe, using a special tuning that allows him to use the E tone as a constant drone in the background. By almost turning it into an Indian raga, he seems to describe the Monsoon climate, as represented by the heat and humidity of life in nineteenth century Louisiana. This is something that was simply not in Hall's style to conceive or play.

With Hall sticking to the same sound throughout, there is good contrast between tracks like Steve Swallow's *Falling Grace*, where the two men take turns to vamp for each other's solos on very similar sounding equipment, and *Birds and the Bees*, in which a soothing balance of tones is obtained by Pat's change to acoustic guitar.

At 74 minutes, the CD is clearly crammed with music. It remains to be argued whether it would have been a better album without the Improvisations.

Michael Brecker: *Time is Of the Essence* – 1999 (***)

Michael Brecker was himself an accomplished drummer. He had always been fascinated by the different properties that unusual time could add to his music, and for this album he decided to explore it further. The tunes mostly have titles that reflect an aspect of time, and although there are no complex metres as such, there is a lot of successful experimentation with syncopation and the superimposition of one rhythm over another.

Michael hired Pat Metheny and Larry Goldings for the project, as well as three expert drummers: Elvin Jones, Jeff 'Tain' Watts, and Bill Stewart. In a sense, Jones was Brecker's 'dream drummer', whilst Watts had played alongside Brecker over the past three years or so. He was less familiar with Stewart, but selected him because Stewart and Goldings were used to playing together.

Of Pat Metheny, Michael told West, "I welcome any opportunity I can ever possibly get to play with Pat Metheny. He's, you know, probably my favourite musician playing right now. I can't say enough about him; I love his playing. Obviously, I love his sound, and his conception, I think, really transcends the instrument. He's an artist in every sense of the word, and, as you said, a fantastic composer. So I asked him to come up with a couple of tunes for the record, because the idea of playing with Pat and not playing his compositions seemed crazy. Fortunately, he brought in a couple of tunes, one of which he had previously recorded on his quartet record, the ballad *As I Am*. And then, he had kind of half-finished *Timeline* and we realized that it would be a great vehicle for Elvin, so Pat finished it quickly, and I think it was the perfect vehicle." [21]

Pat's playing on these two tracks is to the fore, of course. *As I Am* is a very legato ballad that is played as a pseudo-duet between Michael and Pat with almost no emphasised beats at all. Its melody follows a twisted path with just a gentle swash of backing from organ and Stewart's drums. *Timeline* has a tricky syncopated counter rhythm built into the melody, but is otherwise a lively 12-bar blues.

With a strong focus on time for this album and a straight-ahead melodic format, Pat sticks to his Ibanez sound throughout and is mostly a second string behind Goldings' strong organ presence. However, Pat does play on every track. He plays heads in unison with Michael on some tracks, and takes several good solos. His sentimental melodic qualities are left locked inside the guitar case for this project with Brecker whose melodic style is more like a Porsche than a Chevvy.

In selecting Larry Goldings to play the organ, it was Michael's first venture with this instrument, which has the unique feature by which organists play their own bass lines by means of foot pedals. Brecker did consider using a separate bass player for the album, but decided to let Goldings supply the bass lines and was pleased with the result. Goldings own compositional skills are most suitably represented by the second track, *Sound Off*, for which Pat just comps in the background. Larry gets to really fly in the tune *Renaissance Man*, a soulful number that would have been strong on a David Sanborn album.

As for the drumming, well, the nine tracks are split evenly amongst the three men, and the turns are in strict rotation on the album. All three give fine performances, although it is inevitable that Jones, being Coltrane's drummer, is the star. He gets a good run out on the last track, *Outrance*, which is a showcase big blow for Michael and Elvin, with Pat and Larry making up the numbers.

Pat Metheny *Trio: 99-00* – 2000 (***)

In 1999 Pat spent a lot of time playing in a trio with bassist Larry Grenadier and drummer Bill Stewart. A two-month summer tour was followed by two days of recording during which the tracks for this album were laid down.

Travels is a truly wonderful version of the beautiful ballad that is the title track of the live 1983 album. Whereas on that album we were treated to a gorgeous electric version with full band support, here Pat does not have Lyle's shoulder to lean on. Just sit back and listen to the fabulous skill with which he plays this piece on his acoustic guitar. Everything is here, luscious chords and delicate melody, with a full array of embellishments and harmonics. At times it's hard to believe there's only one guitar here, but this is a consummate guitarist at his peak.

Get It is a straight-ahead jazz flier with a bop melody line. Composed by Pat, it sears along at terrific speed – about 300 beats per minute – and Pat is often playing his standard sound electric guitar at about ten notes per second, controlled and crisp.

Giant Steps is a classic from the jazz repertoire, written by saxophone colossus John Coltrane. It's the kind of number all serious jazz musicians will play at some point in their careers so we can expect all three musicians to be pretty comfortable with it. Again, it's a straight-ahead rendition with Pat's normal electric sound and, apart from some excellent improvisations, no real surprises. Larry Grenadier has a splendid solo that demonstrates the depth of talent he possesses.

Just Like the Day is another great ballad from Pat's pen, played on acoustic 12-string guitar and rich in impressionistic sounds and textures. Just focus on the melody line and the way it gently rocks through a number of different modulations. The melody is at all times completely integrated with its harmonic context, and the symbiosis with bass and drums is utterly masterful. At 3.40 the band comes to a superb break as they enter the gorgeous coda, and Bill

Stewart's use of cymbal is withering. It's on pieces like this that you become very aware of the quality of modern recording methods by which every twitch and breath on the instruments can be heard with crystal clarity. Pat's delicate harmonics are a joy, but play the track through again and just listen to the drums.

With *Soul Cowboy* it's back to the mainstream jazz format, this time at a more measured pace to play a 12-bar blues that occasionally moves off in angled directions, but always seems to find it's way back to the path ahead. Grenadier gets a generous solo that sticks to the usual twelve-bar sequence, though Stewart's solo is digressive and spread over three rounds alternated with Pat and Larry.

The Sun in Montreal begins with Pat's electric guitar presenting the theme solo and apparently in 4/4 rhythm, but then the others join him we find the piece is actually based in 6/8. Throughout this piece, the trio toys with us, first trying to make us feel sixes then fours. The phrasing is therefore complex and it goes without saying that the band is playing with extreme skill to bring off all these effects whilst keeping the theme delicate and the feel of the piece so seamless.

Capricorn is a composition by Wayne Shorter played as another straight-ahead jazz trio piece with an up-tempo swing rhythm. The theme soon becomes history as the boys are grooving along at a fair pace with Pat improvising at speed. There's a pretty stunning run around the frets of his guitar at 2.52 and another at 3.25 that leave me feeling inadequate.

We Had a Sister is a title that gives a fair impression of the kind of feel this piece transmits. The first part of this poignant ballad on acoustic guitar is solo and freely played. When Larry and Bill join in at 1.35 the rhythm becomes formalised, but the melody develops in ways that require several hearings to give us orientation. What is clear from the first hearing is Bill Stewart's very imaginative percussive accompaniment, which is a real highlight of this track.

With the track *What Do You Want* we are right back on the standard jazz trio format once more, with an up-tempo swing piece written by Pat. This is a serious improvisational number that will inspire the jazz traditionalists.

You may recognise the title *A Lot of Livin' To Do* and it is indeed the 'standard' that is regularly played over the popular airwaves. From the show *Bye, Bye, Birdie* (1960), Charles Strouse wrote the music and Lee Adams the lyrics. It's always rare when Pat does a cover number like this, but it serves as a reminder of just how versatile he is.

Lone Jack first appeared as the final track of the 'White' album and here it is over thirty years later drawing a great album to a close. The pace is breakneck and Pat's playing utterly amazing. The theme starts immediately, played in single notes. Listen to the great change of rhythm into a waltz for the middle eight at 0.30. At 0.48 listen to the great way he plays the sequence of chords that defines the end of the main theme; they just fall from his guitar like leaves from a tree. Then it's back into the piece for a blistering solo run through the sequence of changes. Stewart's drumming is fantastic as he constantly seeks new changes that remain in sympathy with Pat's playing, and all executed at such speed. At 2.07 Pat moves into a chordal style of improvising that culminates at 2.30 with a repetition of the chordal motif. Next up is a solo from Larry and just listen to the way he follows the changes. It's not virtuosic but still most impressive. Stewart gets some drum fills after the bass solo before Pat returns to take us through to the end. Stunning! This album has a wealth of variety for all tastes and the undeniable mastery of composition and musicianship makes it a great addition to the Metheny repertoire.

Pat Metheny: *Pat Metheny Trio Live* – 2000 (***)

Another two hours of wonderful jazz from the same trio is available on this double CD, this time recorded live during the tours of 1999-00. And, apart from *Giant Steps* and *Soul Cowboy* it is a genuine bonus with material not on the studio album. The selections are about as varied as they could be, with Pat choosing the title track from his first album *Bright Size Life* to open with. It's as fresh as the day it was written. *Question and Answer* is given an extended treatment that emphasises the delicious freedom that jazz musicians have, for this piece, the title track of his 1990 album with Dave Holland and Roy Haynes and which reappears on the album *Like Minds* (1998), is extended to almost twenty minutes in length. It's not the total freedom that leads to chaos, but the freedom to display masterful qualities within the chosen framework. Having said that, Pat makes the most of the chance to try out new sounds and ideas that he has not applied to this piece before. The trio environment gives Pat the chance to play PMG material in the less formal format of the larger group situation, which is necessarily more orchestrated. *Into the Dream* from *Imaginary Day* is refreshingly treated with a beautiful opening on the 42-string Pikasso guitar. *So May it Secretly Begin* is taken from the *Still Life (Talkin')* album, whilst *The Bat* is from *Offramp* (1982). Both are beautifully presented ballads, though *The Bat* does lose something in the translation from its full format. The first disc is completed with a nippy version of Jerome Kern's *All the Things You Are*, which allows the boys to experiment with some fresh ideas at an unusual pace.

The second disc opens with *James*, another selection from *Offramp*, which sees some transformations, whilst retaining all its original charm. *Unity Village* is a second choice from *Bright Size Life* (1976), again receiving a facelift that remains faithful to the original but allows jazzers to feel refreshed. *Soul Cowboy* enjoys an encore on the live album, as a freewheeling number that the band would have been able to add to their repertoire with the minimum of rehearsal. The next three tracks are original to this album. *Night Turns into Day* is another of Pat's delicious ballads played on acoustic guitar. In total and deliberate contrast, and just in case we thought that Pat had forgotten about his dark side, *Faith Healer* reminds us that he considers himself entirely unrestricted by styles and genres. This extended spontaneous improvisation gives us plenty to think about, even if it's only the decision to jump to the next track. *Counting Texas* begins with the unmistakable sound of Texas and its slide guitar music, but here implanted into the modern jazz combo. You may recognise echoes from some of his other songs, but this is a fairly loose, unformatted number that sounds like it has been well lubricated with Jack Daniels, but hasn't.

If you like to imagine you are present at a gig, you will really enjoy this album for the presence and warmth of the recording are excellent.

Michael Brecker: *Nearness of You – The Ballad Book* – 2001 (***)

In December 2000, Pat turned up at New York's Right Track studios to record an album of 'ballads' for Michael Brecker. Also in the band were Herbie Hancock, Charlie Haden and Jack de Johnette. A ballad is usually sentimental and romantic, containing the kind of feelings we expect lovers to exchange in song and not the typical fare we expect from Michael. Right from the start, the album seems to be positioning itself towards the commercial side of jazz where, hopefully, it might attract rather more attention.

Pat had a big role in the album for it is Metheny Group Productions (Pat and Steve Rodby) that is listed as producing the record. Pat also provided two tunes and a number of arrangements, and of course played on all of the tracks. Another friend of Pat and Michael, Gil Goldstein, took care of other aspects of the arrangements, as well as the onerous job of generating the sheet music for the band.

The first track is *Chan's Song*, a cool, beautiful and logical piece by Herbie Hancock that won Michael a Grammy for the best jazz instrumental solo of the year. It gets the album off to a perfect start and acts as a warm-up for the main event. This is an appearance by Michael's friend James Taylor. Michael played on no less than seven of James' albums from 1972 to 1997, so now it was time for some payback. James' song, *Don't Let Me Be Lonely Tonight* is richly arranged and allows Michael to show right away just how lusciously lyrical he can be when he is not chasing the next unusual chord change. Even James' singing has taken on a kind of new laid-back special-for-jazz tone and if I were a woman I'm sure I'd fancy him madly, even at his age.

Nascente is a well chosen but little-known piece that is not really a ballad, but is certainly a beautiful piece of music. Pat arranged this piece and plays his Roland guitar synthesiser overdubbed onto an acoustic guitar backing, before Herbie solos and finally Michael comes in for some masterful jazz. The music is interesting and delightfully effervescent.

Next, the lights are dimmed and the candles lit for an intimate dinner party with your beloved in *Midnight Mood*, a delicious ballad by Joe Zawinul. Recorded on Joe's first album, *Money in the Pocket* (1966) when he was still very much a cabaret accompanist and before he was converted to electric playing, this is a very sexy piece with minimal playing and maximum feeling that oozes expression.

Then James Taylor returns for a spine-tingling version of *The Nearness of You*. It's a stunning highlight of the album as James embarks on the first verse with just Pat Metheny's gentle Latin rumba accompaniment on acoustic guitar. Then when the band enters for the chorus, it becomes an exquisite whole as bass, drums, guitar and piano all play to perfection. A catchy little lolloping motif is used as a link into Michael's lead solo, played in a higher key that steps the whole piece up a notch, before falling back once more for a final verse from James that Herbie plays in the foxiest of foxtrots. The coda is improvised with a fade of slinky notes from Pat, Herbie and Michael and I feel like applauding out loud.

The idea of this being a *Ballad Book* leads to an arbitrary subdivision of the tracks into the meaningless *Chapter One* (tracks 1-5), *Chapter Two* (tracks 6-10) and *Epilogue* (track 11). Unfortunately, *Chapter One* is far better than the rest, as the album entirely loses its way after track five. The danger of a book of ballads is of course that all the tracks sound the same, and I can state categorically that this album is not guilty of that. It's hard to put a finger on just why the rest is so disappointing, but it always comes down to the selection of pieces. Michael's *Incandescence* returns to his format of chasing the chords, although his theme is not as disjointed as in some of his compositions. Pat's *Sometimes I See* provides a gentle lift, as the conventionally harmonic slow waltz, made up of logical changes, breaks into interesting counter-rhythms. It is the familiar Gil Evans arrangement of *My Ship*, taken from Miles Davis's album *Miles Ahead* (1957) that may excite listeners most amongst *Chapter Two*. Gil Goldstein's adaptation of Evans's arrangement for this band is very good so it must be my familiarity with it that causes my lack of excitement on this occasion.

Irving Berlin's *Always* is an arrangement by Larry Goldings in which Jack de Johnette monotonously plays triplets. Sadly, the arrangement is not enough to save the piece, which is just too much of a musical cliché to be appropriate in this context. Pat Metheny might have saved the album with his own *Seven Days*, but the choice is too morose and the changes too unsettling at this stage in an hour of tender music; the music has an inappropriate presence here. Then, finally, Michael leads all the way through his own composition *I Can See Your Dreams*. With mostly just Herbie for accompaniment, this piece too fails to deliver with its schizophrenic design of short moody sections. Thus, the album ends in significant anti-climax, which is a great pity considering the obvious love and care that went into the making of it.

There's a little taste of Michael's humour on the cover of this CD, with a tiny human speck in the midst of a vast wilderness. I'm sure he laughed when he thought of that one!

Pat Metheny Group: *Speaking of Now* – 2002 (****)

The recent history of the band has seen it attract the highest level of talent currently available. The brightest new star is undoubtedly Richard Bona, a true musical prodigy discovered by Joe Zawinul. Here is a musician with limitless potential, able to pick up any instrument he chooses and play as if he were born doing it. An electric bass player with the same level of dexterity as John Patitucci, it would seem pointless having him in the band with Steve Rodby. Sadly, this fantastic skill has not been demonstrated on a PMG album, though it can be heard (and seen) on the finale of the *Speaking of Now Live* DVD, entitled *Song for Bilbao*. Bona's contribution to this album is in every other area except bass, for he provides vocal colour to the Metheny compositions, as well as guitar backings and percussion. Cuong Vu is the other young member, a gifted trumpet player as well as a backing vocalist. Since the early albums such as *The First Circle* when Lyle Mays provided trumpet sounds, Pat has always liked the sound that the vibrato-less trumpet contributed to his musical pastiches. Cuong Vu succeeds by adding a subtle flavour to the mix, never obtrusive, always enhancing the textures. Finally, Antonio Sanchez is yet another example of how skilled are today's jazz drummers. In the freer context of a gig, his solos are breathtaking. On record, as well as on stage, he is the consummate band member, always intimately involved with the piece whilst never dominating it.

The 2002 album *Speaking of Now* was an initial disappointment for many, for it seemed that PMG had finally lost the cutting edge creativity we had grown to expect. The Amazon website was filled with comments, some complimentary, but many not. Yet the World Tour that followed the record's release was a great success and, as time passed, it became clear that the album fell into the category of "grower". The World Tour gigs were varied, and, rather than just promote the new album, included many pieces from the back catalogue. Most surprisingly, in the gig filmed for the DVD, Pat actually included a cover number of the Bossa Nova number from the 1960s, *Insensatez*. A rare event indeed! There were also two dramatically reformed versions of *Last Train Home* and *Are You Going With Me?*

The album, however, contained all new material of the standard PMG type. Pat's success in PMG is clearer now than before. The winning formula is continued and evolved throughout the sequence of albums. With PMG, Pat remains very loyal to his audiences who are given what they desire: a collection of thoughtful, melodic, thoroughly crafted and imaginative compositions played by musicians at the peak of their abilities. The extreme musical purists would argue that jazz should be about constant experiment with sound and form, but sudden changes of direction are deeply unsatisfying to the majority of supporters, as Herbie Hancock found out to his cost. Pat is the rock-star equivalent of his genre, designing his world tours to satisfy the demands of the huge band of loyal fans literally all over the world, but unlike many rock stars, he is constantly evolving and improving the quality of his music.

As It Is starts with a great theme that is memorable, singable yet extremely tantalising. It twists through some great changes and the basic rhythm is constantly changing, the emphases on certain beats switching subtly like a weather vane swinging in the breeze. You really need to see the score to appreciate what is going on here. The introductory theme is short and the sequence of beats is 6, 5, 4, 6, 4, 4. After only thirty seconds a great groove kicks in that has a really beautiful deep-seated swing at its root. As with all great grooves, it's undemonstrative, yet gutsy and wholly cool. It takes just four bars of four. Then comes the main theme with a couple of seven beat bars to throw us off the scent, the sitar guitar with its eastern twang, and a few harmonics thrown in for good measure, but again the subtleties of the rhythm are puzzling.

The last part of the main theme is going to be made into the hook that sticks in our memories. From 1.40 to 2.00 its bars contain the sequence of beats 6, 5, 4, 3, 2, 4. This is so unusual there must be a queue of academics ready to explain to us that this is in fact a secret coded message. Unless you are interested in these things, you can remain blissfully unaware of the complexities and simply relax to this undulating and smooth chocolatey sound. This would be quite enough in one piece for most musicians, but for PMG the piece is only getting to half way. An entirely new section starts at 2.22 that shakes us out of our lethargy. We're ready for take-off as it adopts a driving rhythm that builds on the phrases already presented, yet is new. This is an example of what Pat calls improvisation based on the song but is not in the song. First Lyle's piano gives us the new direction. Then Pat's guitar synth is insistent. And after a brief ascendancy into the stratosphere, where the ice crystals glisten on the wings and the air is bitingly cold, our vehicle returns to solid ground with a wordless vocal. The undercarriage is down and we're hurtling along the runway, brake pads glowing hot as they bite hard. But the momentum is such that we take a long time to stop. Fortunately, there's plenty of space ahead so the band eases us out gently with several encores of the coded hook.

Proof is another mysterious composition. It starts well, but at once seems to have conflicting rhythms, with Sanchez's drums unrelated to what Pat and Lyle are playing. At 1.45 we enter a section of improvisation, but in this case, it's not clear what the basis of the improvisation is. There's coherence provided by a chord sequence that holds the band together and the rhythm is now settled into a groove that is urgent but not breathless. At 4.22 the trumpet of Cuong Vu enters the picture. Vu has a wonderful tone born in the modern era, but with echoes of the great trumpeters of the twentieth century. Yet it is his beautiful tone, assisted no doubt by the digital recording that is remarkable. His playing is assured and full of emotion as he tightens his lips and drives the notes ever upwards in tense intervals. The dramatic effect of his solo is a wonderful lead into a Mays solo on acoustic piano that also goes through the changes and explores every corner of this complex theme. Finally a theme that is now rather familiar reappears to indicate the approaching finale, which is an explosion of competitive musical activity. The drumming in this piece is exceptionally creative and is an example of what Pat meant when he said that Sanchez had enabled the band to do new things.

Another Life begins with a melody sung by Richard Bona that is typical of the contents of his solo album, *Reverence* (2001). The theme is brief at first, and overtaken by a beautiful laid-back slow samba over which Pat lays out another of his delightful melodies. Bona's melody reappears and then Pat starts his improvisation on an electrified Spanish guitar. The melody is developed and then the song is back, but more integrated than before. What began almost as two pieces spliced together is now a homogeneous unity. The end section starts at 5.40 and we seem to float on air. Lyle's solo is so delicate and the band provides the brocade cushion on which we sit as his wonderful magic carpet glides out into the dusk.

The Gathering Sky is an exquisite tapestry of rhythm, sound and melody. It begins with a six beat rhythmic flourish of African percussion invisibly woven into a fabric of acoustic guitar textures. Soon the theme is upon us and, though the rhythm remains tight, the theme is quite liberated as it twists and turns in the musical up-draughts. A peal of chimes introduces the Metheny guitar and the inevitable complexity begins. Then at 2.30 there is a fracture in the piece. The six-beat light-heartedness is exchanged for a much more business-like delivery in fours, but this doesn't last long before everything just gets too complicated to analyse here. We just sit back and marvel at everything that is going on. At 6.05 there is yet another complex section of composed and seriously orchestrated music that is taken over by a Sanchez drum solo. This dissolves at 7.05 into a dark, storm cloud that we can assume is representative of a gathering sky. By 8.10, the gloom and despondency dissolves into a wonderful sunshine-laden coda and a climactic ending is the only sensible resolution to this superb piece of music.

You is a love song in which a beautiful Metheny melody is sung by Richard Bona and blended with delicious guitar work. The wordless phrases are long, and expansive as the chordal accompaniment increments beneath it. Guitar and piano provide a delicate accompaniment during this wistful section. The lover sets out his stall for his amour and is clearly desperate to win her attention. As he sings, his desire for her grows ever more demanding. Soon the melody rises to higher and higher pitch where at 3.32 Lyle's synthesiser overwhelms its plaintive cry with a PMG-branded sound. Then Pat takes on an improvised section in the centre of the piece, and Mays takes over with a bright piano sound that, by changing key, is fresh and invigorating when the music seems to be going a little astray. The moods he paints cover the whole spectrum of feelings and emotions that lovers feel, until finally Bona returns and the band takes on a full sound for the final statement of his theme. There are long-held breathy notes as the chords descend and then at 7.00 a long crescendo of chords that dissolve into a quiet contemplation that is as beautiful as love should be.

In view of the emotional tension of the last song, *On Her Way* is an instant relief. The title almost implies that everything is well with the lovers after all, and the music would appear to confirm that. This piece begins as a hymn of celebration, packed full of joy and love that demands to be sung aloud. Of course, being jazz, this rarely goes exactly according to plan. We move into a section of guitar improvisation, with Pat spinning his way amidst the showers of brightly coloured confetti, fluttering to the ground in the sun-filled morning light. Then a change of key sets this wonderful song up for a final section of development. A new theme enters the picture and forms the backdrop for the fiesta of jazz that spews out of the speakers until the song fades out. It's a happy ending, as it should be.

A Place in the World begins with a guitar theme that seems serious and ambitious. The motif wants to be free. Under development amongst the instruments, it echoes and reverberates across the bar lines for two minutes or so. Then at 2.05 the guys in suits come knocking. "Please get into the limo, sir." By 3.15, the music sounds like a quiet engine, ticking over at low revs in top gear as the scenery glides by. Lyle sits in the driver's seat and puts the motor through it paces. The engine is so powerful that little gas is required at first, but Mays soon shows us what he can do with a V8. Cuong Vu, with shades on his trumpet is supremely relaxed riding shotgun, but soon the opposition arrives at the rear and Pat is forced to show them the colour of his guitar from the back seat. Fortunately for us all, they back off and we glide smoothly on to the rendezvous.

It is *Afternoon*. The deal is done and it's time for a cool vodka and lime by the pool. We're feeling pleased with ourselves. The flight back to LA is in a couple of hours so we can sit back and watch the pretty girls. Richard Bona feels lucky and his patter seems to work. This is a melody that sure works with the girls. Pat tries the same approach. It works just the same. The girls just come running, no matter which way he twists the lines. It's time to be ambitious. Several modulations are on the edge between respectability and being 'in your face', but the guys pull it off. They finish their drinks and head off to the airport with smiles on their faces and telephone numbers in their pockets.

Wherever You Go is a piece that conforms pretty much to the formula that has been developing. The main theme is first presented on Pat's solo guitar and then Lyle and Steve join in. The theme is developed into new shapes and then re-presented with different combinations of instruments. At 2.27 a quiet section begins based around Pat improvising over the chords. By 4.10 the brisk tempo is pretty much re-established and the piece starts to acquire a new enthusiasm. At 5.13, the main theme returns now with the trademarked voices coupled to Lyle's synthesised flute. Like a piece of origami, the music folds endlessly into itself and finally transforms into a shape that is recognisable as a sophisticated version of the initial theme.

Speaking of Now is a very good album, and it is now that we begin to consider it a disappointment if it is not awarded five stars. Sadly, this is not possible, for when compared to the ones that did receive the award, this album really does not quite reach the same pinnacle of brilliance. That should not put you off from buying it, however.

Pat Metheny: *One Quiet Night* – 2003 (****)

Pat's solo album is unusual by any circumstances and a delight for connoisseurs of solo guitar. Pat explains on the album notes how, in late November 2001, he spent a quiet night at home enjoying a recently discovered tuning on a newly acquired baritone guitar. The combination of new sounds stimulated him to create quite a lot of new material. Fortunately for us all, he decided to press the 'record' button and songs such as *One Quiet Night*, *Another Chance*, *I Will Find the Way*, *Peace Memory* and *Time Goes On* were saved forever. A year or so later, he completed the album in the same way, this time by adding some extra pieces by other composers. Thus Keith Jarrett's *My Song*, the gorgeous Norah Jones song *Don't Know Why* (written by Harris) and Gerry Marsden's *Ferry Across the Mersey* were added to his own *Song for the Boys* and *Over on 4th Street*. His old favourite *Last Train Home* completed the list. This is about as pure as a record can get – just one man and his instrument with no overdubs, artificiality or edits. I waited a long time before buying this album and I regret that now. It's not jazz-fusion, but it has enriched my life.

Pat Metheny Group: *The Way Up* – 2005 (*****)

In the 2005 album, *The Way Up*, PMG have taken their musical journey to its farthest reaches yet by dispensing with the traditional multi-track album format. A single Metheny/Mays composition lasting 68 minutes and 10 seconds is arbitrarily separated into *Opening* plus three further unnamed parts that are, according to Pat, purely for the convenience of the listener who wants to find his way around the composition.

Pat must be the record company's dream client, for he satisfies the commercial demands to make money whilst never compromising his art. Clearly, Pat's ambitions are more likely to be satisfied if he is a commercial success. The history of art is well populated with those who martyred themselves in order to be unique. What point is served if a musician refuses to make albums that sell in favour of those that further some idealistic goal yet are so strange and disorientated that no-one wants to hear them? Pat enjoys being a star, yet he appears modest and approachable. His popularity has never been greater in Europe and Asia, but the UK now exhibits the disinterest in Pat that is being presently shown to all jazz. As a result the 2005 World Tour contained only one date in the UK (London), whilst other EU countries were much visited. I was lucky enough to be present at two performances of *The Way Up*, first in Paris on 3 June and then London on 12 June.

Officially billed as a 'protest record' according to the tour programme notes, there was a deeper motive for the big change that occurred with this album. After the Paris gig I spoke to Lyle Mays and asked him about the significance of the album's title. He told me that, although there was not too much direct meaning, it was a result of the dissatisfaction that he and Pat both shared about the current state of music in which everything had to be short, simple and dumber. He said they both believed that it was necessary to create something with more substance and therefore they set out to write a single composition in which ideas were developed in depth. Pat himself said, "It used to be, they told you that you had to write three-minute songs to be a success. Now the question is: will it make a ring tone?"

Pat told Courtney Pine: "The thing about this record – I think we've been leading towards this for a while without actually going all the way – is that this record is not a suite record. This record is not a loosely organised group of semi-related things that we call one thing. This is really a single composition that is 68 minutes long that goes from the beginning to the end, and was written and scored and conceived to be that. As a navigational courtesy to the people that are going to have the CD in hand, we did put four IDs on it, just so you could get around the record, but it's one continuous piece of music and that's a pretty big hill to climb. I think the experience that Lyle and I have as writers over the years, it's taken us this amount of time to really get to the point that we felt that we could address that particular subject. It was absolutely the right band to do that with. We have this amazing new drummer Antonio Sanchez who's just opened up a whole new range of possibilities and potentials for what the group can be, and we just went right at those things. We're pretty excited about it. It's an unusual part of our story to have a record that functions like that and it's going to be a challenge to play it live. That's the next thing for us." [16]

So, with this record Metheny and Mays moved on from their earlier formats in favour of music that is even more sophisticated in texture, multi-layering and complex structure. The traditional PMG 'tunes' are fewer in number and those that remain are generally undergoing continuous transformation inside the broader tapestry, more in the style of Wayne Shorter's recent work but less improvised. There are recurring references and themes throughout the piece that form links and hooks to help listeners discover the music more quickly than they might otherwise have done, but don't expect this to be an easy listen. This significant step in the band's musical evolution comes at a cost, and this is paid in listener concentration. It runs totally contrary to current culture to expect audiences to concentrate for long periods of time, let alone to give them something of such consistent complexity. Casual listeners meeting this music for the first time may not be prepared to pay such a price. In my own case, I have listened to the music some thirty times, five of which have been detailed dissections. How many of us regularly sit down to listen to a single piece of music lasting for 68 minutes? Yet to get the most out of this stuff we need to do this many times, but most of us would claim not to have the time to spare.

Such demanding music is really to be found only in the classical world. I asked Lyle if it could be compared to a symphony and he did not deny the description. However, a symphony composed of four movements does not necessarily have repetitions of the themes and phrases across the movements. On the whole, classical music has greater longevity and can be appreciated over a lifetime, but a composition such as this is born in a disposable culture and will struggle to survive unless it achieves a new kind of status rarely accorded to jazz compositions. I'm sure Pat and Lyle don't care too much about that and Pat has taken the gamble that this record *will* stand the test of time.

Structurally the music is very complex and difficult to break down without reference to the score. Some of the themes are disguised or reinvented, but never repeated verbatim. The context is constantly changing and the whole piece varies considerably from the very quiet to the very loud, from the peaceful to the frantic. There certainly do appear to be natural breaks in the music that might correspond to symphonic movements. Pat is changing guitars constantly throughout to keep up with the constantly changing demands of the backdrop and, in a live context, the crew is kept busy furnishing him with the ever-changing array of guitars, some of them mounted on the fixed stands he likes to employ. Other features of the changing soundscape are the battery of electronic effects employed by Cuong Vu, nominally playing trumpet, though you would not realise it at times. Pat requires so much guitar work on stage through the layering of the composition that Nando Lauria is used pretty much as a second guitarist supporting Pat with the rhythm guitar sections he needs. Throughout are the majestic, ever-present drums of Antonio Sanchez who provides a level of accompaniment unsurpassed on any other PMG album. Rodby too makes a major contribution, especially in providing some of the most sonorous and resonant playing on any PMG record when he uses his bow on the bottom end of his lovely double bass during *Part Two*.

As for Pat's playing, well, this man simply gets better and better. Every aspect of his playing is more finely honed than it has ever been. The band takes on some of the fastest tempos you are likely to hear. In *Part Two*, one astonishing section has Metheny, Mays and Vu playing a melody in unison at amazing speed. And Pat's facility over the guitar's fret-board is better by orders of magnitude, a clear benefit derived simply from the large proportion of his life that he spends playing.

Overall the success is astonishing. From the very first bar, it is obvious how much of a step up in sound quality has been achieved above that of previous albums. A few years ago, PMG albums did not sound significantly different if you listened to the earliest ones. That is no longer the case. However, they do not sound dated – simply different. My analysis seems to indicate a small step change in the level of all-round musical quality and sophistication between *Letter From Home* and *We Live Here;* the change may even have occurred at *Still Life (Talking)*. It is clear that the sound of Metheny fusion has moved on and *The Way Up* has taken PMG listeners to a new third level of attainment. The music is so original that it surely cannot date.

Another interesting point is to be made when comparing the recorded music with the live version. It is true to say that the music is highly orchestrated, as it usually is with PMG. This at once raises questions of validity with the serious jazz connoisseurs who criticise music that is not substantially improvised. An obvious comparison to the overall concept of the work might be made with saxophonist Joshua Redman's composition, *Passage of Time*, of which the performance might last anything from 20 minutes to several hours, depending on the band's 'take' on the piece at the time. We could conclude that Redman's composition is more based upon improvisation than the inevitably more orchestrated Metheny/Mays piece. This is not to distract from the success of the PMG recording, which satisfies the listener to a high level. Here, jazz is at last presented in the same shape that classical music has been for centuries. Here is one in the eye for the classical music 'snobs' who see jazz musicians as pop musicians in anoraks; this is the classical music of the 21st century.

One criticism might be that the piece seems to be front-loaded. Its major impact occurs early on and the final third seems to sell us rather short. However, this criticism does depend on musical interpretation. The atmospheric ending is full of echoes of the earlier themes and motifs and the listener who seeks to understand the underlying structure finds continual pleasure. One interpretation is that the piece describes an entire life, from a joyful birth (*The Opening*), through the excitement and challenge of childhood and youth (*Part One*), to the highs and lows of having a family (*Part Two*), a rewarding but stressful time for most of us. The work progresses with an increasing awareness of the march of time and an approaching appointment with destiny. A growing sadness starts to pervade the music that seems to describe retirement, in which the pain gradually outweighs pleasure. Finally come old age, death and the progression to a life after death (*Part Three*). Is this literally, *The Way Up?* Is the work really so philosophical? At present we don't know, but PMG does have a track record of using music to represent earthly experiences.

A feature of the album music that was even more pronounced in the live performances I witnessed was the use of a single repeated note on guitar that varied in loudness and the speed of repetition. It sounds like a resonance or an effect in physics known as 'beats', which is what you hear when two different acoustic waves interfere with one another. This was used twice, each time against a solo. The first time occurred at the very beginning of the gigs. Pat walked on stage and began to play solo guitar against this background. There appeared to be no relationship between the two and the result was that the beauty of his solo was severely curtailed by this unrelated resonating pulse. On the album, the most obvious place to hear it is in *Part Two* when it is used against Lyle's beautiful solo. For some time I was very annoyed by this, because it impeded the listener's appreciation of the solo. It also bothered me because it was clearly intentional. It later occurred to me that, if we take Pat's explanation for the album's concept as a protest by Metheny/Mays against the current musical establishment, we could actually view this musical effect as a description of the battle between Metheny/Mays, on the one hand creating beautiful music with their solos, and the musical environment portrayed as a kind of degrading Matrix. I do not know if this explanation is correct or not, but it helps me greatly with my appreciation of the music.

Opening begins with an atmosphere of the outdoors, of people and traffic. A high pitched hum materialises from the void, resonating as a rapid four-beat rhythm that transforms into and out of triplets, that is, each beat is turned into three. Then each beat becomes two, then three, then four again. Then, thirty-six seconds into the piece, the bass drumbeat begins. It seems to follow what has already been established, but the drumsticks begin something entirely new. Oh, and there's some percussion in the background that is playing in yet another rhythm. (This is an example of what Pat was referring to when he said that Sanchez had greatly widened the scope of the band's music. Sanchez also demonstrated this skill in the track *Proof* on *Speaking of Now*.) When the guitar and piano enter at forty seconds I give up trying to count the components of this polyrhythm because Lyle and Pat begin a dialogue that is simply stunning. Soon, every musical activity is feeding off every other. It's the ultimate in interaction, perfectly orchestrated and brilliantly executed. The sound is lush, and very sophisticated. It has presence and demands your attention. Within the first minute of this work we know that PMG have embarked upon a musical enterprise of startling density and imagination. This is in quite a different league from all that has gone before. Here is an all-pervasive musical Matrix of the twenty-first century, permeating everything that is going on around it, sustaining it, driving it, feeding it, and allowing us brief glimpses of what we believe to be the real world beyond.

At 1.34 Pat comes in with the first theme, a strong Metheny melody, delivered to the backing of the Matrix. But don't expect it to last long, for in this masterwork change is never far around the corner. There will be many echoes and reminiscences to come, but the basic piece constantly evolves, stuck like the arrow of time in forward gear. In some ways this is Pat's answer to Miles Davis's premise that jazz is living in the moment and moving on. At 2.11 a sustained guitar begins to slither around like a hungry anaconda. Some heavy footfalls at 2.42 introduce a short transition into a different rhythm at 2.50, reminiscent of a little girl skipping briefly down the road in the spring sunshine. The Matrix pulls us back into its clutches while the snake still circles around.

At 3.40 the next rhythm begins softly in the background. A quick-fire series of three-note motifs is delivered in a cascade across all the instruments. This is used to build a tension and a warning of imminent change of direction. The short climax ends at 4.24 with a materialisation from the Matrix. We burst into reality like a diver coming up for air. The complex rhythms dissolve away, but the pulse remains in the background as Pat plays some soothing acoustic sounds to relax our taut nerves. The *Opening* closes at 5.16.

With only the slightest break *Part One* takes us on a new journey with one of the main themes of the album. It is a rhythmic chevron made up of three notes assembled in slightly different ways, some angled up, some pointing down, randomly permutated. They are used to create a melody that will be a highlight of the album. The method used is the one I have described previously in which the band plays a whole series of modulations behind the repeated line of melody that soon becomes memorised. Here, the line begins on xylophone and continues on guitar. Soon a new cascade of three-note motifs appears, as it did in the *Opening*. Second time around, the melody itself is developed into a new richer, more mature version. At 1.18, Pat begins a short solo that grows into some gorgeous heavy rock guitar sounds, whilst Cuong Vu's electronic trumpet sounds create atmosphere. At 1.35, the theme returns with a few nice twists.

At 2.05 we switch to a bitterly cold winter's day. Pull your coat around you. We're walking along the banks of a great river that is completely frozen. From far away across the great expanse of white wilderness we hear the distant sounds of wildlife, struggling to survive the cold. What promised to be a beautiful start to the day as the sun tried to break through the dark clouds, starts to turn against us as the wind picks up and a remorseless, bitingly cold blast cuts a swathe all the way from the Arctic. Pat applies his standard technique of developing a hard-driving guitar solo from the slightest base. By 5.08 we're back to the warmth of the main theme. Now it embraces us with its familiarity, and at 5.26, just to make sure, transforms by modulation into a definitive statement. The cascade of triplets ripples through the band once more, rising to a fantastic climax before a final glorious pass through the theme. The overwhelming sense of security it transmits is about to dissolve, as does everything else in this complex piece, but just for now it sweeps us off our feet. Let it. Enjoy this moment of magic.

At 6.22 a completely new mood begins with Pat and Lyle leaving the comfort of their cosy cottage and stepping out into the deep snow. It's a hesitant foray, and the band joins in to emphasise the uncertainty. The Matrix starts to resonate before the band begins a very fast tempo theme at 8.50. At 10.18 the band are playing a section of resonance that seems to be passed around from one musician to the next. Then at 11.08, guitar and trumpet play a new line, again at very fast tempo, which ends in a sequence of sharp shouts.

At 12.04 there is an intro to a second major new theme that kicks in at 12.29. Once again, this theme is comprised of a series of three-note phrases, but played over a lazy 5/4 (five beats to a bar) rhythm. This is almost impossible to pick up on if you don't know it's there, but the key is to wait until the theme ends when the triplets die away leaving the same underlying beat. The other indicator is to listen to Steve Rodby's bass, which plays the five-beat rhythm whilst everyone else is playing fifteens. This is a masterpiece of musical complexity. Then at 13.18 what seems like it should be a middle-eight occurs and we rightly expect the piece to return to the complex theme, but it doesn't. Instead, the resonance returns at 14.12 and lasts until 14.21. Now it's time for a decent solo in 4/4 played at breakneck speed, about 320 beats per minute! At times, Pat is playing ten notes per second through this passage. This is a fantastic passage of mainstream jazz that many jazz guitarists could only dream of playing. As he moves forward into it, at 16.22 he enters a sequence of short cadenzas played solo with drums, interspersed with ensemble playing. From 16.43 to 16.57 there's a crescendo and then comes a superb change of tempo as Lyle comes in to take up the theme at half speed. He's feeling extremely animated for this solo and his playing is superbly varied, typically lyrical one moment and imperious the next. First his fingers flow impeccably up and down the keyboard and then, from 18.05, he is expounding a series of percussive chords.

At 18.30 Cuong Vu takes a solo and this is a highlight of the album, for the theme he plays over the same chords that Lyle has just used progresses through a wonderful series of modulations that drag him upwards to ever more creativity. The tension builds in the most spine-tingling fashion until at 20.00 we are literally screaming with delight. This is a very fine moment on the album. The second theme returns at 20.06 in its five-beat glory, undisguised by flying triplets. It's the same theme we heard eight minutes ago and it's familiar, but so much has happened since then!

Now it's time for another change, so this super theme concludes with a long sequence of chords that slowly releases the tension all the way back to zero. By 20.50 all that is left is Pat's lovely acoustic guitar soothing away the stress. At 21.18, his standard electric guitar starts a lovely melody that takes a gentle step up at 21.48, a sign that this is the start of something more profound. At 22.30 the three-note motifs echo around in the background again and this is a sign that the first major three-note theme is making a comeback. It's not the full theme because we've moved on, but at least the chords are at the bottom of the music now and so it feels like familiar ground. From 24.20 we move into a final section based on the very fast 4/4 tempo used earlier. At 25.30 Antonio Sanchez begins a sequence of drum fills that rise to a crescendo. The band fades leaving the drums in full flow, but soon they too fade and peace is once more restored.

Part Two begins in a sombre mood. The Matrix is resonating once more to a melancholy solo played on acoustic bass. At 0.55 the trumpet takes up the cry and tries to add some optimism as the music starts to build. At 1.37, Lyle comes in to play a middle section over Steve's continuing bass. The optimism seems dampened slightly, and bass agrees, but by 2 minutes the mood is changing once more. Darkness becomes light and at 2.15 the sun emerges to shed warmth and love on all present. A third major theme in 4/4 now begins, and each note is again played in triplets to create a woven tapestry of rhythm. At 3.00 the bass returns with its tale of woe. The Matrix continues behind throughout, but at 3.43 a special thing starts to happen as the Matrix starts to resonate with itself. Lyle commences an extended solo on acoustic piano, but the Matrix is ever-present, tugging the music first one way, then another, slowing to a pulse, throbbing through Lyle's beautiful song, a piano on life-support. At 6.25, the pulse becomes irresistible and the Matrix demands the same complex rhythms that were used at the start of *Opening*, but now used to accompany Cuong's solo. This serves to introduce a five-and-a-half-minute section of extended band improvisation over constantly rising chords that will drive us to the very edge of nervous breakdown. This is fearsome music, organised pandemonium, but thoroughly wonderful up to the point of collapse at 12.03 when the crescendo is almost too much to bear. Free jazz fans eat your hearts out! This is what Miles Davis and his disciples dreamed of playing in the early 1970s and didn't.

A calming link passage on Pat's acoustic guitar introduces a beautiful extended melody played on Grégoire's harmonica at 13.00. Even now, the Matrix is wafting in and out of the phrases. Unhurried and spectacularly cool, this luscious line seeps sweet juices like a fresh-cut pineapple. Listen out for the lovely blue notes around 15.38. At 16.45 a coda begins for this song in the form of a sequence of cymbal flourishes and drum rolls. Then we are caught up by the Matrix that bursts out into the open. Again, it's a rhythm of three, this time encapsulated into 9/8 time. The harmonica tries to make itself heard but is drowning in the wave that rushes along and sweeps all in its path. At 19.58

things get very serious as we draw to a close with a short set of sharp, two-note motifs accompanied by thrashing strings. After a brief climax *Part Two* ends at 20.29.

The two-note motifs set the mood for the start of *Part Three* and a lively up-tempo theme. By fifty seconds the original three-note phrases echo through the accompaniment once more. Pat and Cuong play the melody, brief as it is. At 1.16 a middle section starts. At 2.22 a super new theme begins from which Pat starts to solo up to 3.38 on standard electric guitar. A short bridge from Lyle on acoustic allows Pat to pick up his guitar synth at 4.00 and lay down a section that twists and turns. At 4.35, another section begins that covers the space up to the return of the main theme at 5.14. Now voices join the full band. That starts to wind itself up. This is PMG as we know it so well with everything burning and turning. Melody and harmony turned up to max and everything expected to end in a climax as it must. At 7.12, the Matrix takes over again. From 7.47 the two-note motifs combine with the three-note theme from *Opening* and another mouth-watering climax builds slowly to a fade at 9.19. But now there is an unusual turn of events as the very first theme returns to wither and die in front of us. The realisation that we are to fall victim to a terrible loss is a bolt from the heavens. From 10.00 we pass the point of no return. There is to be no joyous end to this wonderful piece. We must seek our final resting place in the stark frozen wasteland – desolate, lonely and desperately sad. All the echoes and resonances are there from the beautiful music of the past hour, but the Matrix is all consuming. Is this the way up? It's icy white and, Oh! So coooold!

This is an exquisite combination of the simplest and the most complex music. Here are some of the most complex musical constructions and rhythms ever put together for a jazz performance, but the themes could hardly be simpler based on two and three note phrases. We should all celebrate this music as a milestone in music history. How can I not award it five stars?

Michael Brecker: *Pilgrimage* – 2006 (****)

By August 2005, it was clear that Michael Brecker, who had been diagnosed with a rare illness a couple of years earlier, was a very sick man. But Michael was a fighter and determined to go ahead with the recording of a new album. With the help of Gil Goldstein as an associate producer, he drew together a band of friends to take part in the project: Pat, Herbie Hancock, Jack de Johnette, and John Patitucci. Herbie wasn't able to be present on all of the tracks so his place was taken by the young superstar, Brad Mehldau, who had been recently working with Pat.

There is no doubt that, in its own genre, this is a very good record. As someone who has specialised in composition, as well as being one of the greatest sax players who ever lived, Brecker could not have been associated with anything second rate. Unfortunately, I must report that the album is heavily constructed on modal harmonies and no matter how many times I play it, the music succeeds only in making me steely-hearted. There is nothing that I can sing, little inspiration for my feet to move and absolutely nothing to make me smile or feel warm about. My musical knowledge tells me that there are masterpieces of both composition and performance on this disc, but my heart simply doesn't want me to play it. Perhaps it is my imagination, but I also feel that Pat is more inclined to play clichés when he plays in the modes. His inspiration seems to lack the usual high level of creativity. Perhaps it is because he is a musician used to playing from the heart and there isn't much of a connection to that organ from this kind of jazz.

In February 2007, the album attracted a lot of attention at the Grammy awards ceremony and the track *Anagram* was given the award for the Best Jazz composition. Unfortunately, Michael was not there to receive it, for he died on 31 January 2007. If there is anything warm about this album it is the poignancy of Michael's smile in his final portrait on the artwork, and the memory of one of the finest musicians ever to pick up a saxophone.

Pat Metheny and Brad Mehldau: *Metheny Mehldau* – 2006 (****)

Brad Mehldau was born in 1970 in Jacksonville, Florida. He moved to New York in 1988 to attend The New School and study jazz and piano with Fred Hersch, Junior Mance and Kenny Werner. It was in 1993 that Pat Metheny first heard about the young pianist who had already developed his own unique style of playing. Pat had been recording and touring with Joshua Redman when an excited Joshua came to a gig one night and told Pat about the wonderful new young pianist he had just seen and who he was going to hire for his band. This he did, and, after Pat had left the band, Redman and Mehldau (with Christian McBride and Brian Blade) recorded *Mood Swing* (1994). Although Pat knew that he would one day play with Brad, and their paths did cross from time to time, it wasn't until late in 2005 that he was able to bring it about, by which time Brad had built a formidable reputation for himself as one of the brightest young stars of jazz piano.

From very early in his career Mehldau gravitated towards small group jazz, preferring the trio format most of all. This interest resulted in the recording of a project in five volumes (CDs) all entitled *The Art of the Trio*, a rather odd enterprise for someone still in the early phase of his career. Whilst clearly a jazzer at his core, there remains a strong formal side to his playing that maintains links with the traditional European classical style of music. Consequently he has been involved in numerous projects beyond the world of jazz. For example, two new works for voice and piano entitled The Blue Estuaries and The Book of Hours: Love Poems to God were commissioned by Carnegie Hall and performed in 2005 with the classical soprano, Renée Fleming. Both were released on the album *The Love Sublime* (2006). Mehldau has also written music for films, including Stanley Kubrick's *Eyes Wide Shut* and an original soundtrack for the French film, *Ma Femme Est Une Actrice*.

These two quite different aspects of Mehldau's musical ethos often compete in his music and the result has been well described as "something like controlled chaos." [22] This is perfectly illustrated in parts of the two albums he recorded with Pat in December 2005 in New York's Right Track studios. The first album is 80% duets with two of the ten tracks using their two mutual friends Larry Grenadier and Jeff Ballard. The second album, recorded at the same time but released a year later than the first, is comprised of 20% duets and 80% quartet.

The opening track is *Unrequited*, a Mehldau composition that is appropriately melancholic and is played as precisely and sensitively as a piece of classical chamber music. The interplay between the two players is remarkable from around 2.00 as they engage in Bach-style counterpoint, diving and weaving like opposing football players. The structure of the music develops throughout its five minutes of existence as deliberately as a sonata form and is a fine exposition of Mehldau's mix of rigid classics and loose jazz.

Ahmid-6 is a bright, lively Metheny composition that would stretch most musicians as it romps through a fast sequence of changes, a chordal origami that makes *Giant Steps* look like ballet practice. Yet Brad never shows the slightest sign of hesitancy with this complex piece written by his partner.

Brad's playing over Pat's beautiful ballad *Summer Day* is stunning. Pat uses the first 1.20 to outline his theme that includes a four-chord phrase that spans four bars with a clever use of triplets. Then Brad takes over and displays his "controlled chaos" – a blend of cheeky motifs and harmonic raspberries with soul-probing prose. Pat's music is a welcome reminder of his PMG melodic style without being in any way a re-hash. Through the latter stages of this album highlight, the four-chord phrase gently rocks like a rowing boat on a mooring. Then, after a final spell of friendly jousting, the two players come together in a series of perfectly timed hops and bring this wonderful piece to a crisp close.

Pat's tune *Ring of Life* is a perfect contrast as the quartet is fired up for this incredible piece that stands out from this clutch of great compositions. This piece is a rarely rivalled display of rhythmic fireworks and Ballard has his work cut out to manage the proceedings, which he does with honours. The basis is a cycle of sixteen beats delineated by a give-away cymbal crash. But that doesn't mean it's simply four bars of four because the players – Brad in particular – superimpose the changes in a sequence of downbeats that seem randomly spaced. For his solo, Brad deals with all this in his stride and appears to continue the random accents with his left hand whilst extemporising with his right. It's a simply stunning display of music at the highest levels of both composition and performance. Instead of the simple symmetry of the Ring in the title, this music seems to me more like the complexity of a double helical spiral of DNA, its two twisted strands linked through the constantly varying sequence of four amino acids.

Rhythm is also strongly featured in the second composition from Brad entitled *Legend*. This piece is mostly about a six-beat cycle comprised of a two and a four. It does, however, break down into the simpler 3 + 3 from time to time. The harmonic elements twist and turn like a path through a forest that is as unclear as the origins of many a legend of popular culture.

Pat returns to the theme of the love song for *Find Me in Your Dreams*, an exquisite 21st century expression of love between two people. In a previous era and in a simpler format, Billie Holiday, Sarah Vaughan or Dinah Washington might have sung Pat's lines to a cocktail bar piano accompaniment, but this is 2005 and we have moved on a long way, thanks to the efforts of musicians like Pat. What would have once been ordinary lines are now embellished with the many subtle changes that Pat crafts into his music. Yet again, Brad's creativity shines brightly through his brilliant solo from 3.15, with a delicious cadence thrown in at 3.45, and it is as clear as the tone from both instruments why Pat was so keen to duet with this original and articulate musician.

Say the Brother's Name is the second of the two quartet pieces, played in a gentle Latin tempo. The piece first appeared on Pat's album with John Scofield, *I Can See Your House from Here* (1994) and was a stunner there. Once again, it is an echo of former PMG glories.

Bachelors III is a blues waltz by Pat in the spirit of Gershwin. It's a simple enough piece that Pat and Brad would have rattled off in no time, yet Brad's soloing once more steals the limelight as his lines repeatedly step off the kerb into the murkier parts of this Louisiana roadside. Pat uses his beautiful electro-acoustic guitar to find some clear tonal space for Brad's bright solo and as Brad breaks loose again towards the end, the comping is delightfully dusky.

Annies Bittersweet Cake is the third piece from Brad and is aptly named for this slice has many complex flavours. It's got a fairly regular shape but the ingredients are unusual, with lots of rare goodies picked from the fields and forests around Annie's traditional palisaded house in the country.

The final track is *Make Peace*. It's almost impossible to imagine the last track on a Metheny album being a throw-away item, as is the case on some other artists' work. Last tracks are frequently the ones played least because we so often interrupt our listening sessions before we reach them. However, when we buy a Metheny album, we can be sure that great thought has been put into both the content and the sequence of the album and that the final track is as important as the first.

The melody is focussed on a three-note motif that takes on the kind of significance that the five-note motif did in Spielberg's film *Close Encounters of* the Third Kind. There's nothing alien about this music, however. On the contrary, it embraces the whole of humanity. It could easily be an anthem for pacifists, although it may be a little too complex to be played over loudspeakers at a rally. That shouldn't matter however. The fact is that, as this exquisite music proceeds, the clear message in the title becomes first an exhortation and then an order issued by Pat's insistent guitar strumming and Brad's robust left hand chords. But there is a final 'Please!' at the end. Magnificent!

Pat Metheny and Brad Mehldau: *Metheny Mehldau Quartet* – 2007 (***)

It's difficult not to arrive at the conclusion that this Quartet album is an album too far. It's the old example of a poor double album that could have been cut down to a better single album. Yet the music is strangely divided between a good first album and a poor second. It's a bit like matter and anti-matter; a bit like two contra-rotating rings of protons ready to smash into each other. Just as the first album was a collection of duos with some quartets, this is a collection of quartets with some duos.

The first track gives a false impression. *A Night Away* is light and bright, a medium tempo simple melody that heads off into straightforward, familiar territory, led by a Brad solo in his usual step-off harmony. It's a memorable piece and will have you whistling the tune after a few plays. Then comes *The Sound of Water*, which is a duo with Pat on his 42-string Pikasso guitar. You might guess that this is intended to be a somewhat descriptive musical sketch, and it is, yet it really does not add anything to the wider world of music and is disappointing. *Fear and Trembling* has a heavily distorted guitar sound and clearly intends to purvey some darker idea, but matched against the pure sound of Brad's piano it doesn't come off. Now I find myself starting ask why Lyle is not playing this on his synthesisers and I realise that I am beginning to miss his presence on Pat's albums. Track 4 is *Don't Wait*, another inspirational acoustic melody with a special moment at 5.48, but this excellent piece is the only genuine highlight of this album.

Towards the Light adopts Pat's now familiar format of taking a muse and turning it into a whirlwind in the style of *Are You Going With Me?* However, even allowing for a good transition into a strumming section around 6.18, the feeling of déjà vu is starting to detract from what should have been a stirring experience. I guess, if you have not heard much of Pat's music before, you can still enjoy this.

The second half of the album is, frankly, poor. *Long Before* is another of Pat's cocktail lounge songs, now played as a duet when you think it would be more appropriate for a bass and drums to be present. It's Pat trying to sound like Jim Hall and really not improving on what might have been achieved fifty years ago. However, the quality of the composition is poor.

En La Tierra Que No Olvida is clearly designed to have a Spanish style and sound, but this is just lip service and Pat is now starting to sound as if he only has clichés in his guitar case during this entirely vacuous piece. Things do not improve during Brad's piece *Santa Cruz Slacker*, despite his looser style of harmony. Things are starting to look like they are disappearing down one of CERN's black holes.

By the time I get to *Secret Beach* I am losing the will to live. This very ordinary piece, with some echoes of Autumn Leaves, has a slight slow bossa nova feel and chord changes that contribute to the feeling that I am looking at a beach through an alcoholic stupor. Everything is hazy, including the point of doing this piece, and the final burst of guitar synthesiser serves only to highlight the fact that they've run out of ideas during this dustbin piece. Nothing improves during the curiously sterile *Silent Movie*. When the inspiration dries up, all that is left are the clichés. The addition of *Marta's Theme* at track 11, breaks the physical symmetry and, to some extent, the boredom, but it's a tiny concession, a postscript apology for the poor quality of eight preceding tracks.

As a fan of bass, I find myself asking the question, "Where is the bass?" It seems such a long time since I remember hearing some really memorable bass playing on a Metheny album. It's not that he doesn't use good players, but simply that their playing does not seem to contribute much to the overall result. I have not mentioned Larry Grenadier once in my critique, and the only reason for that is that nothing stands out for me on either of these two albums.

The Tao of Physics

As I sit to write this, it is a momentous day in the history of mankind. It is the very day in September 2008 when scientists commenced their largest experiment. Today could prove to be more significant than the 1945 day of the Trinity explosion in the New Mexico desert, more fundamental than the publication of Einstein's Theory of Relativity, more relevant to our understanding of the Universe, because it leads to the answer to the greatest question of all – where did the Universe come from?

Deep below the mountainous terrain on the borders of France and Switzerland, a great international project has been underway since 1995 to build the world's largest and highest energy particle accelerator known as the Large Hadron Collider (LHC). Today is the day they switched it on. Some people thought it would result in the end of the world as its powerful contra-rotating beams came together to create a tiny black hole into which the Earth would disappear. We're still here.

So, what has all this to do with Pat Metheny? Pat is a highly intelligent human being who thinks as deeply about what he is doing as any musician alive. Furthermore, he is never afraid to try to communicate his ideas, no matter how difficult they are to describe. A particularly philosophical session occurred in an interview with Richard Niles of the BBC during a radio programme broadcast in 2007. It is daunting enough to talk about music because language doesn't easily deal with descriptions of sounds or feelings. Even more difficult is to use words to describe that deep place in the human soul occupied by music. Pat should be applauded for trying. As a scientist, I see remarkable parallels between the ultimate physics, as represented by the experiments at the LHC, and Pat's brace of albums with Brad Mehldau.

With these two albums, it is as if Pat is distilling his music down to an ever-purer form. It is as if, after nearly forty years as a professional musician he has now uncovered and refined all the elements of his trade that he needs in order to present his ultimate thesis. Rhythm and harmony are comparatively easy to master, and Pat does this in almost everything he plays. Saxophonist Michael Brecker once said that he felt he had mastered all the technicalities of his instrument in the early days of his career and that when he practised he was not trying to improve that. Most intriguing for him were the relationships between the notes, and he was always seeking new ways of combining and presenting them. The actual playing of the instrument was not of concern to him; the deeper significance of the music that came out was what mattered most. Pat Metheny has a similar mastery of his instrument; he is able to play anything he (or others) can conceive. Although he modestly maintains that he doesn't play the guitar as well as others, for Pat, it is the complete package that matters most when we describe his contributions to music. Not only does he play the guitar brilliantly but he delivers packages of musical intuition that are as deeply beautiful as anyone has ever done. Musical ideas are paramount for Pat, but along the way, there happens to be that great indefinable parameter, melody.

He told Niles: "Melody is the most impossible aspect of music to nail down. With chords, if you play these sets of tones under these conditions, there's no denying it – that's a Bb7#11 – that's what it is. There's no discussion necessary. The attempts to quantify melody ...in classical studies, certain kinds of intervals invoke lyricism, certain kinds of intervals invoke romance – that's all well and good, but when you hear Lester Young or Stan Getz or Clifford Brown, there's a genuine melodic quality at work there...that goes way beyond anything that you can quantify. And as much as you try to break down what is a melody, it ultimately becomes a poetic definition. You can't really break it down. It's also the rarest thing. It's the thing that you almost don't hear any more – somebody who's a really good melodic improviser. It's possible to become a really good abstract improviser, and it's possible to become a good bebop improviser, but for somebody to really devote their efforts as a musician or their practice time to becoming a good melodic player, you know, what do you even tell 'em to practice? What is it exactly? You can't really break it down. It's something that goes beyond the nuts and bolts of any discussion that we can have." [23]

Asked why it is that a musical interval like the perfect fifth can have an undeniable common effect, Pat said he believes that there is a relationship between music and physics at the deepest level. I agree. Physicists have discovered many wonderfully symmetrical relationships in nature and it is entirely possible that human evolution has incorporated the beauty of physics into the emotional responses caused by musical sound. "It does seem like on the most minute level of our existence, that relationship – the thing that makes a fifth sound good to all of us – exists. My favourite way of describing this is that music is actually this gigantic mistake that we're not actually supposed to know about. Somehow in our sense of the Universe around us there's these tiny little cracks that give us a window into everything that we can't possibly understand because we're not equipped...we don't have the tools for them. But somehow the music seeps into those cracks and it's something that reminds us or indicates to us these imperceivable things that are in fact around us all the time. I tend to think of music as something that's an incredible variation away from the rest of most human experiences and for that reason value it even more." [23]

The Metheny-Mehldau project, represented by these two albums is a remarkable achievement for they complement each other like those two contra-rotating proton rings at the LHC. In this Alpine underworld *(En La Tierra Que No Olvida)* we stand in awesome anticipation, *A Night Away* from the moment of truth. We wait for the electrical breaker to be thrown to power up the 27 km of superconducting magnets that will set them in motion (*Don't Wait*). This is an endeavour that probes the Tao of physics. These two rings of life are yin and yang – almost mirror images of each other in terms of the balance of duets and quartets. As they circulate at speeds approaching the speed of light (*Towards the Light*) we stand in *Fear and Trembling*, waiting for the impact that results in the release of great quantities of energy. Will we all die tonight? Apparently not. These albums represent a voyage of discovery for Pat as he seeks to probe ever deeper into the source of his musical inspiration, looking for his own answers to things that happened *Long Before*.

The more physicists probe into the nature of matter and the Universe, the more symmetry they uncover. Studies of the fundamental particles have produced results so remarkable that some people suspect a divine architect at work. But, like the eleventh track, *Marta's Theme*, the symmetry is imperfect. Scientists have long wondered whether nature is able to differentiate left from right-handedness. For a long time it appeared that nature could not; every positive had a negative, every pole an anti-pole, every right a wrong. Then it was proved that Nature *can* tell the difference between right and left. This has a profound effect in the philosophy of humankind. Gravity really does operate in only one sense. Perhaps the amount of good in the World really does outweigh the amount of evil? *Make Peace*.

Pat Metheny Trio: *Day Trip* – 2008 (****)

In my early days as a fan of Pat Metheny, I had become used to – perhaps 'spoilt by' is a better phrase – the grand output of PMG. Collections like the 'White' album, *First Circle* and *Offramp* were so expansive and colourful that I believed the music to be the finest I had ever heard. It came as a shock when I bought albums like *Rejoicing* and *Question and Answer* in which the scope of the music had changed so dramatically. There is still a danger of that for fans today who rush off to buy Pat Metheny Trio albums thinking they are going to get something like *Imaginary Day* or *The Way Up*.

Over the years, Pat has become so philosophical about his music – so purposeful about his creations that there is a danger that he will overdo the thinking bit and disappear down his own paradox, like the peculiar creature in the Beatles film *Yellow Submarine* that sucked itself out of existence. It takes a very committed fan of jazz to want to sit for nearly two hours (if you take this album together with the next *Live* trio album) and listen to a guitar, string bass and drums. However, this is not just any old jazz trio. The *Metheny Mehldau* album of duets was remarkable, but the *Quartet* album failed to satisfy. Could this Trio album deliver the goods to satisfy my very high level of expectation?

There's not a lot you can change in such a format and there's a great danger that the listener will not get past track four before moving on in boredom. For a trio album to be a success, it has to be about the music, the music and the music. When the Pat Metheny Group's seven musicians are all burning and turning, it's about as dramatic as you can get, but how do you inspire folks with a standard electric guitar, a string bass and drums? For most listeners this is black and white compared to the Technicolor of *The Way Up*. I can't think of many musicians who could do it, but Pat does on both this record and the *Day Trip Trio Live* album and I'm going to describe how.

Pat may be taking a look at himself with the opening track, *Son of Thirteen*, for (it is said) he was 13 years old when he took up the guitar. Perhaps he is considering just how far he has come, for this composition is the freshest piece of jazz on the album and as fresh as anything else he has written. Pat may also be wondering just how good a guitar player he has become, for he has said openly that he thinks he is not a great player. My answer is that he is far better than he gives himself credit for. Just listen to this piece and how fleet he is at this fast tempo. Hear how brightly he creates new sounds. Yes, he's using what I call his 'standard' guitar sound – the one jazz listeners expect a jazz guitar to sound like – but hear how remarkably dissimilar his lines are to anything he has played before, and not for a half minute or so, but for most of the track's length. The complete cycle of melody does not repeat until over a minute has passed. It's not until 3.54 that he gives way to a drum lead, and even then he continues to create superb lines that include harmonics and slick chords. There is not a single hesitation, nor the hint of a poor choice of note. This is a remarkable achievement of both composition and execution, with Pat's overall contribution quite exceptional.

Likewise, the next track *At Last You're Here* meets all the criteria for interest, excitement and quality in composition. This beautifully recorded track (as, indeed, they all are) has nowhere to hide and all three players are outstanding. It's a superbly relaxed tune that, for once, does not stray too close to the sentimental side of Pat's nature. This one is more like a happy-go-lucky traveller, shambling along on foot without a care in the world, smiling at everyone he passes. From 4.31, McBride's bass sings its solo like a wise old song thrush looking down from above. Sanchez is constantly in attendance, impeccably accurate, remarkably fresh as he leads and complements in equal measure. Pat, meanwhile, just plays his jazz waltz with his 'standard' sound as well as he has ever played in his life.

Then comes *Let's Move* at a ridiculously fast pace. Unflinchingly, they tackle the crazily difficult orchestration at the tune's head as if they've played it for years and then at 0.54 move on to their solos, completely unfazed. To tackle such a pace when you play an instrument that has a fundamentally slow action like the double bass is intimidating to all but the very best players. Here, Christian just sweeps aside the difficulty and delivers amazing lines throughout, but especially from the commencement of his solo at 2.50. But to talk of solos is limiting and inaccurate for all three players interact at a supreme level. Just listen to the complexity of the music that comes after the bass solo from 4.10 onwards. Pat seems to have shifted to an even higher gear from the overdrive in which he started, whilst the bass and drums interaction with him from 4.42 to the end is quite breathtaking.

Snova is, I guess, a kind of bossa nova contraction, its melody wriggling sexily through a series of unpredictable chords like a dusky dancer's hips. Christian plays another solo and demonstrates the gulf between a properly melodic improvisation and just another bass line. Overall, there's not a lot to write about as the piece is not far beyond the ordinary, given the high standard of the rest of this album.

Calvin's Keys is a Blues Plus, a very user-friendly piece that will please many listeners with its familiar tones and unexpected twists. It begins with eight bars of blues that sound like they'll get repeated to sixteen but from 0.32 to 1.01 is supplemented by a second 16-bar section of harmonic gymnastics. Given that novelty, this piece is as mainstream as you can get and neither Sanchez nor McBride are asked to play anything demanding apart from keeping together for Pat's floorshow. However, there is a great deal of audience satisfaction to be gained from this good piece.

The second half of the album starts with *Is This America*? a tribute to the 2005 devastation by Hurricane Katrina of New Orleans, the jazz capital of the world. Sentimentality is exactly appropriate for this topic and Pat's weeping acoustic guitar is a clear expression of distaste, not just for the physical destruction but, presumably, for the apparent apathy of the Federal authorities in dealing with the humanitarian outcome. I've a feeling, Pat's question in the title was answered in his own earlier piece, sung by David Bowie on their hit record from *The Falcon and the Snowman*. To Antonio's brushes, Christian translates his own feelings into a beautiful bowed solo and this psalm for a beautiful city is completed with a poignant, composed ending.

Track 7 is *When We Were Free*, a return to mainstream jazz with a straightforward melody. Cemented by a solid bass phrase that introduces this 3 / 4 jazz waltz, it's an opportunity for Antonio to occupy the spotlight. His work is intricate and multi-layered, and leads to a good accompanied solo from 4.10. Pat switches to guitar synth from 6.00, a move that we discovered in *Metheny Mehldau Quartet* is not without risk in an otherwise acoustic environment, but it is more successful here, if still rather unnecessary. At 7.35 there is a final decay into a short bass lead followed by a creative coda and an atmospheric *diminuendo* to close.

With *Dreaming Trees*, another of Pat's acoustic ballads, there is now a risk of rendering this aspect of Pat's repertoire into a cliché of his own design. A country melody with chords that drift through the scales like smoke through the tree branches, there's a chance that the lack of logic in the chord sequences will lose the listener's loyalty at this point. What makes sense to Pat has to make sense to Christian too, and his solo is a valiant effort to deal with Pat's curious thinking. It's a serious and workable idea, but viewed over the broad spectrum of albums, there have been rather too many tracks of this ilk. In the end, it is the sheer musicianship of the three musicians that pulls it off, assisted once again by the warmth of the recording.

In total contrast is the excellent track *The Red One*, that first appeared on Pat's album with John Scofield, *I Can See Your House From Here* (1994). Here we have a wholly original take on the concept of jazz-rock, and the fact that McBride succeeds with his string bass when up against Pat's heavily distorted, hairy guitar and Antonio's raunchy jazz-rock drum beat is itself amazing. From 2.20, there's even a reggae feel to the beat, but it's the constant folding of jazz into rock and rock into jazz that is a joy on this unique track, with a lot of action squeezed inside the 4.47 duration.

The final track is *Day Trip*, in which Pat reverts to the straight-ahead format that underpins the album's focus. This is another clever Metheny composition that explores yet another part of this musical pool. It's a move away from the more usual weepie to finish, but perfectly fits the album's concept. Indeed, the cover art for the album presents some of the many aspects of ordinary daily life and the choice of title seems to refer to the recording of this entire album on the single day of 19 October 2005. This is a remarkable achievement in itself for, even allowing for some essential rehearsal time, it would be a rare event to lay down so much high quality music in a single day. The music is beautifully recorded with excellent clarity, and played to perfection. Christian's solid, capable bright tone is so confident and novel accompaniment to Pat's tunes, whilst Antonio's drumming is of the highest quality. It would be very easy to put this CD on as background music and feel a good measure of satisfaction when it ends, but that listener would entirely fail to appreciate what an excellent piece of work this album is.

Pat Metheny Trio: *Tokyo Day Trip Live* (EP) – 2008 (****)

The release of this mini-album – five tracks recorded live during the Trio's tour of Japan – was a significant contribution to the risks described above, but again, the challenge is overcome by this bonus disc. As if *Day Trip* was not enough, here are five more of the same, but this is not a live version of tracks from the studio album. Instead, these are five more wholly original Metheny tunes.

Tromsø is almost a reversion to the days of *New Chautauqua* whereby he creates an effect with a particular guitar sound and develops it into an impressionist sound painting. Curiously, there appear to be additional musicians playing on this live recording, with both additional bass and percussion apparent. Unfortunately, there's no information on the disc's notes. This isn't a normal jazz style, but an improvised approach to a tone poem describing a lovely Norwegian landscape of fjords and ice sheets.

Travelling Fast is predictably quick with a traditional melody from the drawers of Pat's PMG past. A long development spanning eleven minutes, it gives Sanchez the chance to play a very good solo, showing his mettle without losing touch of the rhythm – listen to the steady hi-hat. This is an excellent piece delivered at a stunning pace.

Inori is another acoustic melody in which the normal intimacy of the studio is reduced by the hiss from the live venue. It's an unfortunate effect that diminishes the warmth of this straight-through tune.

Back Arm and Blackcharge is another of the extraordinary pieces that Pat conjures up from time to time. Just as in *The Red One*, Pat adopts a harsh sound for this jazz-rock piece that has echoes of *Offramp*. It's a full-on in-yer-face piece played at a pace that no rocker would care to tackle and entirely unexpected for a trio of this kind. The string bass seems entirely inadequate in such a scenario, yet is not! When you feel the piece is all done, it is only halfway through and the piece encompasses a brave bass solo and ends in triumph.

For the last track, *The Night Becomes You*, it is back to the acoustic melodic form with Pat subtly incorporating some delightful harmonics into the melody. However, the piece is not quite there and leaves a slight question mark about the way forward for Pat's small group work. Is he going to rely upon the jazz devotee getting excited because of any new projects alongside this or that jazz star? Well, there are few left for him to work with that he has not already done so. Working alongside jazz stars of the future, such as Brad Mehldau, perhaps. An album with John McLaughlin would be interesting, for example. But where else is there to go?

Pat Metheny, Anna Maria Jopek: *Upojenie* – 2008 (****)

Whilst on tour in Europe in 2001, Pat was contacted by Polish singer-songwriter Anna Maria Jopek who suggested a project with Pat that involved a mixture of her own music, and other Polish music, as well as some reinterpretations of Pat's music. The context was to be strongly Polish and to offer an opportunity to some of the best local musicians. After listening to her ideas in more detail, Pat agreed to take part and the result is this beautiful CD. The album's title *Upojenie*, which means *Ecstasy*, is an indication that this music is luscious in all respects and not just the title of one of the tracks. Anna Maria sings the selections from Pat's songbook to new lyrics that, in Polish, do not detract from the originals because, to non-Polish speakers like me, the effect is similar to the wordless vocals that have been used on PMG tracks for many years. As for her original songs, they bear certain similarities with Pat's music and the two groups of pieces fit snugly around each other. All of the music is set within a range of musical contexts, giving the album a lot of variety, without destroying the artistic envelope. As usual, Pat's playing is varied throughout and ranges across his spread of guitars, from the atmospherics of his 42-string Pikasso through another of Linda Manzer's specials – a soprano guitar, to his favourite Roland synthesiser and Ibanez 'standard' sounds.

The album opens with a traditional Polish prayer that tries to set the scene, but perhaps is slightly too downbeat to be a true indicator for what is to come. On the other hand, this is followed with a glorious version of Pat's *So May it Secretly Begin*, the highlight for me being the band's rich orchestration. Pat and Anna Maria perform a duet together in *Biel (Whiteness)*, with Pat showcasing his baritone guitar, overdubbed with an acoustic solo on classical guitar. Another of Pat's sad melodies is *Tell Her You Saw Me* (from *Secret Story*). Here it is imaginatively transformed into a wonderfully fragile, precious creation. Next is the PMG classic *Are You Going With Me?* which is presented in a great new arrangement that remains close to the original. Pat plays on his Roland, as per the original. Anna Maria performs her own song *Black Words* in which Pat ambitiously balances the contrasting sounds of both his Pikasso guitar and his Roland. Track 7 is a traditional Polish carol whose familiar sounds have been given new shades of jazzy white by Pat's arrangement. Anna Maria penned the title tune too, and this is almost a classic cool jazz Latin number, with Pat on his Ibanez guitar and the seductive female voice at its most enchanting. This is a fine piece of jazz, notable for some very good soprano saxophone playing by Henryk Miskiewicz, who repeats his presence on the next track *Zupelnie Inna Ja* (Originally: *Always and Forever*) – one of Pat's great melodies.

Track ten is *A Song for Stas*, penned by the producer, who tells us he was first inspired by Pat's *Lonely Woman* on his *Rejoicing* (1984) album. Next comes a short version of *Letter from Home*, a solo, well played by the omnipresent pianist Leszek Mozdzer. Twelve is a reworking of Pat's *Another Life* with Pat playing guitar synth, whilst the next is the heart-melting melody *Farmer's Trust*. It begins as an intimate combination of voice and classical guitar, with piano bass and drums joining this very slow jazz waltz by invitation. A lovely piano solo brings a depth of satisfaction to the piece. Next is the short *Polish Paths*, a pretty ballad with Pat unusually playing a Manzer custom soprano guitar and with just acoustic bass for accompaniment. The piece originally chosen to close the album is *Follow Me*, played in an arrangement similar to the original except for the wonderful substitution of mesmerising vocals where Pat played before. Finally come two bonus tracks, recorded live at a gig in Warsaw in 2002. A short cameo duet of Anna Maria and Pat is followed by an energetic locally written piece *Whispers and Tears* that sounds very much like PMG except for more good vocals.

Since most listeners will have no experience of Poland or its musical heritage, the atmosphere of the album comes across as a statement of musical ambition for an entire nation, with Pat's impressionist ethos being carried forward through images that contrast a warm summer land of lush, fertile farmland and a cold winter land blanketed in large deposits of friendly snow. It's a place where all the familiar dreams and relationships of humankind are played out in the same old ways, despite a somewhat impenetrable relationship between the Polish language and the alphabet. In a language that looks on paper to be as harsh as the winter winds from Siberia, there is a welcome gentleness in Jopek's lyrics and enunciation. Though there is a world of difference between the countries, the climates and the cultures, I am struck (even before listening to the title track) by the similarities between this project and the occasion when Stan Getz absorbed himself into the music of Brazil and the bossa nova, as performed by Antonio Carlos Jobim, Joao Gilberto and his wife, singer Astrud Gilberto, whose voice was similarly sweet and mostly vibratoless. Jopek's voice most certainly fits her style of music, and, like Gilberto, her voice is by no means exceptional, but does carry a great deal of charm and combines a certain confident maturity with a touch of childlike naivety. It remains to be seen whether Jopek also becomes an international star in her own right, as perhaps she deserves to. This is a very good album that possibly tends more towards the yang than the yin.

Gary Burton, Pat Metheny, Steve Swallow, Antonio Sanchez: *Quartet Live* – 2009 (***)

Looking back is a risk for any jazz musician. It was anathema to Miles Davis, who went so far as to suggest that when he looked back he would die. [24] To work in an art form that is based upon creative expression requires an openness of mind that sponsors innovation, whilst innovation itself is, by definition, progressive, not regressive. But Pat Metheny remembered working with Gary Burton as a pinnacle in his professional career. "For me, getting to join that band in 1974 was the rough equivalent of getting to join the Beatles. It was the greatest thing that could ever have happened to me. If nothing else had ever occurred in my musical life but that, I would have been happy forever." [25] Revisiting such a creative and inspiring period of his life seemed a natural move for Pat.

According to Gary Burton, Pat called him in 2006 and suggested that they reform a quartet similar to the one they had in the mid 1970s. [26] They agreed on a one-year project that would play at the Montreal Jazz Festival. However, the new band performed so successfully in Montreal that both Pat and Gary were excited enough to want to continue its existence, and to encompass an extended tour despite their busy schedules. Towards the end of the tour, on June 10-11 2007, a couple of performances were recorded at Yoshi's Jazz Club in Oakland California and an album was made from the cuts that was called *Quartet Live* (2009). Just seconds away from 80 minutes in length, the single CD album is rammed with eleven tracks of high quality jazz, much of it transmitting echoes from the past.

Sea Journey opened their album *Passengers* (1977) and is a welcoming introduction to this one. The second track, *Olhos de Gato (Cat's Eyes)*, is a moody, modal piece composed by Carla Bley in the early 1970s and which first appeared in the Quartet's repertoire before Pat joined. The band's version with Mick Goodrick on guitar appeared on ECM's *The New Quartet* (1973), an album that was reissued in 2008.

Falling Grace is a piece of Steve's, again, retrieved from the days of the early quartet. Here he takes the lead solo, playing with a joyful, sprightly spirit that sets Gary and Pat up for a work-out that is like a smooth running, well-oiled engine. This is followed by *Coral*, a Keith Jarrett composition that is the gentlest of pieces. Besides being a companion to *Olhos de Gato* on *The New Quartet* album, it was also recorded for another Burton Quartet album, *Times Square* (1978).

A composition of Gary's, *Walter L* has a special place in Pat's heart as one of the tunes that Pat jammed on at Wichita in 1972 when he first asked Gary if he could sit in with the band. The music bears all the hallmarks of the late 1960s when Gary was first experimenting with electric rock guitarist Jerry Hahn. The main theme is an early jazz-rock template that combines the jumping bebop sensibilities with funk bass and distorted guitar. For once, Sanchez, who is too young to remember the days in question, sounds slightly uncomfortable. It is one track on the album that might be used as proof that Miles Davis was right after all, but the energetic reactions of the live audience seem to show otherwise.

B&G (Midwestern Night's Dream) is a favourite Metheny tune taken from *Bright Size Life* and the Burton Quartet's album *Passengers*. Its title is yet another example of human inability to cope with the apostrophe. Though essentially unchanged musically, this song has undoubtedly benefitted from the many years between the band's two versions of it. Similar can be said about its companion from *Bright Size Life*, the urgent *Missouri Uncompromised* which drives forward like an eager shopper in the January Sales, encouraged from the rear by the force of a Sanchez drum solo.

Fleurette Africaine was originally written in 1962 by Duke Ellington as part of a collection of material to be recorded by his trio with Charles Mingus and Max Roach. The album that resulted was *Money Jungle* (1963). It is a lovely melodic composition that has been fed like steak into a food mixer, the output from which is clearly present in other recordings from this period of the Burton Quartet. *Hullo Bolinas* is another sweet chestnut, this time from Swallow's pen. Bolinas, a town in Marin County, California must be a fun place to live. However, the much slower 1973 recording of this tune by Bill Evans in Tokyo is very difficult to beat.

Syndrome is another Carla Bley number that derives from the early 1960s, when it was recorded by Paul Bley. Since then it has occasionally resurfaced on a number of albums, including those by Gary's various quartets: *Dreams So Real* (1975), *Real Life Hits* (1984) and *Generations* (2004), no doubt kept in the band's focus by Steve Swallow's life partnership with Carla Bley. The final track is Pat's classic composition, *Question and Answer*. This music oozes class and is given a generous consideration, its thirteen minutes filling the back end of this CD with very meaningful, expertly-played jazz.

One surprising fact that Gary chose to share on the sleeve notes was that Pat had borrowed a vibraphone soon after arriving at Berklee and that he had made the transition from beginner to accomplished player in a few months. To this day, Pat plays vibes at home.

The contents of this very good album show that looking back was clearly not as bad an idea as Miles Davis had predicted. Steve Swallow, who initially had doubts about many aspects of the plan to re-form the band, summed it up as follows. "What we're doing doesn't involve nostalgia: we're still trying to get it right, and I sense that our audience is responding to this, not to a familiar melody or a trademark sound." [27] However, I'm not sure that Pat could honestly say that nostalgia was not involved in this part of his career.

Pat Metheny: *Orchestrion* – 2010 (****)

Having spent a significant period of time revisiting his past with Gary Burton, it was beginning to look as if Pat was having a problem with the idea of another project with his own band. Five years had passed since the brilliant success with PMG and *The Way Up*, and it seemed that the problem posed by the old axiom "How do you follow that?" was becoming increasingly intractable. Fans wondered whether he had truly exhausted the envelope of the PMG formula. Perhaps there *was* no other place to go? Pat took his band touring in 2010 under the banner of *The Pat Metheny Songbook Tour*, but there was no new album to promote. Just as an over-the-shoulder look back to the days of Burton's 1974 band might have been looked upon by some as risky for a creative artist, so also a decision to once again work with PMG could also been seen as simply nostalgic. But Pat had never been afraid of nostalgia and didn't for a moment see his 2009/10 output as anything other than cementing his already solid presence in the steady currents of the jazz mainstream. In any case, Pat had for some time been planning an entirely new project that excited him enormously – one that would satisfy a curiosity about mechanical music machines and apply them in a way that used some of the latest technologies, just as he had done with synthesisers in the 1980s. Pat called this his *Orchestrion* project.

The idea of the one-man band is familiar to most of us from amongst the many popular street entertainers we meet in our city centres. The desire of a musician to play many instruments simultaneously can be traced back to the 13th century. A no-man band was first achieved using the so-called player piano (also called a pianola or autopiano). This is a more recent device in which the piano keys are operated by pneumatic or electro-mechanical mechanisms in the overall control of a rotating roll of perforated paper. Pianolas allowed people to create live music in a time before the age of gramophones and recorded music, and in situations where no-one present possessed the skills to play the piano.

Pat's interest in these player pianos was stimulated when, as a child, he had a lot of fun with one in his grandfather's basement. His interest grew when he realised that other devices could be attached to create mini-orchestras, known as orchestrions, using methods that were worked upon during the late 19th and early 20th centuries. One place where visitors can enjoy these devices is at a Wisconsin tourist attraction called *The House on the Rock* where, since 1968, there has been a marvellous collection of mechanical and electromechanical instruments on display. At the insertion of a coin, whole rooms burst into life with joyous music apparently played robotically by large arrays of orchestral instruments. Although a certain amount of deception is involved whereby the sounds of the strings and woodwinds are actually created by organ pipes, the effect of each 'mini orchestra' is mesmerising and hugely entertaining.

Building upon his own significant experience with musical electronics, Pat realised that there was much scope for new music by combining these old ideas with the latest technologies. Over a period of time, he collected devices that he could assemble into his own orchestrion and then worked up a method of control that allowed him, not just to play the guitar, but also to improvise over an accompaniment of rich sounds from his band of robots. First he assembled his collection in his Manhattan apartment, but later moved them to a nearby empty church as the collection came together into his state-of-the-art orchestrion.

One contributor was Ken Caulkins who had spent nearly forty years making robotic instruments. (A tour of an orchestrion in his factory is available on a You-Tube video where, without Pat, it plays a unique version of *One Note Samba*.) A Chicago-based company called Peterson Electro-Musical Products manufactured a bottle organ in which air was blown across the open mouths of a range of bottles to produce the well-known sounds most of us made as kids. Eric Singer, a musical inventor and artist from Pittsburgh, provided his own designs of guitar-bot. Together, all these devices, and more, were assembled into a fantastic new musical machine that Pat not only mastered for his own musical purposes, but then proceeded to take on a world tour.

The remarkable thing about this record, epitomised by the opening track *Orchestrion*, is that there is an immediate level of disbelief that Pat could possibly create so many sounds simultaneously. This music is in essence the same as a performance by Pat Metheny Group, complete with piano, bass and drums, and a variety of other sounds that might otherwise have been made by Cuong Vu. In a TV programme, Pat demonstrated how these instruments followed his guitar finger-work, note-for-note, at whatever speed he wished to play. [28] That alone is very remarkable, but that's the simple bit, for in performance he goes on to play just as a soloist does, separately from the band. How can this be? How can the percussion continue on playing apparently independently from his own? At this point it seems more like a case of Pat Metheny meets Penn and Teller. The answers are by no means clear. Clearly foot pedals play some role, although they are not in evidence. There is a clear lack of explanation as to how it all works, though it appears to be no secret. As Pat told an audience in Vienna, "It takes hours to explain, and whatever you think it is, it's that and many other things." [29]

The audio CD contains five tracks. The title track is followed by *Entry Point*, *Expansion*, *Soul Search* and *Spirit of the Air* and all of them could be played by PMG. It is a wonderful musical experience that parallels Pat's high quality music from the past, but surely the point of this project is for listeners to actually see the music being performed? The audiences at his *Orchestrion* Tour concerts were treated to fabulous performances of the newly released material, but also heard some of his classic songs in this new context. Pat had already pointed out that he had experimented extensively with the one-man band ideas on *New*

Chautauqua. Without the benefit of an orchestrion, he had achieved the results using the standard recording methods of multi-tracking. He was well satisfied with the results, but he noted that it was an especially suitable technique to take on tour. Now, his live gigs allowed him to revisit songs like *Sueño Con Mexico*, for example.

It's unthinkable to suggest that Pat and his orchestrion could ever replace the Pat Metheny Group, yet to many listeners, the sounds on this disc will appear remarkably similar. Likewise, we could hardly imagine that Pat would subject his playing with these devices to worldwide exposure if he were not artistically satisfied with the results. You might think there was a danger of it all being branded rather Heath-Robinson, but no. Pat has successfully created a musical environment that is as sophisticated and powerful as he could wish for. So, despite the apparent contradictions, the *Orchestrion* Project must be pronounced a total success. However, the absence of an official DVD showing in detail his remarkable work in this unique project is regrettable and something that Pat's publishing company should consider carefully.

Pat Metheny: *What's It All About* – 2011 (****)

At the time of writing, Pat's latest release is an album of his favourite 1960s and early 1970s songs, played solo on a range of guitars. As in his earlier project *One Quiet Night*, Pat concentrates on the rich sounds of the baritone guitar, but here he broadens his work on that instrument to include three tunes played on the acoustic nylon and steel 6-string guitars, as well as his now famous Pikasso instrument. The sum of the parts is a definitive guide to Guitarists' Heaven.

The album begins with the famous Simon and Garfunkel tune, *The Sound of Silence*, played on the 42-string Pikasso guitar, a selection that is very appropriate for both the instrument and the song. Pat plays it both imaginatively and impeccably. *Cherish* is a beautiful melody written by Terry Kirkman that was a #1 hit in 1966. It is followed by a stunning version of the Bacharach and David theme to the film *Alfie* (1966). *Pipeline* was written by two members of a band called The Chantays and reached #4 in the US in May 1963. Pat's interpretation of *The Girl From Ipanema* will surprise (and perhaps disappoint) many listeners as he creates an entirely different mood from the joyful expressions of love from a distance that were used by others, including the composer. We get back on track with *Rainy Days and Mondays*, a wistful portrait of that will entrance listeners and show what a great artist Pat is when it comes to re-interpretation. *That's the Way I've Always Heard It Should Be* is an early example of the compositions of Carly Simon who used it as the opening track on her self-titled first album in February 1971. The album continues with an impressionistic version of *Slow Hot Wind* (1976) by Henry Mancini, followed by *Betcha By Golly, Wow*, which was a hit for The Stylistics in 1972, and more recently recorded by Prince in 1996. As with the other tracks, Pat plays it slow and sexy, and then rounds off with a delightful rendition of the Beatles' *And I Love Her.*

This beautifully recorded and played album makes an excellent companion to *One Quiet Night*, with all its associated atmosphere and attention to the minutest detail of sound and performance. There's no serious attempt to change the relaxed mood throughout, so it's a challenge to listen to the whole album in one sitting because, however much you love Pat's music, these sixty minutes are a perfect remedy for insomnia.

Some Other Stuff

In September 1974, Wayne Shorter had recorded an album called *Native Dancer* that was promoted as a new interpretation of the fusion of jazz with the rhythmic and joyful music of Brazil. The focus of attention was a young Brazilian called Milton Nascimento, whom Wayne and Herbie Hancock had heard about. In 1968, Herbie went to Brazil for his honeymoon where he had been introduced to Milton an amazing musician who naturally could not speak English. It was natural for Wayne, with Portuguese wife Ana Maria – the perfect person for translating – to be brought into the excitement right from the start. Nascimento had a style that was quite different from the one that had excited non-Brazilian listeners in the 1960s. Herbie Hancock, in particular, was keen to bring Milton back to LA, which he did with the help of Brazilians Flora Purim and Airto Moreira who were already living in the US. Events culminated in the 1974 recording. With his reputation established, he continued with a solo recording career of his own, and this included *Encontros e Despidadas* (1986) on which Pat appeared.

In 1983, at the end of July, whilst on tour in Japan, Pat was given the opportunity to play alongside the great tenor saxophone player Sonny Rollins in a quartet completed by Alphonso Johnson (bass) and Jack de Johnette (drums). Sources show that this session was recorded and released on discs that have long since disappeared from view. [30] Later, after he had recorded *Rejoicing* with Charlie Haden and Billy Higgins, Pat was once again joined by Sonny for a session captured on a recording in Ravenna Italy on 3 July 1986.

In 1986, Pat played on an album led by his brother, Mike, entitled *Day In – Night Out* (1986) The music, with Mike on flugelhorn, EVI and trumpet, also included Dick Odgren (piano), Rufus Reid (bass) and Tommy Ruskin (drums).

At the end of September 1987, Pat joined Steve Reich (b1936), a composer of so-called 'minimalist' music to record a commission that Reich had been awarded by the Brooklyn Academy of Music's *Next Wave* Festival. For some years, Reich had been experimenting with soloists playing against pre-recorded tapes of themselves. Pat's input was to a piece called *Electric Counterpoint* (1987), of which there had been two previous ones – *Vermont Counterpoint* (1982) for Ransom Wilson (flute) and *New York Counterpoint* (1985) for

Richard Stoltzman (clarinet). Pat's piece was written in three short movements and consisted of a variety of repeating guitar sounds from as many as "nine guitars in canon", all carefully choreographed in conventional harmonies and rhythms to create interesting new sounds. Published in conjunction with another work for tape and string quartet, the fifteen-minute *Electric Counterpoint* is still available on a CD that leads with the highly acclaimed response to the holocaust entitled *Different Trains* (1989).

As a close friend of Charlie Haden, Pat contributed to one track on Haden's album *Nocturne* (2001). This is a collection of gentle Latin ballads or *boleros*, played by Haden with pianist Gonzalo Rubalcaba and percussionist Ignacio Berroa. Pat was one of a number of guest musicians, along with Joe Lovano and David Sanchez (saxophone) and Federico Britos Ruiz (violin). Pat expertly played the role of solo Mexican guitar (known as *requinto*) on the second track, *Noche de Ronda* (Night of Wandering).

Pat's Guitars

Like most guitarists, Pat has played and owned many different guitars over the years. However, there are a relatively small number that have featured significantly in his playing, both live and on record. As a jazz guitarist primarily, Pat's musical persona is carved from the more traditional stock of players such as Wes Montgomery, Jim Hall, Kenny Burrell and Joe Pass, players located in what might be called the first generation of electric jazz guitarists. Such musicians went about their business with the minimum of equipment. They played mostly on just one instrument and did not generally feel the need to vary their sound, and they were certainly never to be seen playing Spanish-style or folk-style jumbo acoustic instruments. In Pat's case, not only is he comfortable playing almost any kind of guitar, but he plays some kinds that most of us have never seen before.

It was with a 1958 model Gibson ES 175 that Pat started his jazz career. Not surprisingly, however, his original instrument sustained sufficient damage to render it fragile, so the guitar was replaced with an Ibanez PM100 that looks and sounds very similar to his much-loved Gibson. Both instruments are of yellow hollow-bodied construction, with f-holes and single pickups. Pat normally uses flat-wound strings and turns the tone control to minimum, although the newer Ibanez is louder and less tone-sensitive.

I would describe Pat as a second-generation electric guitarist, by which I mean a child of the era of rock music who is comfortable with solid body guitars and electronic effects. But that is not a sufficient description. Whilst Pat is not known for his use of conventional solid bodied guitars, since the very early 1980s he has become a serious user of the Roland GR-300 guitar synthesiser, one of the earliest types and now long discontinued. Over all this time, starting with *Offramp* (1982), he has treated this walnut-coloured solid instrument, and –

more importantly – just one of its sounds, as a major tool in his instrument box, by which he has established one aspect of the sound he now owns. Pat has stated that he prefers to treat one sound as an instrument and to master it, rather than to jump feely from one sound to another as some other guitar synthesiser players have done.

There are few guitarists who never use an acoustic instrument at some time or another, and Pat is no exception. As we have seen repeatedly, Pat has always been as much at home with acoustic as he has with electric sounds, another characteristic of his membership of the second generation of jazz guitarists, except that in Pat's case, he seems to be equally at home on both.

Since about 1986, Pat has been supplied with a range of acoustic instruments made by a Canadian luthier called Linda Manzer. When he first tried one, Pat was knocked out by the effect it had on him. "With Linda's guitars, something happened that made me hear things differently. They really fit with my conception of sound, and I can't begin to explain why. The necks were easily playable for me." [31] Besides the usual six string models – with both nylon and steel strings, the Pikasso guitar is particularly noticeable because of its unique design and extreme looks. There is some commonality here with the Abraham Wechter guitars owned and played by John McLaughlin whereby a principle adopted from Eastern music is employed. In such case, there are two different kinds of strings – one that is played normally by stopping different lengths with the fingers on a fingerboard (that may be fretted or not, as the case may be) and a second group of strings that simply resonate or are strummed periodically to form a rich backdrop of sound over which the first group are played. This is particularly suitable for Indian music that commonly employs drones or ragas, which, in western terminology, are based in one key centre.

Some time between *Offramp* and *First Circle*, Pat's outlook on the nylon-stringed Spanish acoustic guitar changed when he came upon such an instrument made by Linda Manzer. Both the sound and feel of the six-string instrument had a big effect on him and suddenly he found himself inspired to play in a completely acoustic environment as he found a whole new vista of opportunity opened up for him.

Linda told me that Pat first asked her to build him a special guitar in 1984. It was to have "as many strings as possible" and their collaboration resulted in Manzer building Pat the Pikasso guitar. With its back and sides made of Indian Rosewood and a German Spruce top, this amazing guitar has four necks of mahogany with ebony fingerboards to manage the 42 strings (3 of 12-strings plus 1 of 6-strings.) There are two sound holes, and two access doors to the internal equipment, one on the upper player's side and one at the tail block. Another innovation was Manzer's design, specifically for this instrument, called the 'Wedge', in which the body is tapered, with the side closest to the player thinner than the side that rests on the player's knee. This allows the top to lean back towards the player for an improved view. A state-of-the-art piezoelectric pickup system by Mark Herbert of Boston was added, as well as a hexaphonic pickup on the 6-string section that allowed Pat to connect the guitar to his Synclavier synthesiser. Finally, there are two mounting holes with brass insets on the treble side (knee side) of the guitar so that the instrument can be mounted on a stand. The instrument took Manzer almost two years and approximately 1000 hours to build and weighs 6.7 kg.

Obviously, it is not possible to finger all 42 strings at once, so Pat uses a technique whereby he strums on one or more sets of strings and uses a different set to play over the top of each set as it resonates. [32] Pat first used it in December 1985 for the recording of *Mob Job* on his album *Song X* with Ornette Coleman, but it is barely audible as a couple of notes towards the end of the piece. This unique instrument made its first significant appearance on *As a Flower Blossoms* on *Secret Story* (1992).

Concluding Remarks

During the course of this book, amongst other things, I have outlined the shape of Pat Metheny's remarkable career. I intend to complete this work with a final summary of Pat's outstanding contributions to music. The headlines are as follows. Pat Metheny has:

- Invented a new form of jazz-fusion that is not based upon the usual blend of jazz with electric rock sounds;
- Created an entirely new legacy for jazz electric guitar;
- Substantially extended the legacy of contemporary music on acoustic guitar and associated instruments;
- Greatly extended the range of techniques for composition of both jazz and contemporary music.

Pat's vision for the art of guitar playing

When he started out, there were several ideas Pat wanted to explore regarding the role of the guitar in a jazz group. He realised there were many guitar sounds and techniques that were not used in jazz, and it is because Pat's work focussed on drawing these ideas into jazz that he is widely regarded as a jazz-fusion musician. The problem is that, in Pat's case, the term is a poor description of what he does. We shall see why that is so.

All of the top 'first generation' jazz guitar players such as Wes Montgomery, Jim Hall and Barney Kessell used the electric guitar simply as a tool with which to make their music. Since that tool was pretty much the same in each pair of hands, the sounds that the guitars made were similar too. When jazz-fusion came along, contemporary guitarists made little effort to sound like anything other than rock guitarists. One exception was John McLaughlin, who had already distinguished himself as more than just another 'jazz-rocker'. McLaughlin's career, like Pat's, is complex and I have discussed it in another book. [33] McLaughlin was – and still is – a superb guitarist: I have argued that he is one of the best ever. Like Pat, he was responsible for creating his own kind of jazz-fusion – with Indian music. However, in origin and style, the two guitarists are entirely different, and there was no overlap between them. This left the field wide open for Pat to exploit. Like John, Pat was helped by the contemporary developments in electronics that, as I have described elsewhere, were revolutionising the piano and keyboard. The same advances were soon offered to guitar, in the designs of instruments, amplifiers, and effects, whether stand-alone or built into the mixing desks of the recording studios. Pat was able to make the most of the opportunity presented to him by deliberately looking for new kinds of sounds on the guitar, and thus to generate original colours and textures. This is what I define as making him a 'second generation' jazz guitarist: he was heavily influenced by his favourites in the first generation, and could play like them, but he also added entirely new features to the art of guitar playing that they did not have. Pat's playing featured him on a variety of six-string acoustic and electric guitars, 12-string and nylon-string guitars, as well as guitar synthesiser, and some special 'custom' instruments. Pat said: "No one had really explored the textural aspects of guitar playing in jazz. I began a process of trying to expand the role of guitar in jazz that is ongoing. Guitar had a lot to offer the music. The whole idea of incorporating these sounds in a small group in an orchestrational and soloistic fashion is a big part of what I've been working to address for years." [1]

Pat had this immense vision, even as a young man, at the very beginning of his career with Gary Burton, for example. While recording *Bright Size Life*, *Watercolors*, the 'White' album, *American Garage*, and *As Falls Wichita, So Falls Wichita Falls*, he highlighted these sounds as he began also to develop his own special brand of jazz-fusion. Then, on his *80/81* album, Pat prominently featured wild acoustic guitar strumming and finger-picked selections in the company of jazz stalwarts such as Jack De Johnette (drums), Dewey Redman and Michael Brecker (saxophones), and Charlie Haden (bass). Pat says: "That was new territory. Having the guitar function in a rhythm section that way and join in the polyrhythmic aspects of drumming through strumming had not been applied much in jazz before that. I am still very interested in exploring it further." [1] (You can hear a similarly impressive section of strumming in *First Circle* and *Approaching the Light* on *Metheny Mehldau Quartet* (2007)).

After *American Garage*, Pat was still experimenting and he used a different format for his next two albums. He seemed almost to dispense with bass and drums in favour of developing the music along the more tightly constrained lines of guitar and keyboard. This work set him up for further developments in solo, duet and trio work that was to come much later. Richard Niles outlined just a small part of the scope of his playing: "He used acoustic and electric twelve string guitars in unusual tunings (*The Search*); he developed the Synclavier and Roland Guitar synthesiser (*Are you Going With Me? Yolanda, You Learn, The Good Life*); he developed the fretless nylon string guitar (*Imaginary Day*), the sitar guitar (*Facing West, Last Train Home*) and the 42-string Pikasso guitar (*Into the Dream, The Sound of Water*)." [23]

The formula for PMG fusion

So, beginning with *Bright Size Life*, Pat was starting to develop his own kind of jazz-fusion, but it clearly had little to do with jazz-rock fusion and much more to do with the assimilation of his own musical roots into jazz. In a sense, it was an intensely personal kind of jazz-fusion and, because a lot of it was done with Lyle, a man from a similar background as himself, the PMG brand of fusion was even stronger, homogeneous, and unlike anything done by other musicians. Let's look in more detail at how this was done. There are a number of cross-linked elements involved.

Pat made clear in a 2005 BBC Radio 2 interview that the exploration of new forms for his compositions was a primary goal. "I think from very early on the idea was to take the whole idea of what a jazz quartet could be and really just push it as far we could go. In the early days so much of the sound of guitar piano bass and drums had already been pretty clearly defined in jazz. We wanted to do everything that we could do to rub against that, and also to push it to areas that really hadn't been explored that much, and a lot of that had to do with form. So much of the music that we've worked on over the years has been about taking what at the core is really a tune and finding an environment and a way of presenting it that takes it beyond just being a tune. That may be to write other sections, to have different material that comes and goes, to have the improvising built on material that's generated from the song itself, but isn't exactly the song itself. And, of course, the obvious stuff like using different elements of what we have available to us in terms of orchestration, like odd guitars and weird tunings, obviously the electronic elements that we've used, eventually the vocal stuff that came in. We really wanted to do everything that we could do to expand the whole idea of what a quartet could be. Eventually the band started getting bigger, then it was five, then six then seven and it's kind of ranged between six and seven guys over the years, but all the way through one thing that's been a prominent goal for us has been form, to try to expand form as much as we can." [16]

In fact, Pat's analysis is greatly simplified to fit the short space available during an interview. As so often happens, Pat is also being very understated and modest about his achievements. I don't need to hold back so I intend you give you both barrels about why PMG is the finest band in music today. PMG have excelled at creating these new forms for their tunes, and it is one of the great features of their music that the listener is treated to a constantly changing musical menu.

Interviewer Richard Niles observed that Pat came up with a new style of jazz-fusion by a means that was evolutionary, not revolutionary. Pat agreed. "I was conservative. What they now call fusion – the impulse to combine heavy backbeats, really loud distorted guitar and electric bass with jazz didn't quite seem to work to me. It seemed to negate many of the qualities that were most attractive about jazz." What Pat wanted to achieve seemed to be entirely independent of this or that kind of band. It was the ideas and the music itself that determined what line-up he would use – not the other way around. There was "a certain kind of drama and orchestration in the rock and pop world that no-one had thought of going towards." [23]

There are a number of basic ingredients to PMG jazz-fusion. First, there is a very strong emphasis on harmony and melody, and across the wide spectrum of possibilities, the compositions can take on any aspect of mood from the lightest to the darkest. Great importance is assigned to the creation of beauty through fine melody. Metheny and Mays are deeply committed to the creation of lasting works of art and a strong belief that beautiful harmonic and melodic constructions will outlive ugly ones. They have never shrunk from presenting the most *avant-garde*, as in for example, *Offramp* or *Dismantling Utopia*, usually in the context of a narrative rather than stand-alone abstraction. However, their preference always seems to be towards the glory of natural, exotic harmonies and melodies, rather than the unnatural. Songs such as *If I Could* from *First Circle* or *Something to Remind You* from *We Live Here* are typical of this. Pat's greatest strength is his "magical" ability to create powerful melody. However, Pat is a weaker musician when he ventures into the soulless world of modal harmony. He is always more than competent, of course, but because he is a truly soulful musician, there is something missing from his playing when the musical environment does not allow communication to or from the innermost parts of the human psyche.

Second, is the crucial exploration of new rhythmic structures, gained from unusual time signatures, but always retaining the natural feel of a rhythm. John McLaughlin also realised the power of this from the start of his recording career on *Extrapolation* (1968) and extended it into extremely complex metres with the first three Mahavishnu Orchestra albums. Listeners to PMG are often aware that there is something special about the music but don't necessarily realise how the effect has been achieved. The secret often lies in the unusual metric constructions they use. As with the Mahavishnu Orchestra, this has always been a key element of the PMG fusion and there are many examples, such as the main theme from *Phase Dance* from the 'White' album and *5-5-7* from *Letter From Home*.

Third is the use of new textures. Clearly, this was first to be obtained from Pat's own main instrument, the guitar. He achieved this right from the beginning of his career and has continued to do so, not just on one guitar, but on many. Pat has been universally lauded for his contributions to the general art of the guitar. Many guitar sounds have been explored using both electronics and technique in combination. He has employed traditional guitar sounds as well as synthesised and rock sounds. Along with McLaughlin, he trail-blazed the use of the guitar synthesiser from the time of *Offramp* (1981), but where McLaughlin attracted criticism for failing to distinguish himself from a keyboard synthesiser, Pat retained the essence of guitar playing in his own use of the guitar synthesiser. He is quoted as saying that he considers each different synthesiser sound to be like playing a new instrument, and that he prefers to master the playing of one instrument before moving to another. [34] So successful has he been that for twenty years or more, he has been entirely identifiable as having his own 'sound'.

Style has been another element, co-ordinated with Lyle on keyboards. One of PMG's most successful pieces is *Are You Going With Me?* from *Offramp*. It begins with a groove that is erotically different. The playing is as simple as possible and blends a two-note phrase with a subtly changing chordal backdrop. These are played with such smoothness as to eliminate the sound of the playing of individual notes – an extreme form of the musical term, *legato*. The technique is to separate the music from the sound associated with the making of the note. When you ordinarily press a piano key or pluck a guitar string you hear a sound of the action, as well as the note itself. Both Mays and Metheny go to great lengths to generate the pure musical sounds with no trace of the mechanical noises that are usually present, hence the extraordinary *legato* sounds in *Are You Going With Me?*

New textures were to be employed from every possible source, and this is where the use of percussion became so important to the band. Nana Vasconcelos demonstrated just how much scope could be obtained from good percussion and it has been a crucial part of every PMG album since. All of the sidemen employed in the band since Vasconcelos have been multi-instrumentalist, doubling on guitars, wind instruments, bass and keyboards, and even voice, as well as percussion. This great versatility amongst the band members has been a major part of the success story and their contributions in this area should not be underestimated.

Metheny and Mays have always been inspired by the world around them. It's not so much a fusion with rock as with rocks: the Big Country that is America. In contrast to Steely Dan's packages of cynical sideswipes at the seedy side of city life on the other side of the tracks, PMG have focussed on the finest traditions of beauty, Mother Nature, the natural world and good old-fashioned love. Cook describes (or perhaps I should say, accuses) Pat's music of being sentimental – as if there's something wrong with that. [6] It's an indictment of society – not music – that makes it old-fashioned or even distasteful to create things of beauty based on love instead of hate. The common image of electric guitar players is that they strut their stuff with all genes blazing and then, like Hendrix or Townsend, smash their guitars into pieces when they reach orgasm. Apparently, real men don't eat apple pie – they stomp on it! Pat's music, on the other hand, is the music of the wide-open spaces and of natural phenomena that will be around long after the brief whim of fashion is history.

Generally, both Pat and Lyle assign meaningful titles to their compositions, so from the liberal scattering of geographical names amongst the titles of their songs, landscapes from Kansas and Wyoming, Oklahoma and Colorado open up before you as you listen. In later works their musical paintings have attracted the hues of Southeast Asia. From the very fine melody *Travels* which elicits a tear from the meanest eye, to the impressionism and sheer beauty of *The Bat* to the field full of gentle creatures depicted in *Farmer's Trust*, PMG music is based on all of the best things about America. Should real men cry? Well, if they don't, they should! If ever there was music to enrich the soul, this is it. It is so trivial simply to discuss this music as fusion or jazz or even contemporary music, or to discuss the mechanical aspects of technique or style. All of this is rendered utterly pointless in the context of the value of this work to a statement or description of the human condition. If ever there were fine art, this is it, and the music is as important as Monet's Water Lilies, Van Gogh's sunflowers, Turner's landscapes, or the Mona Lisa.

This last, most vital quality of Pat's music is very hard to pin down. It focuses on the intangible, but essential, effect that music can have on our souls. His own words are best used to sum it up. "We can talk about melody, rhythm, and chords all day, but in many ways none of them really matter. What does matter is the effect that music or any human endeavour can have on other people. For me, that's what it is all about. It's about trying to manifest in sound the qualities, ideas, and features that are the good things that make being part of life on earth such a privilege. Trying to come up with things that accurately reflect the details of what I've seen and experienced has been more of a focus for me than the process of how you do that. The point of all this is to offer to others the same things that I have gotten as a fan of music. You give them a mirror to find something about themselves through what you offer. There is a quality that some music has that accomplishes that. With instrumental music, jazz, classical, or other music, since there is no text, people can really find things in it. Instrumental music transcends every language and is very international. I think the best instrumental music offers people a real window into something that they can't find elsewhere." [1]

Pat's last point is very important. We have become so obsessed with vocal music that instrumental music has been pushed right into the background. Yet, instrumental music has the potential to offer us a lot more. Pat also believes there is another quality in music that he calls an inevitability, without which the music has no meaning or purpose for him. "There are certain kinds of resolutions, harmonies, melodies, and ways of improvising that, for me as a player, are perfect examples of the things I love most about music. Some of the choices in a piece like *Map of the World* couldn't go any other way. The piece has to go that way. That quality of inevitability in music is what I really respond to. Certain things make some music very compelling to me as a listener, and they are prerequisites for gaining my enthusiasm. Oddly, most jazz does not have that for me, but when I think of the music that has it the most for me, it's jazz. It doesn't occur that often in jazz, but it does happen in the music of Miles, Wayne Shorter, Sonny Rollins, and the other greats; I find the compelling qualities – that inevitability – there in abundance. It's rare in jazz, and a lot of jazz just goes in one ear and out the other for me. It almost doesn't matter if the players are great if it doesn't have qualities that say to me this music could only go this way. That's universal in all the music that I love." [1]

The band

Pat defines the group as fundamentally a quartet (Pat, Lyle, Steve plus a drummer), though he admits that it has, from time to time, increased to five, six or seven players, depending on the projects he is trying to create. In this long essay describing Pat's contribution to jazz, let us not forget the fantastic support of his friend and keyboard player, Lyle Mays. It is clear that Pat's relationship with Lyle is the keystone to PMG, and it is *not* inappropriate to compare that relationship with the other great musical partnerships such as Ellington and Strayhorn, Rogers and Hammerstein and even Lennon and McCartney.

A pianist of the finest class, Lyle is a player of the modern generation who is equally at home on a Steinway grand or a Korg synthesiser and can play both at the same time. In the music I have described that is accredited to the Metheny/Mays partnership, it is difficult to attribute any particular composition to one or other of them. Lyle must have contributed substantially to these extraordinary musical compositions. Even if Pat wrote a piece, the luscious sounds that Mays creates are a perfect match for everything Pat does, a fact that can only have come about as a result of a collaboration that has lasted over 30 years. Lyle's playing is always sublime, his long fingers effortlessly finding the perfect harmonies and probably having a strong role in creating the stunning atmospherics of many of the orchestrations and performances.

However, Lyle's voracious appetite for music does not appear to be of the same order as Pat's. As a leader, Lyle has made only a few albums: *Lyle Mays* (1986), *Street Dreams* (1988), *Fictionary* (1993) and *Improvisations for Expanded Piano* (2000). Lyle has also composed the music for *In the Shadow of a Miracle* (1996), a suite of classical music recorded and performed by The Debussy Trio.

His first album was a popular collection of material considered by some to be similar to his work in PMG. However, Lyle also has ambitions that lie outside PMG fusion and in *Fictionary* he assembled a collection of straight-ahead jazz pieces to be played by Marc Johnson and Jack de Johnette. With the whole world of musicians now within range of his radar, Pat continues to regard Lyle very highly indeed and he has made it quite clear that all options for PMG with Lyle on the piano stool remain open.

I should say too that my analysis of PMG fusion is in no way intended to diminish Steve Rodby's contributions. I have summarised the sound of PMG fusion as essentially guitar/string dominated, without recourse to significant use of wind instruments, and not dominated by electric bass. The magnificent textures offered by string bass in the hands of Steve Rodby are as good as from any other player, but I do not believe that Steve's bass is a unique sound without which PMG fusion would not exist. He has certainly become the third 'permanent' member of the band, but has now taken on the role of producer of the PMG records and it is in this capacity, away from the instrument and behind the desk where Pat views Steve Rodby's contribution as unique. Nevertheless, bass was clearly an important part of the PMG sound, as Pat proved with the hiring of Steve Rodby in 1980. For Steve, it was a dream come true. "When I met Pat I was an unformed nobody from small town Illinois, who didn't even know what chords were, and he was already the future of music – he was 18 and had it all figured out. He was so far ahead of the game it was unbelievable. But when we played there was something about the style of the music that I felt that I could understand that I couldn't account for. It may have been similar backgrounds and a shared love of pop music, the Beatles. It just made sense. I used to listen to the first couple of PMG albums and say to myself, 'that's my music'. It really was my dream group." [10]

Breadth

Pat Metheny has now established himself as one of the greatest all-round jazz musicians by means of a twin-track approach to his career – he himself would say "Well, there's the Group and then there's the other stuff." Clearly, it was a most successful strategy, if only because he has been able to avoid a lot of the bad press that inevitably was associated with playing in the genre labelled as jazz-fusion. His commercial success has been due to his leadership of the Pat Metheny Group and the creation of music that actually touches souls. In that band he has developed a unique sound and style that is instantly recognisable. Perhaps it was his success with PMG that enabled him to pursue the mainstream projects with virtually every other leading jazz musician (except John McLaughlin!) No matter how his work is perceived by others, Pat doesn't see much delineation between his work with the Group and "the other stuff. There's way too much overlap!" Pat thinks his route was to "come up with a narrative, storytelling quality that adds up. That's what I'm looking for." [23]

For a musician clearly operating at the top of his tree, he has never been afraid to join other musicians on their albums. The logic of this was simply for the experience and fun of playing with this or that musician. His time spent with Joshua Redman comes to mind, for here was a young musician – some fifteen years his junior, with no significant profile, but one who Pat had identified as special. It was enough for Pat to join Joshua's band and not just play on an album but to go out on the road with him. That says much for Pat's selflessness and humility. Having said that, Pat is no shrinking violet and, once he is inside a musical context, he has never refrained from stamping his presence all over the project. The album he made with John Scofield springs to mind, where, even in the company of another jazz guitar heavyweight, Pat was able to almost to dominate the recording to the point where Sco looked inadequate. Even the renowned composer Steve Reich gracefully accepted Pat's "improvements" to his own composition. [35] How many others would do the same?

Pat has worked on high profile recordings such as *Like Minds* (1998), or his old friend Michael Brecker's last album *Pilgrimage* (2007). But he has also appeared on lower profile projects such as Jack de Johnette's *Parallel Realities* (1990) or Marc Johnson's *The Sound of Summer Running* (1999). Then there are the complete wildcard appearances, for example, on a vocal album of Brazilian music with Milton Nascimento, or some cameo appearances with Bruce Hornsby. The sheer expanse of Pat's musical imagination and desire is without comparison in the jazz world.

Desire to play

Pat's personality has had a lot to do with his success. He is a warm, friendly, positive individual who, like Burton, adopts a serious scholarly approach to music and really knows what he wants to achieve. Totally dedicated to the furtherance of music as an art form, Pat is indefatigable, prepared to expend countless hours in practice and preparation, as well as the many days spent each year in the studio and on the road. For Pat, it is literally the road to success.

"We tour non-stop and by virtue of playing live have had personal contact with millions of people. We play between 200 and 300 nights a year, and there are between 2,000 and 5,000 people each time. If you add that up, it's a lot of people and a certain percentage of that audience wants to have a record, which sells a lot of records. We deliver the goods live; we play really long and hard and it shows, even though we sound much better live than on records." [8]

Gary Burton: "Pat is one of the most successful jazz musicians in history... He is a very melodic player and I think that's a key ingredient for any successful jazz musician, but above all else he has a terrific natural charisma. He really communicates to the audience extremely well." [23]

But Pat is his own best (and worst) critic. "I'm always happy to hear that people like the music of course, when they do, and, you know, that's great, but on the other hand, my relationship to music is a very personal one. Pretty much everything that I do I'm doing between me and it. I think as soon as you cross that line when you're worrying about what other people are saying about you, you're in big trouble because then you're always guessing, you know? I've never really cared that much what people thought. Of course, a lot of people have liked it. There have been other situations people haven't liked it. In a way, both are irrelevant to me because, believe me, every night when I go home I know how well I played compared to how well I want to play and on a critical level I'm extremely critical of my own playing, and the band and everything else, in a way that would probably scare most people. (He laughs.) You know, it's very serious for me, this thing we're trying to do, and to get it to be the best it can be is an on-going quest for me. If somebody likes it, that's great, but on the other hand, it doesn't really alter what I'm doing that much. It's more just sort of a feeling of support from people which is important." [36]

Pat, the guitarist

Pat does not rate his position in the league table of guitar players too highly. Many others disagree, however, and Pat is absolutely not qualified to judge on this matter. Jay Azzolina of Spyro Gyra was a student of Pat's at Berklee. For him, Pat's playing is very special indeed. "He made the guitar a new instrument in terms of his uniqueness and sound and phrasing ... just the way he played the instrument and what he brought to it, it was like a reinvented guitar. How many people can you say that about?" That's a remarkable accolade for someone who says, "The truth is I don't really play the instrument that well – relative to several hundred thousand other people." It seems that the explanation to this dichotomy is in the way he views his overall role as a musician. For Pat the instrument is just the means for conveying an idea. "The idea is completely the dominant factor. The playing of the instrument is almost incidental – the instrument is like fifth or sixth or seventh or eighth on the priority level. Now somebody who's playing the instrument from an instrument standpoint – this whole issue of ideas often is not even in the top ten. What I notice is, a lot of jazz lacks ideas." Pat believes that very often musicians who concentrate on technique or style alone don't pay any attention to the deeper values of the music they strive to play. [23]

You hear many players, on all instruments, making mistakes when playing live. Miles Davis, for example, is well known for being an inaccurate player. Pat, however, plays with extraordinary accuracy. He has an extraordinary memory to retain in his head so much complicated music pertaining to such a large repertoire. His style involves sliding in and out of his notes and the frequent use of devices like repeated single notes or repeated short motifs during solos. There is no style in which he does not participate, although his use of the blues is limited and his solos in blues forms are not as innovative as in other styles. He also has remarkable stamina, with the ability, no doubt acquired from years of practice, to play hard for long periods.

Although he has obviously acquired his own branded sound, there are plenty of occasions when you hear guitar sounds that you cannot attribute to him. His style has been in perfect concordance with the Miles Davis law of cliché-free music. Consequently, I suggest he is the musician with the broadest range of styles on record. For example, he could be writing, playing and producing music for film scores of the type he made for *Map of the World* – a very sweet, homely style that upsets jazz puritans. He could also be emitting the kinds of sounds that I find to be mere indescribable noise, as on his own *Zero Tolerance of Silence* (1994) or as a part of Derek Bailey's 3-CD project *The Sign of 4* (1996). In between there are albums with mainstream jazz giants such as Ornette Coleman, Charlie Haden, Chick Corea, Herbie Hancock and Dave Liebman.

When you watch Pat play, you become aware that he is a very special musician. He stands centre stage, legs slightly apart, with his selected guitar braced across his chest. His head is tilted downwards towards the guitar and lolls incessantly, his face and mouth in constant motion. Depending on the stage the music is at will determine whether his knees bend as he leans backwards, or whether he broadens his stance to brace himself for a great physical effort.

At first, the sight of his rolling head and facial contortion can be rather off-putting. However, the more you appreciate what is going on, the more awestruck you become. In electric mode, his right hand is gripping a pick or plectrum, a small unsymmetrical oval piece of flat plastic with which he plucks the strings. This hand doesn't generally move a lot, unless he is playing a piece like *First Circle*, as on the *We Live Here* DVD, for example, when he strums the strings extraordinarily quickly for long periods of time. This, of course, requires extreme physical effort and the fact that he keeps it up for so long is remarkable in itself. His left hand, however, moves with remarkable dexterity, up down and across the fingerboard. Just watch the incredibly rapid and precise finger movements. Perhaps you remain unimpressed? Well, consider this. He rarely looks at the fingerboard – he generally doesn't need to. His eyes are mostly closed. When he plays at speeds in excess of ten notes every second, he is making instantaneous decisions, first on what note to play, and then to match the plucking of the correct string with the fingering of the correct note. At any given moment, if he needs a G he might have three different places to play it on the keyboard and the one he chooses will depend on what he expects to play next, so as to try to reduce the amount of left hand movement as much as possible. Superimpose on this the smallest of decisions of nuance, for it is this that makes the difference between a great artist and someone who just plays the guitar. He must decide whether he will embellish a note with the slightest of inflections that will affect its tone or texture, and whether it will be held for a short or long time before he plays the next. Will there be a gap between this note and the next, or will it flow smoothly into the next? All of these decisions are being made in tiny fractions of a second. It makes him sound like a very smoothly operating, efficient piece of machinery, but, of course, humans are much more complicated than that.

Pat Metheny has developed his skills to such an extent that the guitar becomes a part of his body. And it is not just his hands and his brain – it is his entire body! That is why his playing affects his body movements. He has spent his life teaching his brain to control not only his body but to make the guitar an integral part of it and to turn the whole entity into a perfectly functioning music machine. Thus, to describe his music as pure mechanics, as I have just done, is far too simplistic.

Pat himself describes his playing like this. "Well, for me, playing, at its best, is a lot like talking with somebody that you know really well – that you feel very comfortable with – and you sort of forget about time and space and everything kind of inside the ideas that you have, really living each moment in a very particular way that's very unique to what the process of playing is all about. For me, honestly, I can say, when I'm playing really good, I'm not really thinking about anything. I'm just listening, and in fact, more and more, as the time has gone on, I realised that playing is really more about listening than it is about playing. Now what I really mean by that is that if I play one note and then I really hear how that note fits with what everybody else is playing, then there's a person inside me who's a fan of music, who's a listener. And then I just kind of ask the listener, 'OK, if you were listening to this (which you are) what would you like to hear next?' And then I play that. So really, it becomes the listening part of you that's the leader of the melodic phrase, or whatever, so really I'm just kind of listening. I mean, that's the best thing I could say: that I'm trying to really hear the whole sound of the band and just kind of participate in it." [36]

So Pat is saying that he is totally at one with his guitar: his brain is in control and the act of mechanically making the sounds is subconscious, whilst his conscious mind listens. He has reached the point where he doesn't have to consciously think about the mechanics of playing. He is in a completely different mental state in which he can almost relax and interactively enjoy the music as it is being created. What a fantastic description of skill at the highest level!

Pat, the composer

So, with the mechanics of playing the guitar so far down the list of *his* priorities, what about composition, an art that Pat places higher up the list? Pat has now established a reputation as being one of the great jazz composers. Comfortable across the entire spectrum of styles, Pat can conceive music that is constantly probing new corners, but use his guitar merely as the vehicle for transmitting this stunning array of new ideas to an eager audience. Many of my descriptions over the previous pages have attempted to emphasise the constant inspiration his music provides, the way it nucleates a stream of wonderful imagery in the listener's mind.

Throughout all these albums the musical formulae have become increasingly open to analysis, yet, as with Einstein's deceptively simple equation, a great depth of sophistication lies within the envelope of a long series of musical pieces. In a similar manner to the output from Chick Corea, here is music in which each piece has been crafted with supreme care, composed to an extent that each musician is required to play written music, often in complex time and with very sophisticated rhythmic patterns. Yet, throughout the majority of PMG pieces, the bars are infused with melodies that are far more lyrical than the hard bop-inspired lines of Corea's tunes. Melody is a musical parameter that Pat has always focussed on, but which, as I wrote in my section called "The Tao of Physics", he finds most mysterious and helps steer him towards deeper thoughts.

Coda

There can be no doubt that Pat is one of the most extraordinary jazz musicians of all time. Very little of his success has been due to chance of fortune, but instead Pat has largely carved out his own destiny and set a fine example for a new generation of musicians. From the very beginning Pat had a clear idea of what he wanted to achieve. His first success resulted from a deliberate encounter with Gary Burton, at which he attempted (unsuccessfully at first) to impress Gary with his guitar skills. This was an extremely important early decision, for Burton was no ordinary mentor but himself a jazz musician of the highest standing. Through perseverance, he succeeded in attracting Burton's attention and gaining an invitation to join his band. During his three-year apprenticeship, Pat was able to draw from the great depth of musical wisdom and expertise that Burton possessed. He was also able to meet and play alongside many of the best jazz musicians, and to make friendships that would last throughout his career. Since then he has gone from strength to strength, building a long line of successful and very different projects.

This book set out to describe Pat's contribution to jazz-fusion, which is clearly very significant indeed. The organisation of his peers responsible for awarding Grammys gave "Best" awards to no fewer than eight albums by the Pat Metheny Group: *Offramp* (1982), *First Circle* (1984), *Still Life (Talking)* (1987), *Letter From Home* (1989), *We Live Here* (1995), *Imaginary Day* (1997), *Speaking of Now* (2002) and *The Way Up* (2005). Perhaps we should now pose the question, what would Pat's work have amounted to without the PMG? Well, even by the yardstick offered by the Grammys, Pat would still have won ten – that's more awards than most other musicians for his work in the wider jazz arena, which I have extensively documented in these pages. That is an astonishing achievement by any measure.

Now in his fifties, Pat is a master composer, as well as a brilliant guitarist who lives to play. His compositions are rich in colour, complex in rhythm, and vary widely between angular tones and tear-jerking melody. It is truly music of the soul and will undoubtedly endure. By describing Pat Metheny and his music at such length, I intended to justify the assertion that he should be regarded as the foremost living jazz musician. When I started to write this, I wondered if that was an extravagant claim. Now that I have finished I am certain it is not.

References

To complete this work I have had to use information obtained from album sleeve notes, Internet sources, and interviews on radio and video. I wish to acknowledge all of the sources quoted below for helping to provide background material. All other opinions are my own.

[1] Mark Small, http://www.thescreamonline.com/music/music4-3/metheny/metheny.html
[2] Intervista Pat Metheny a Umbria Jazz 2008, http://www.YouTube.com
[3] Bill Milkowski, *Jaco: The Extraordinary and Tragic Life of Jaco Pastorius 'The World's Greatest Bass Player'*, Backbeat Books, San Francisco, CA (1995) p63.
[4] Bill Milkowski, Jaco, p58.
[5] Paul Stump, *Go Ahead John, The Music of John McLaughlin*, SAF Publishing (2000) p68.
[6] Richard Cook, *Jazz Encyclopedia*, Penguin Books (2005) p424.
[7] Allan Holdsworth, *5 to 10* from the album *Wardenclyffe Tower*, Restless Records (1992).
[8] Pat Metheny: Interview with Nicholas Webb, *Guitar Magazine* (1985) http://www.joness.com/gr300/metheny.htm
[9] Wayne Scott Joness at http://www.joness.com
[10] Steve Rodby: Interview with Steve Lawson, *Bassist* Magazine 1999; http://www.stevelawson.net/wordpress/2007/11/steve_rodby_int/
[11] Michael Brecker, sleeve notes to *Michael Brecker*, GRP Records (1987).
[12] Gary Burton, sleeve notes to *Reunion*, GRP Records (1990).
[13] Neil Tesser, sleeve notes to *Reunion*, GRP Records (1990).
[14] De Johnette, Hancock, Holland, Metheny, *Live in Concert*, Arthaus Musik (1990) directed by Clark Santee, Exec producer Ted Kurland.
[15] Barry Miles, *Paul McCartney*, Secker and Warburg, 1997.
[16] Pat Metheny, 14 February 2005, Interview with Courtney Pine, *Jazz Crusade*, BBC Radio 2.
[17] Tony Williams, Interview with *Downbeat* magazine, April 1997.
[18] Tony Williams, sleeve notes to Wilderness (1996).
[19] Charlie Haden, sleeve notes to *Beyond the Missouri Skies*, Verve (1997).
[20] Gary Burton, sleeve notes to *Like Minds*, Concord Records (1998).
[21] Michael Brecker talking to Jason West (1999): http://www.allaboutjazz.com/
[22] http://www.nonesuch.com/artists/brad-mehldau
[23] Richard Niles, *Bright Size Life (Episode 3)*, BBC Radio 2, 2007.
[24] Paul Tingen, *Miles Beyond*, Billboard Books (2001) p25.
[25] Pat Metheny, sleeve notes to *Quartet Live*, Concord Records (2009).
[26] Gary Burton, sleeve notes to *Quartet Live*, Concord Records (2009).
[27] Steve Swallow, sleeve notes to *Quartet Live*, Concord Records (2009).
[28] *Strike up the Band*, CBS Sunday Morning 3 April 2011.
[29] Pat Metheny, *Orchestrion Tour Concert in Vienna*, You Tube video recorded 25 Feb 2010.
[30] Pat Metheny Complete Discography, http://www.jazzdisco.org/pat-metheny/discography
[31] http://guitar.about.com/library/weekly/aa060500c.htm
[32] Linda Manzer, http://www.manzer.com
[33] Ken Trethewey, *John McLaughlin: The Emerald Beyond*, Jazz-Fusion Books (2008).
[34] *Wikipedia*: Pat Metheny.
[35] Steve Reich, sleeve notes to Electric Counterpoint, Nonesuch Records (1989).
[36] Pat Metheny, Interview on *We Live Here, DVD*, 1995.

Pat Metheny (left) playing the *Speaking of Now* gig in May 2002 at the Lighthouse Centre, Poole, UK with Antonio Sanchez (centre) and Richard Bona (right). Photo: Ken Trethewey.

Discography

Pat Metheny is a musician who has performed and recorded prolifically. The following discography is not complete, but covers many of the more significant albums he has appeared on. Besides the 'officially' published albums, Pat's popularity means that, as with many other artists, there are recordings (mostly obtained at live performances without permission) that are impossible to ignore. Some of these are listed here. There are also many appearances made on albums by other artists and a large proportion of these are also included. Only during the later part of my research did I make use of the discography at:

http://www.jazzdisco.org/pat-metheny/discography

I wish to state that the discography reproduced below was compiled by me exclusively from sleeve notes to albums in my possession and that I am therefore wholly responsible for any errors that may occur.

Pat Metheny as Leader:

Pat Metheny

*** 1976 Bright Size Life

CD: ECM 1073 827 133; Album length (37.06)

Musicians: Pat Metheny (guitar), Jaco Pastorius (bass), Bob Moses (drums)

Tracks: 1 Bright Size Life (4.45), 2 Sirabhorn (5.29), 3 Unity Village (3.40), 4 Missouri Uncompromised (4.21), 5 Midwestern Nights Dream (6.00), 6 Unquity Road (3.35), 7 Omaha Celebration (4.18), 8 Round Trip/ Broadway Blues (4.58)

Notes: Recorded: Ludwigsberg, Germany.

Pat Metheny

*** 1977 Watercolors

CD: ECM 1097 827; Album length (41.48)

Musicians: Pat Metheny (guitar), Lyle Mays (keyboard), Eberhard Weber (bass), Danny Gottlieb (drums)

Tracks: 1 Watercolors (6.29), 2 Icefire (6.06), 3 Oasis (4.02), 4 Lakes (4.43), 5 River Quay (4.57), 6 Florida Greeting Song (2.31), 7 Legend of the Fountain (2.29), 8 Sea Song (10.17)

Notes: Recorded in Oslo, Norway.

Pat Metheny Group

***** 1978 Pat Metheny Group

CD: ECM 1114 422 825; Album length (41.28)

Musicians: Pat Metheny (guitar), Lyle Mays (keyboard), Mark Egan (bass), Danny Gottlieb (drums)

Tracks: 1 San Lorenzo (10.12), 2 Phase Dance (8.17), 3 Jaco (5.35), 4 Aprilwind (2.08), 5 April Joy (8.12), 6 Lone Jack (6.40)

Notes: Recorded at Oslo, Norway.

Pat Metheny Group

**** 1979 American Garage

CD: ECM 1155 827 134; Album length (35.21)

Musicians: Pat Metheny (guitar), Lyle Mays (keyboard), Mark Egan (bass), Danny Gottlieb (drums)

Tracks: 1 (Cross the) Heartland (6.55), 2 Airstream (6.20), 3 The Search (4.54), 4 American Garage (4.13), 5 The Epic (12.59)

Notes: Recorded at the Super Guitar Festival, Brookfield, MA, June, 1979.

Pat Metheny

*** 1979 New Chautauqua

CD: ECM 1131 825 471; Album length (38.28)

Musicians: Pat Metheny (guitar)

Tracks: 1 New Chautauqua (5.19), 2 Country Poem (2.34), 3 Long Ago Child/Fallen Star (10.19), 4 Hermitage (5.39), 5 Sueño con Mexico (5.59), 6 Daybreak (8.38)

Notes: Recorded at Oslo, Norway.

Pat Metheny

*** 1980 80/81

2 CD: ECM 1180/81 422; Album length (80.26)

Musicians: Pat Metheny (guitar), Dewey Redman (saxophone), Michael Brecker (saxophone), Charlie Haden (bass), Jack De Johnette (drums)

Tracks: 1 Two Folk Songs (20.45), 2 80/81 (7.27), 3 The Bat (5.58), 4 Turnaround (7.05), 5 Open (14.26), 6 Pretty Scattered (6.56), 7 Every Day (I Thank You) (13.16), 8 Goin' Ahead (3.51)

Notes: Recorded at Oslo, Norway, May 26-29, 1980. Brecker plays on 1 and 7; Redman plays on 2. Both play on 3, 5

Pat Metheny and Lyle Mays

**** 1981 As Falls Wichita, So Falls Wichita Falls

CD: ECM 1190 821 416; Album length (43.34)

Musicians: Pat Metheny (guitar), Lyle Mays (keyboard), Nana Vasconcelos (percussion)

Tracks: 1 As Falls Wichita, So Falls Wichita Falls (20.45), 2 Ozark (4.03), 3 September Fifteenth (dedicated to Bill Evans) (7.45), 4 "It's For You" (8.20), 5 Estupenda Graça (2.41)

Notes: Recorded at Oslo, Norway, September, 1980

Pat Metheny Group

***** 1982 Offramp

CD: ECM 1216 422 817; Album length (42.22)

Musicians: Pat Metheny (guitar), Lyle Mays (keyboard), Steve Rodby (bass), Danny Gottlieb (drums), Nana Vasconcelos (percussion)

Tracks: 1 Barcarole (3.15), 2 Are You Going With Me? (8.47), 3 Au Lait (8.28), 4 Eighteen (5.05), 5 Offramp (5.55), 6 James (6.41), 7 The Bat Pt II (3.50)

Notes: Recorded NYC, October 1981. Album won Grammy for Best Jazz Fusion Performance, Vocal Or Instrumental

Pat Metheny Group

**** 1983 Travels

2 CD: ECM 1252/3 810 622 2; Album length (96.24)

Musicians: Pat Metheny (guitar), Lyle Mays (keyboard), Steve Rodby (bass), Danny Gottlieb (drums), Nana Vasconcelos (percussion)

Tracks: 1 Are You Going With Me? (9.18), 2 The Fields, The Sky (7.46), 3 Goodbye (8.16), 4 Phase Dance (8.03), 5 Straight on Red (7.26), 6 Farmer's Trust (6.25), 7 Extradition (5.44), 8 Goin' Ahead (4.20), 9 As Falls Wichita, So Falls Wichita Falls (5.00), 10 Travels (4.00), 11 Song For Bilbao (8.26), 12 San Lorenzo (13.35)

Notes: 1983: Album won Grammy for Best Jazz Fusion Performance, Vocal Or Instrumental, 1983.

Pat Metheny Trio

*** 1984 Rejoicing

CD: ECM 1271; Album length (43.51)

Musicians: Pat Metheny (guitar), Charlie Haden (bass), Billy Higgins (drums)

Tracks: 1 Lonely Woman (6.50), 2 Tears Inside (3.50), 3 Humpty Dumpty (5.42), 4 Blues for Pat (6.05), 5 Rejoicing (3.23), 6 Story from a Stranger (5.53), 7 The Calling (9.51), 8 Waiting for an Answer (2.17)

Notes: Recorded NYC, November 29/30, 1983.

Pat Metheny Group

***** 1984 First Circle

CD: ECM 1278 422 823; Album length (49.54)

Musicians: Pat Metheny (guitar), Lyle Mays (keyboard), Steve Rodby (bass), Pedro Aznar (voice), Paul Wertico (drums)

Tracks: 1 Forward March (2.49), 2 Yolanda You Learn (4.49), 3 The First Circle (9.16), 4 If I Could (7.01), 5 Tell It All (7.59), 6 End of the Game (8.02), 7 Mas Alla (Beyond) (5.40), 8 Praise (4.18)

Notes: Recorded NYC, February 15-19, 1984. Album won Grammy for Best Jazz Fusion Performance, Vocal Or Instrumental Year, 1984.

Pat Metheny Group

*** 1985 The Falcon and the Snowman

CD: EMI Manhattan CDP748411-2; Album length (38.55)

Musicians: Pat Metheny (guitar), Lyle Mays (keyboard), Steve Rodby (bass), Paul Wertico (drums), Pedro Aznar (voice), David Bowie (voice)

Tracks: 1 Psalm 121/Flight of the Falcon (4.08), 2 Daulton Lee (5.56), 3 Chris (3.16), 4 The Falcon (4.59), 5 This is Not America (3.53), 6 Extent of the Lie (4.15), 7 Level of Deception (5.45), 8 Capture (3.57), 9 Epilogue Psalm 121 (2.14)

Notes: Special guest David Bowie sang the vocal for the track "This is not America", which made the top twenty of the pop record charts in 1985. Recorded London, September, 1984

Pat Metheny

* 2005 Song X: Twentieth Anniversary

CD: Nonesuch 7559-79918-2; Album length (66.36)

Musicians: Pat Metheny (guitar), Ornette Coleman (saxophone), Charlie Haden (bass), Jack De Johnette (drums), Denardo Coleman (drums)

Tracks: 1 Police People (4.57), 2 All of Us (0.15), 3 The Good Life (3.25), 4 Word From Bird (3.48), 5 Compute (2.03), 6 The Veil (3.42), 7 Song X (5.34), 8 Mob Job (4.11), 9 Endangered Species (13.18), 10 Video Games (5.20), 11 Kathelin Gray (4.31), 12 Trigonometry (5.05), 13 Song X Duo (3.07), 14 Long Time No See (7.38)

Notes: The original edition of this album was published in 1986 as Geffen GEFD 924086 2; recorded NYC, December 12-14, 1985. The first six tracks on this album were added by Metheny in 2005 from the original tapes.

Pat Metheny Group

***** 1987 Still Life (Talking)

CD: Geffen GEFMD 24145; Album length (42.28)

Musicians: Pat Metheny (guitar), Lyle Mays (keyboard), Steve Rodby (bass), Paul Wertico (drums), Armando Marçal (percussion), Mark Ledford (voice), David Blamires (voice)

Tracks: 1 Minuano (Six Eight) (9.27), 2 So May it Secretly Begin (6.25), 3 Last Train Home (5.41), 4 (It's Just) Talk (6.17), 5 Third Wind (8.37), 6 Distance (2.45), 7 In Her Family (3.16)

Notes: Recorded NYC, March, April, 1987. Album won Grammy for Best Jazz Fusion Performance, Vocal Or Instrumental

Pat Metheny Group

**** 1989 Letter From Home

CD: Geffen GEFD 24245; Album length (61.45)

Musicians: Pat Metheny (guitar), Lyle Mays (keyboard), Steve Rodby (bass), Paul Wertico (drums), Armando Marçal (percussion), Pedro Aznar (voice)

Tracks: 1 Have You Heard (6.25), 2 Every Summer Night (7.13), 3 Better Days Ahead (3.03), 4 Spring Ain't Here (6.55), 5 45/8 (0.57), 6 5-5-7-7 (7.54), 7 Beat 70 (4.55), 8 Dream of the Return (5.26), 9 Are We There Yet (7.55), 10 Vidala (3.03), 11 Slip Away (5.25), 12 Letter From Home (2.34)

Notes: Recorded NYC, spring 1989. Album won Grammy for The album won the Grammy for Best Jazz Fusion

Pat Metheny Trio

*** 1990 Question and Answer

CD: Geffen 9-24293-2; Album length (62.49)

Musicians: Pat Metheny (guitar), Dave Holland (bass), Roy Haynes (drums)

Tracks: 1 Solar (8.27), 2 Question and Answer (7.07), 3 H and H (6.51), 4 Never Too Far Away (5.52), 5 Law Years (6.51), 6 Change of Heart (6.14), 7 All the Things You Are (8.26), 8 Old Folks (6.38), 9 Three Flights Up (6.10)

Notes: Recorded Power Station, NYC, December 21, 1989. The track, Change of Heart won the Grammy for Best Instrumental Composition, 1990.

Pat Metheny Group

**** 1991 The Road To You

CD: Nonesuch 7559-79941-2; Album length (73.57)

Musicians: Pat Metheny (guitar), Lyle Mays (keyboard), Steve Rodby (bass), Paul Wertico (drums), Pedro Aznar (voice), Armando Marçal (percussion)

Tracks: 1 Have You Heard (6.07), 2 First Circle (8.39), 3 The Road To You (5.29), 4 Half Life of Absolution (15.22), 5 Last Train Home (5.10), 6 Better Days Ahead (4.55), 7 Naked Moon (5.18), 8 Beat 70 (4.40), 9 Letter From Home (2.18), 10 Third Wind (8.39), 11 Solo from More Travels (3.35)

Notes: Recorded live in Italy and France, July, 1991 as Geffen GEFD 24601. The album won the Grammy for Best Contemporary Jazz Performance (Instrumental), 1993.

Pat Metheny

***** 1992 Secret Story

CD: Geffen GED 24468; Album length (76.21)

Musicians: Pat Metheny (guitar), Charlie Haden (bass), Nana Vasconcelos (percussion), Lyle Mays (keyboard), Danny Gottlieb (drums), Mark Ledford (voice), Steve Rodby (bass), Will Lee (bass), Steve Ferrone (drums), Paul Wertico (drums), Gil Goldstein (keyboard), Sammy Merendino (drums), Andy Findon (flute), Toots Thielemans (harmonica), Michael Mossman (trumpet), Mike Metheny (trumpet), Ryan Kisor (trumpet), Tom Malone (trombone), Dave Taylor (trombone), Dave Bargeron (trombone), John Clark (french horn), Anthony Jackson Jr (bass), Akiko Yano (voice), Skaila Kanga (harp), Armando Marçal (percussion)

Tracks: 1 Above the Treetops (2.44), 2 Facing West (6.05), 3 Cathedral in a Suitcase (4.52), 4 Finding and Believing (10.00), 5 The Longest Summer (6.34), 6 Sunlight (3.53), 7 Rain River (7.09), 8 Always and Forever (5.26), 9 See the World (4.48), 10 As a Flower Blossoms (I am Running to You) (1.53), 11 Antonia (6.11), 12 The Truth Will Always Be (9.15), 13 Tell Her You Saw Me (5.11), 14 Not to be Forgotten (Our Final Hour) (2.20), 15 Back in Time (5.18), 16 Understanding (2.14), 17 A Change in Circumstance (1.15), 18 Look Ahead (4.10), 19 Et Si C'Etait La fin (As If It Were the End) (3.39)

Notes: Recorded NYC, autumn-winter 1991. Pat Metheny won Grammy for Best Contemporary Jazz Performance (Instrumental) 1992. Tacks 15-19 issued on a bonus CD: in the Special De Luxe Edition, Nonesuch 7559

Pat Metheny

* 1994 Zero Tolerance for Silence

CD: Geffen GED 24626; Album length (39.15)

Musicians: Pat Metheny (guitar)

Tracks: 1 Part 1 (18.18), 2 Part 2 (5.10), 3 Part 3 (4.19), 4 Part 4 (5.07), 5 Part 5 (5.54)

Notes: Recorded Power Station, NYC, December 16, 1992.

Pat Metheny Group

***** 1995 We Live Here

CD: Geffen GED 24729; Album length (67.02)

Musicians: Pat Metheny (guitar), Lyle Mays (keyboard), Steve Rodby (bass), Paul Wertico (drums), David Blamires (voice), Mark Ledford (voice), Luis Conte (percussion)

Tracks: 1 Here To Stay (7.39), 2 And Then I Knew (7.52), 3 The Girls Next Door (5.29), 4 To the End of the World (12.14), 5 We Live Here (4.12), 6 Episode d'Azur (8.45), 7 Something To Remind You (7.03), 8 Red Sky (7.35), 9 Stranger in Town (6.13)

Notes: Recorded NYC, 1994. Album won Grammy for Best Contemporary Jazz Performance, 1995.

Pat Metheny

*** 1996 Passaggio per il Paradiso

CD: Geffen GED 77007; Album length (47.24)

Musicians: Pat Metheny (guitar)

Tracks: 1 Theme from Passaggio per il Paradiso (3.08), 2 Marta's Theme (1.47), 3 The Roads of Marche (3.09), 4 Marta's House Story (1.44), 5 Wolf Story (1.11), 6 Marta's Stag Story (3.43), 7 Learning on the Road (5.07), 8 Private Eye (1.16), 9 Marta on the Bus, Marta in the Fields (3.12), 10 Remembering Home, Meeting the Kids (3.43), 11 Renato's Theme (2.37), 12 Finale: It's Always Worth the Trouble (13.35), 13 Don't Forget (Renato's Theme) (3.12)

Notes: Recorded at Private Studios, NYC, January, 1996.

Pat Metheny Group

** 1996 Quartet

CD: Geffen GEFSD 24978; Album length (66.08)

Musicians: Pat Metheny (guitar), Lyle Mays (keyboard), Steve Rodby (bass), Paul Wertico (drums)

Tracks: 1 Introduction (0.57), 2 When We Were Free (5.39), 3 Montevideo (2.55), 4 Take Me There (3.39), 5 Seven Days (4.04), 6 Oceania (3.47), 7 Dismantling Utopia (6.52), 8 Double Blind (4.15), 9 Second Thought (2.50), 10 Mojave (3.37), 11 Badland (7.30), 12 Glacier (1.25), 13 Language of Time (7.33), 14 Sometimes I See (6.01), 15 As I Am (5.04)

Notes: Recorded at Right Track Studios, NYC, May, 1996.

Pat Metheny Group

***** 1997 Imaginary Day

CD: Warner Bros 9362-46791-2; Album length (64.35)

Musicians: Pat Metheny (guitar), Lyle Mays (keyboard), Steve Rodby (bass), Paul Wertico (drums), Mark Ledford (voice), David Blamires (voice), Mino Cinelu (percussion), Dave Samuels (vibraphone), Glen Velez (percussion), Don Alias (percussion)

Tracks: 1 Imaginary Day (10.11), 2 Follow Me (5.56), 3 Into the Dream (2.27), 4 A Story Within the Story (8.01), 5 The Heat of the Day (9.44), 6 Across the Sky (5.13), 7 The Roots of Coincidence (7.48), 8 Too Soon Tomorrow (5.47), 9 The Awakening (9.28)

Notes: Recorded at Right Track Studios, NYC, spring 1997. Album won Grammy for Best Contemporary Jazz Performance, 1997.Track, Roots of Coincidence won Grammy for Best Rock Instrumental Performance, 1997.

Pat Metheny Group

*** 1997 Across the Sky

CD: Warner Bros 9362-44545-2; Album length (27.20)

Musicians: Pat Metheny (guitar), Lyle Mays (keyboard), Steve Rodby (bass), Paul Wertico (drums), Mark Ledford (voice), David Blamires (voice), Mino Cinelu (percussion), Dave Samuels (vibraphone), Glen Velez (percussion)

Tracks: 1 Across the Sky (4.49), 2 Across the Sky (Goldie Remix) (6.36), 3 Roots of Coincidence (8.05), 4 Roots of Coincidence (Mr. Spring's Filter Kings 1.1 Mix) (7.50)

Pat Metheny

** 1999 A Map of the World

CD: Warner Bros 9362-47366-2; Album length (66.25)

Musicians: Pat Metheny (guitar), Gil Goldstein (keyboard)

Tracks: 1 A Map of the World (5.36), 2 Family (2.10), 3 North (4.17), 4 Home (0.42), 5 Sisters (4.05), 6 Childhood (1.25), 7 Fall from Grace (2.35), 8 Memory (0.53), 9 Gone (6.28), 10 Flight (0.51), 11 Alone (1.18), 12 Outcasts (1.31), 13 Sunday (1.39), 14 Discovery (2.31), 15 Acceptance (1.12), 16 Realization (1.18), 17 Soliloquy (2.49), 18 Night (1.54), 19 Sunrise (0.46), 20 Resolution (3.45), 21 Pictures (0.20), 22 Patience (1.20), 23 Transition (0.53), 24 Reunion (1.13), 25 Renewal (1.52), 26 Homecoming (3.17), 27 Forgiving (4.34), 28 Holding Us (4.09)

Notes: Recorded at Right Track Studios, NYC, February, 1999.

Pat Metheny Trio

*** 2000 Trio 99-00

CD: Warner 9362-47632-2; Album length (65.16)

Musicians: Pat Metheny (guitar), Larry Grenadier (bass), Bill Stewart (drums)

Tracks: 1 Travels (5.37), 2 (Go) Get It (7.53), 3 Giant Steps (4.43), 4 Just Like the Day (8.28), 5 Soul Cowboy (4.35), 6 The Sun in Montreal (6.19), 7 Capricorn (5.30), 8 We Had a Sister (5.24), 9 What Do You Want (5.29), 10 A Lot of Livin' to Do (5.30), 11 Lone Jack (5.48)

Notes: Recorded at Right Track Recording, NYC, August, 1999. The track (Go) Get It won the Grammy for Best Jazz Instrumental Solo Year 2000.

Pat Metheny Trio

*** 2000 Trio Live

2 CD: Warner Bros 9362-47907-2; Album length (119.54)

Musicians: Pat Metheny (guitar), Larry Grenadier (bass), Bill Stewart (drums)

Tracks: 1 Bright Size Life (4.18), 2 Question and Answer (19.53), 3 Giant Steps (9.51), 4 Into the Dream (4.27), 5 So May It Secretly Begin (7.10), 6 Bat (7.28), 7 All the Things You Are (9.37), 8 James (6.08), 9 Unity Village (5.18), 10 Soul Cowboy (11.06), 11 Night Turns Into Day (8.20), 12 Faith Healer (18.10), 13 Counting Texas (8.08)

Notes: Recorded live during 1999 and 2000 on tour in Europe, Japan and the United States.

Pat Metheny Group

**** 2002 Speaking of Now

CD: Warner Bros 9362-48025-2; Album length (71.59)

Musicians: Pat Metheny (guitar), Lyle Mays (keyboard), Steve Rodby (bass), Cuong Vu (trumpet), Antonio Sanchez (drums), Richard Bona (multi)

Tracks: 1 As It Is (7.40), 2 Proof (10.13), 3 Another Life (7.08), 4 The Gathering Sky (9.22), 5 You (8.24), 6 On Her Way (6.04), 7 A Place in the World (9.52), 8 Afternoon (4.43), 9 Wherever You Go (8.04)

Notes: Recorded Right Track Studios, NYC, 2001. Album won Grammy for Best Contemporary Jazz Album, 2002.

Pat Metheny

**** 2003 One Quiet Night

CD: Warner Bros 9362-48473-2; Album length (65.35)

Musicians: Pat Metheny (guitar)

Tracks: 1 One Quiet Night (5.01), 2 Song for the boys (4.31), 3 Don't Know Why (3.08), 4 Another Chance (6.54), 5 And Time Goes On (3.19), 6 My Song (4.22), 7 Peace Memory (6.12), 8 Ferry Cross the Mersey (3.58), 9 Over on 4th Street (3.41), 10 I Will find the Way (7.51), 11 North to South, East to West (12.03), 12 Last Train Home (4.35)

Notes: Recorded November, 2001-January, 2003. Won the Grammy for Best New Age Album, 2003.

Pat Metheny Group

***** 2005 The Way Up

CD: Nonesuch 7559-79876-2; Album length (68.07)

Musicians: Pat Metheny (guitar), Lyle Mays (keyboard), Steve Rodby (bass), Cuong Vu (trumpet), Antonio Sanchez (drums), Grégoire Maret (harmonica)

Tracks: 1 Opening (5.17), 2 Part One (26.27), 3 Part Two (20.29), 4 Part Three (15.54)

Notes: 2005: Album won Grammy for Best Contemporary Jazz Performance.

Pat Metheny and Brad Mehldau

**** 2006 Metheny Mehldau

CD: Nonesuch 7559-79964-2; Album length (66.00)

Musicians: Pat Metheny (guitar), Brad Mehldau (piano), Larry Grenadier (bass), Jeff Ballard (drums)

Tracks: 1 Unrequited (5.00), 2 Ahmid-6 (6.35), 3 Summer Day (6.25), 4 Ring of Life (7.35), 5 Legend (7.02), 6 Find Me In Your Dreams (6.07), 7 Say the Brother's Name (7.14), 8 Bachelors III (7.24), 9 Annie's Bittersweet Cake (5.32), 10 Make Peace (7.06)

Notes: Recorded at Right Track Studios, NYC, December, 2005. Grenadier and Ballard play on tracks 4 and 7.

Metheny Mehldau Quartet

*** 2007 Metheny Mehldau Quartet

CD: Nonesuch 7559-79994-0; Album length (73.09).

Musicians: Pat Metheny (guitar), Brad Mehldau (piano), Larry Grenadier (bass), Jeff Ballard (drums)

Tracks: 1 A Night Away (8.01), 2 The Sound of Water (3.57), 3 Fear and Trembling (6.59), 4 Don't Wait (7.13), 5 Towards the Light (8.13), 6 Long Before (7.00), 7 En La Tierra Que No Olvida (7.45), 8 Santa Cruz Slacker (6.12), 9 Secret Beach (9.10), 10 Silent Movie (6.08), 11 Marta's Theme (2.31)

Notes: Recorded at Right Track Studios, NYC, December, 2005.

Pat Metheny

**** 2008 Day Trip

CD: Nonesuch 7559-79956-1; Album length (68.06)

Musicians: Pat Metheny (guitar), Antonio Sanchez (drums), Christian McBride (bass)

Tracks: 1 Son of Thirteen (5.49), 2 At Last You're Here (7.59), 3 Let's Move (5.22), 4 Snova (5.56), 5 Calvin's Keys (7.25), 6 Is This America? (4.34), 7 When We Were Free (9.00), 8 Dreaming Trees (7.46), 9 The Red One (4.47), 10 Day Trip (9.03)

Notes: Recorded at Right Track Recording, NYC, October 19, 2005.

Pat Metheny, Christian McBride, Antonio Sanchez

**** 2008 Tokyo Day Trip

CD: Nonesuch 467580-2; Album length (40.30).

Musicians: Pat Metheny (guitar), Christian McBride (bass), Antonio Sanchez (drums)

Tracks: 1 Tromsø (9.45), 2 Traveling Fast (11.54), 3 Inori (6.04), 4 Back Arm and Black Charge (6.34), 5 The Night Becomes You (6.17)

Notes: Recorded Live in Tokyo.

Pat Metheny, Anna Maria Jopek

**** 2008 Upojenie

CD: Nonesuch 7559 79909-8; Album length (73.05)

Musicians: Pat Metheny (guitar), Anna Maria Jopek (voice), Leszek Mozdzer (piano), Pawel Bzim Zarecki (keyboard), Bernard Maseli (vibes), Darek Oleszkiewicz (bass), Marcin Pospieszalski (bass), Mateusz Pospieszalski (keyboard), Cezary Konrad (drums), Piotr, Nazaruk (flute), Wojciech Kowalewski (percussion), Marek Pospieszalski (turntables), Henryk Miskiewicz (saxophone), Marek Napiorkowski (guitar), Mino Cinelu (percussion), Robert Kubiszyn (bass)

Tracks: 1 Cichy Zapada Zmrok (Here Comes the Silent Dusk. Traditional Polish Evening Prayer) (3.26), 2 Mania Mienia (The Meaning of the Means. Originally: So May it Secretly Begin) (3.40), 3 Biel (Whiteness) (3.22), 4 Przyplyw Odplyw Oddech Czasu (High tide, Low Tide, the Breath of Time. Originally: Tell Her You Saw Me) (4.45), 5 Are You Going With Me? (8.35), 6 Czarne Slowa (Black Words) (5.13), 7 Lulajzejezuniu (Traditional Polish Christmas Carol) (5.14), 8 Upojenie (Ecstasy) (4.44), 9 Zupelnie Inna Ja (The Different Me. Originally: Always and Forever) (3.56), 10 Piosenika Dla Stasia (A Song For Stas) (3.48), 11 Letter From Home (2.46), 12 Me Jedyne Niebo (My Only Heaven. Originally: Another Life) (3.16), 13 By On Byl Tu (Let it Stay. Originally: Farmer's Trust) (6.53), 14 Polskie Drogi (Polish Paths) (2.25), 15 Tam Gdzieniesiega Wzrok (Further than the Eye Can See: Originally: Follow Me) (3.49), 16 Na Calej Polacisnieg (The Snow Falls All Over the Place) (1.47), 17 Szepty I Lzy (Whispers and Tears) (4.47)

Notes: Recorded July-Oct 2002 at S4 and Pueblo People Studios, Warsaw, Poland; Tadeuscz Mieczkowski: Engineer; Produced by Marcin Kydrynski and Pat Metheny.

Gary Burton, Pat Metheny, Steve Swallow, Antonio Sanchez

**** 2009 Quartet Live

CD: Concord Jazz 0888072313033; Album length (79.20)

Musicians: Gary Burton (vibraphone), Pat Metheny (guitar), Steve Swallow (bass), Antonio Sanchez (drums)

Tracks: 1 Sea Journey (9.00), 2 Olhos De Gato (6.36), 3 Falling Grace (7.18), 4 Coral (6.23), 5 Walter L (5.30), 6 B and G (Midwestern Night's Dream) (6.53), 7 Missouri Uncompromised (7.34), 8 Fleurette Africaine (Little African Flower) (7.34), 9 Hullo, Bolinas (4.48), 10 Syndrome (4.42), 11 Question And Answer (13.02)

Pat Metheny

**** 2010 Orchestrion

CD: Nonesuch 7559-79847-3; Album length (51.55)

Musicians: Pat Metheny (guitar)

Tracks: 1 Orchestrion (15.48), 2 Entry Point (10.28), 3 Expansion (8.35), 4 Soul Search (9.19), 5 Spirit of the Air (7.45)

Pat Metheny

**** 2011 What's It All About

CD: Nonesuch 755979647070; Album length (55.53)

Musicians: Pat Metheny (guitar)

Tracks: 1 The Sound of Silence (6.32), 2 Cherish (5.25), 3 Alfie (7.41), 4 Pipeline (3.23), 5 Garota De Ipanema (5.07), 6 Rainy Days And Mondays (7.10), 7 That's The Way I've Always Heard It Should Be (5.57), 8 Slow Hot Wind (4.23), 9 Betcha By Golly, Wow (5.12), 10 And I Love Her (4.22)

Notes: Nominated for a Grammy for Best New Age Album (2011)

Pat Metheny performances on other recordings

Pastorius Metheny Ditmas Bley

** 1974 Jaco

CD: DIW 32DIW312CD; Album length (36.38)

Musicians: Jaco Pastorius (bass), Pat Metheny (guitar), Bruce Ditmas (drums), Paul Bley (piano)

Tracks: 1 Vashkar (9.54), 2 Poconos (1.03), 3 Donkey (6.28), 4 Vampira (7.17), 5 Overtoned (1.43), 6 Jaco (3.30), 7 Batterie (5.05), 8 King Korn (0.30), 9 Blood (1.25)

The Gary Burton Quintet with Eberhard Weber

*** 1974 Ring

CD: ECM 1051; Album length (37.31)

Musicians: Gary Burton (vibraphone), Mick Goodrick (guitar), Pat Metheny (guitar), Steve Swallow (bass), Bob Moses (drums), Eberhard Weber (bass)

Tracks: 1 Mevlevia (6.00), 2 Unfinished Sympathy (3.04), 3 Tunnel of Love (5.33), 4 Intrude (4.52), 5 Silent Spring (10.35), 6 The Colours of Chloe (7.12)

Notes: Recorded: Ludwigsberg, Germany.

Gary Burton Quartet

*** 1976 Dreams So Real: Music of Carla Bley

CD: ECM 1072; Album length (38.35)

Musicians: Gary Burton (vibraphone), Pat Metheny (guitar), Mick Goodrick (guitar), Steve Swallow (bass), Bob Moses (drums)

Tracks: 1 Dreams So Real (6.19), 2 Ictus/ Syndrome/ Wrong Key Donkey (10.23), 3 Jesus Maria (3.44), 4 Vox Humana (7.00), 5 Doctor (4.13), 6 Intermission Music (6.29)

Notes: Recorded: Ludwigsberg, Germany.

Gary Burton Quartet with Eberhard Weber

*** 1977 Passengers

CD: ECM 1092 835 016 2; Album length (40.49)

Musicians: Gary Burton (vibraphone), Pat Metheny (guitar), Steve Swallow (bass), Danny Gottlieb (drums), Eberhard Weber (bass)

Tracks: 1 Sea Journey (9.14), 2 Nacada (4.11), 3 The Whopper (5.28), 4 B and G (Midwestern Nights Dream) (8.22), 5 Yellow Fields (6.58), 6 Claude and Betty (6.16)

Notes: Recorded: Ludwigsberg, Germany.

Joni Mitchell

***** 1980 Shadows and Light

2 CD: Asylum BB 704; Album length (72.16)

Musicians: Joni Mitchell (voice), Michael Brecker (saxophone), Pat Metheny (guitar), Jaco Pastorius (bass), Lyle Mays (keyboard)

Tracks: 1 Introduction (1.51), 2 In France They Kiss on Main Street (4.14), 3 Edith and the Kingpin (4.09), 4 Coyote (4.56), 5 Good-bye Pork Pie Hat (6.04), 6 The Dry Cleaner from Des Moines (4.33), 7 Amelia (6.39), 8 Pat's Solo (3.10), 9 Hejira (7.45), 10 Dreamland (4.38), 11 Band Introduction (0.52), 12 Furry Sings the Blues (5.14), 13 Why Do Fools Fall in Love (2.53), 14 Shadows and Light (5.24), 15 God Must Be a Boogie Man (5.03), 16 Woodstock (5.08)

Notes: Recorded at the County Bowl, Santa Barbara, CA, September, 1979. Available as a DVD. Three other tracks, Black Crow, Don's solo and Free Man in Paris, were omitted from the CD edition.

Michael Brecker

*** 1987 Michael Brecker

CD: GRP 01132; Album length (54.26)

Musicians: Michael Brecker (saxophone), Jack De Johnette (drums), Charlie Haden (bass), Kenny Kirkland (piano), Pat Metheny (guitar)

Tracks: 1 Sea Glass (5.49), 2 Syzygy (9.44), 3 Choices (8.06), 4 Nothing Personal (5.29), 5 The Cost Of Living (7.49), 6 Original Rays (9.04), 7 My One And Only Love (8.16)

Notes: Originally on MCA Impulse! as MCAD 5980. Recorded at Power Station, NYC, 1987.

Steve Reich, Pat Metheny

*** 1989 Different Trains/Electric Counterpoint

CD: Elektra/Nonesuch 7559-79176-2; Album length (14.41)

Electric Counterpoint:

Musicians: Steve Reich (composer), Pat Metheny (guitar)

Tracks: 1 Fast (6.51), 2 Slow (3.21), 3 Fast (4.29)

Notes: Recorded NYC, August 31, September 1, 1987.

Gary Burton

**** 1990 Reunion

CD: GRP GRD-9598; Album length (58.48)

Musicians: Gary Burton (vibraphone), Pat Metheny (guitar), Mitch Forman (keyboard), Will Lee (bass), Peter Erskine (drums)

Tracks: 1 Autumn (4.24), 2 Reunion (5.15), 3 Origin (6.31), 4 Will You Say You Will (4.55), 5 House on the Hill (5.40), 6 Panama (5.38), 7 Chairs and Children (5.55), 8 Wasn't Always Easy (5.06), 9 The Chief (4.16), 10 Tiempos Felice (Happy Times) (4.13), 11 Quick and Running (6.42)

Notes: Recorded NYC, May 6-10, 1989.

de Johnette, Metheny, Hancock, Holland

*** 1990 Parallel Realities Live

2 CD: Jazz Door JD 1251/52; Album length (98.32)

Musicians: Jack De Johnette (drums), Pat Metheny (guitar), Herbie Hancock (keyboard), Dave Holland (bass)

Tracks: 1 Shadow Dance (15.30), 2 Indigo Dreamscapes (7.03), 3 9 Over Reggae (7.35), 4 Solar (13.09), 5 Silver Hollow (8.25), 6 The Good Life (6.08),

7 Blue (7.02), 8 Eye of the Hurricane (15.30), 9 The Bat (8.25), 10 Cantaloupe Island (9.42)

Notes: Recorded live at the Mellon Jazz Festival, Philadelphia PA, 23 June 1990. Also available as a DVD, Arthaus Musik

Gary Thomas

*** 1992 Till We Have Faces

CD: Bamboo POCJ 1130; Album length (61.22)

Musicians: Gary Thomas (saxophone), Pat Metheny (guitar), Tim Murphy (piano), Anthony Cox (bass), Ed Howard (bass), Terri Lynne Carrington (drums), Steve Moss (percussion)

Tracks: 1 Angel Eyes (8.13), 2 The Best Thing for You (7.59), 3 Lush Life (5.29), 4 Bye Bye Baby (6.41), 5 Lament (9.28), 6 Peace (7.18), 7 It's You or no-One (6.36), 8 You Don't Know What Love Is (9.38)

Notes: Recorded NYC, May 8-14, 1992.

Joshua Redman

*** 1993 Wish

CD: Warner 9362-45365-2; Album length (61.38)

Musicians: Joshua Redman (saxophone), Pat Metheny (guitar), Charlie Haden (bass), Billy Higgins (drums)

Tracks: 1 Turnaround (6.24), 2 Soul Dance (6.34), 3 Make Sure You're Sure (5.24), 4 The Deserving Many (5.39), 5 We Had a Sister (5.46), 6 Moose the Mooche (3.32), 7 Tears in Heaven (3.21), 8 Whittlin' (5.21), 9 Wish (Live) (7.26), 10 Blues for Pat (Live) (12.08)

Notes: Recorded Warner Bros. Studios, NYC, 1993.

Bruce Hornsby Band

1993 Harbor Lights

CD: BMG 07863-66114-2; Album length (52.33)

Musicians: Bruce Hornsby (voice), Pat Metheny (guitar), Jeff Lorber (programming), John Bigham (guitar) (guitar), Will Ross (guitar), Jimmy Haslip (bass), John Molo (drums), Phil Collins (drums), Laura Creamer-Dunville (voice), Jean McClain (voice), Bonnie Raitt (voice), Dave Ducan (programming), Branford Marsalis (saxophone), Tony Borg (guitar), Wayne Pooley (guitar), John McLaughlin Williams (violin), Laura Park (violin), Beverly Baker (viola), William Conita (cello), Lamont Coward (percussion), Glenn Wilson (saxophone), Jerry Garcia (guitar), George Harple (french horn), Philip Kaslow (french horn), Adam Leswick (french horn), Alan B Paterson (french horn), John D'Earth (trumpet), Roy Muth (trumpet), Tim Streagle (trombone), George A Gailes III (trumpet)

Tracks: 1 Harbor Lights (7.11), 2 The Talk of the Town (5.11), 3 Long Tall Cool One (4.59), 4 China Doll (5.16), 5 Fields of Gray (4.52), 6 Rainbow's Cadillac (4.37), 7 Passing Through (5.58), 8 The Tide Will Rise (3.55), 9 What a Time (4.53), 10 Pastures of Plenty (6.37)

Notes: Pat Metheny plays on 1, 2, 4, 8

John Scofield and Pat Metheny

**** 1994 I Can See Your House From Here

CD: Blue Note 7243 8 27765 2 9; Album length (69.40)

Musicians: John Scofield (guitar), Pat Metheny (guitar), Steve Swallow (bass), Bill Stewart (drums)

Tracks: 1 I Can See Your House From Here (7.43), 2 The Red One (4.17), 3 No Matter What (7.14), 4 Everybody's Party (6.15), 5 Message To My Friend (6.09), 6 No Way Jose (7.18), 7 Say The Brother's Name (7.18), 8 S.C.O. (4.41), 9 Quiet Rising (5.26), 10 One Way To Be (5.45), 11 You Speak My Language (6.57)

Notes: Recorded Power Station, NYC, December, 1993.

Roy Haynes

*** 1994 Te Vous / Praise

CD: Dreyfuss Jazz FDM 36569-2

Musicians: Roy Haynes (drums), Pat Metheny (guitar), Kenny Garrett (saxophone), Christian McBride (bass), David Kikoski (keyboard)

Tracks: 1 Like This, 2 John McKee, 3 James, 4 If I Could, 5 Blues M45, 6 Trinkle Tinkle, 7 Trigonometry, 8 Good for the Soul

Notes: Recorded Master Sound Astoria Studios, Astoria, NY, ca 1994.

Bruce Hornsby Band

*** 1996 Hot House

CD: RCA 07863 66584-2

Musicians: Bruce Hornsby (voice), Pat Metheny (guitar), Béla Fleck (banjo), Jimmy Haslip (bass), John Molo (drums), Randy Jacobs (guitar), Bobby Read (saxophone), J. V. Collier (bass), Debbie Henry (voice), Chaka Khan (voice), Levi Little (voice), Louis Price (voice), John D'Earth (trumpet)

Tracks: 1 Spider Fingers (6.44), 2 White Wheeled Limousine (5.28), 3 Walk in the Sun (4.58), 4 The Changes (5.49), 5 The Tango King (5.48), 6 Big Rumble

(4.40), 7 Country Doctor (5.57), 8 The Longest Night (5.22), 9 Hot house Ball (4.41), 10 Swing Street (4.36), 11 Cruise Control (5.03)

Notes: Recorded at Bruce Hornsby's House, 1995.

Kenny Garrett Quartet

**** 1996 Pursuance: The Music of John Coltrane

CD: Warner Bros 9362 46209-2; Album length (65.13)

Musicians: Kenny Garrett (saxophone), Pat Metheny (guitar), Brian Blade (drums), Rodney Whitaker (bass)

Tracks: 1 Countdown (3.42), 2 Equinox (7.38), 3 Liberia (7.33), 4 Dear Lord (5.53), 5 Lonnie's Lament (5.23), 6 After The Rain (7.21), 7 Like Sonny (6.13), 8 Pursuance (6.05), 9 Alabama (6.10), 10 Giant Steps (3.23), 11 Latifa (5.47)

Notes: Recorded NYC, early 1996.

Michael Brecker

**** 1996 Tales From the Hudson

CD: Impulse! 11105-1191-2; Album length (60.23)

Musicians: Michael Brecker (saxophone), Pat Metheny (guitar), Jack De Johnette (drums), Dave Holland (bass), Joey Calderazzo (piano), McCoy Tyner (piano), Don Alias (percussion)

Tracks: 1 Slings and Arrows (6.19), 2 Midnight Voyage (7.17), 3 Song for Bilbao (5.44), 4 Beau Rivage (7.38), 5 African Skies (8.12), 6 Introduction to Naked Soul (1.14), 7 Naked Soul (8.43), 8 Willie T (8.13), 9 Cabin Fever (6.59)

Notes: Recorded at Power Station, NYC, January, 1996. Tyner replaces Calderazzo on 3, 5. Alias on 3, 5 only.

Dave Liebman Quartet

** 1997 The Elements – Water

CD: Arkadia Jazz 71043; Album length (57.57)

Musicians: Dave Liebman (saxophone), Pat Metheny (guitar), Cecil McBee (bass), Billy Hart (drums)

Tracks: 1 Water (6.32), 2 White Caps (7.10), 3 Heaven's Gift (4.27), 4 Bass Interlude (2.09), 5 Reflecting Pool (7.06), 6 Storm Surge (8.56), 7 Guitar Interlude (1.19), 8 The Baptismal Font (4.13), 9 Ebb and Flow (5.58), 10 Water Theme (reprise) (1.14), 11 Dave Liebman's Reflections of Water (8.53)

Notes: Recorded at Red Rock Recording Studio, Saylorsburg, PA, January 2-5, 1997.

Tony Williams

**** 1997 Wilderness

CD: ARK 21 7243-8-54571-2-8; Album length (64.59)

Musicians: Tony Williams (drums), Michael Brecker (saxophone), Herbie Hancock (keyboard), Pat Metheny (guitar), Dave Holland (bass)

Tracks: 1 Wilderness Rising (7.35), 2 China Town (8.33), 3 Infant Wilderness (2.31), 4 Harlem Mist '55 (4.03), 5 China Road (2.46), 6 The Night You Were Born (8.05), 7 Wilderness Voyager (2.07), 8 Machu Picchu (6.42), 9 China Moon (3.24), 10 Wilderness Island (2.49), 11 Sea of Wilderness (3.06), 12 Gambia (6.13), 13 Cape Wilderness (7.15).

Charlie Haden and Pat Metheny

**** 1997 Beyond the Missouri Sky (Short Stories)

CD: Verve 537 130 2; Album length (69.26)

Musicians: Pat Metheny (guitar), Charlie Haden (bass)

Tracks: 1 Waltz for Ruth (4.28), 2 Our Spanish Love Song (5.40), 3 Message to a Friend (6.13), 4 Two for the Road (5.16), 5 First Song (6.37), 6 The Moon is a Harsh Mistress (4.05), 7 The Precious Jewel (3.47), 8 He's Gone Away (4.18), 9 The Moon Song (6.56), 10 Tears of Rain (5.30), 11 Cinema Paradiso (love theme) (3.35), 12 Cinema Paradiso (main theme) (4.24), 13 Spiritual (8.22)

Notes: Recorded at Right Track Studios, NYC and Clinton Recording Studios, NYC, April 15, 1996. The album won the Grammy for Best Jazz Instrumental Performance, Individual Or Group, 1997.

Derek Bailey, Pat Metheny, Gregg Bendian, Paul Wertico

* 1997 The Sign of 4

3 CD: Knitting Factory Works KFW 197; Album length (192.21)

Musicians: Derek Bailey (guitar), Pat Metheny (guitar), Paul Wertico (drums), Gregg Bendian (bass)

Tracks: 1 A Study in Scarlet (62.51), 2 Evidently (7.45), 3 Untidy Habits (6.21), 4 The Rule of Three (2.37), 5 Strange Story (4.05), 6 The Aurora (3.38), 7 Tracks (5.37), 8 A Break in the Chain (8.35), 9 One Object (6.12), 10 Euclid (6.31), 11 Fortune (9.53), 12 Poisoned Arrows (14.59), 13 Trichinopoly (7.18), 14 Ransom (19.02), 15 Antecedents (7.26), 16 In Quest of a Solution (19.24)

Notes: Disc 1 title: Statement of the Case (track 1); Disc 2 title: The Science of Deduction (Tracks 2-11); Disc 3 title: The Balance of Probability (Tracks 12-16).

Burton Corea Metheny Haynes Holland

**** 1998 Like Minds

CD: Concord Jazz CCD: 4803 2; Album length (68.19)

Musicians: Gary Burton (vibraphone), Chick Corea (keyboard), Pat Metheny (guitar), Roy Haynes (drums), Dave Holland (bass)

Tracks: 1 Question and Answer (6.23), 2 Elucidation (5.21), 3 Windows (6.17), 4 Futures (10.41), 5 Like Minds (5.50), 6 Country Roads (6.26), 7 Tears of Rain (6.33), 8 Soon (6.24), 9 For a Thousand Years (5.23), 10 Straight Up and Down (9.01)

Notes: Awarded the Grammy for Best Jazz Instrumental Performance, Individual Or Group, 1998.

Jim Hall and Pat Metheny

*** 1999 Jim Hall and Pat Metheny

CD: Telarc CD: 83442; Album length (74.02)

Musicians: Jim Hall (guitar), Pat Metheny (guitar)

Tracks: 1 Lookin' Up (4.34), 2 All the Things You Are (6.58), 3 The Birds and the Bees (5.04), 4 Improvisation No 1 (1.05), 5 Falling Grace (4.39), 6 Ballad Z (4.33), 7 Summertime (5.35), 8 Farmer's Trust (5.29), 9 Cold Spring (6.29), 10 Improvisation No 2 (1.11), 11 Into the Dream (3.05), 12 Don't Forget (4.46), 13 Improvisation No 3 (3.22), 14 Waiting to Dance (4.38), 15 Improvisation No 4 (2.37), 16 Improvisation No 5 (2.08), 17 All Across the City (7.34)

Marc Johnson

*** 1999 The Sound of Summer Running

CD: Verve 539-299-2; Album length (53.19)

Musicians: Marc Johnson (bass), Bill Frisell (guitar), Pat Metheny (guitar), Joey Baron (drums)

Tracks: 1 Faith in You (5.53), 2 Ghost Town (5.35), 3 Summer Running (5.56), 4 With My Boots On (4.25), 5 Union Pacific (5.29), 6 Porch Swing (4.12), 7 Dingy-Dong Day (3.51), 8 The Adventures of Max and Ben (6.08), 9 In a Quiet Place (5.17), 10 For a Thousand Years (6.28)

Michael Brecker

*** 1999 Time is of the Essence

CD: Verve 314547844-2; Album length (69.57)

Musicians: Michael Brecker (saxophone), Pat Metheny (guitar), Larry Goldings (organ), Elvin Jones (drums), Jeff 'Tain' Watts (drums), Bill Stewart (drums)

Tracks: 1 Arc of the Pendulum (8.59), 2 Sound Off (6.04), 3 Half Past Late (7.54), 4 Timeline (6.05), 5 The Morning of This Night (7.42), 6 Renaissance Man (8.36), 7 Dr. Slate (7.40), 8 As I Am (6.49), 9 Outrance (10.08)

Notes: Recorded at Right Track Studios, NYC, 1999.

Charlie Haden

*** 2001 Nocturne

CD: Verve 440 013 611-2; Album length (66.43)

Musicians: Charlie Haden (bass), Pat Metheny (guitar), Joe Lovano (saxophone), David Sanchez (saxophone), Frederico Britos Ruiz (violin), Gonzalo Rubalcaba (piano), Ignacio Berroa (drums)

Tracks: 1 En La Orilla Del Mundo (5.14), 2 Noche De Ronda (5.43), 3 Nocturnal (6.56), 4 Moonlight (Claro de Luna) (5.37), 5 Yo Sin Ti (Me Without You) (6.02), 6 No Te Empenes Mas (Don't Try Anymore) (5.30), 7 Transparence (6.11), 8 El Ciego (The Blind) (5.58), 9 Nightfall (6.40), 10 Tres Palabras (Three Words) (6.18), 11 Contigo En La Distancia / En Nosostros (6.34)

Notes: Recorded at Criteria/The Hit Factory Studios, Miami, FL, August 27-31, 2000. Pat Metheny plays on 2 only.

Michael Brecker

*** 2001 Nearness of You: The Ballad Book

CD: Verve 549 705-2; Album length (60.18)

Musicians: Michael Brecker (saxophone), Pat Metheny (guitar), Herbie Hancock (keyboard), Charlie Haden (bass), Jack De Johnette (drums), James Taylor (voice)

Tracks: 1 Chan's Song (5.15), 2 Don't Let Me Be Lonely Tonight (4.43), 3 Nascente (6.18), 4 Midnight Mood (6.22), 5 The Nearness of You (4.32), 6 Incandescence (5.21), 7 Sometimes I See (5.26), 8 My Ship (7.10), 9 Always (5.37), 10 Seven Days (5.32), 11 I Can See Your Dreams (3.50)

Notes: Recorded at Right Track Recording, NYC, December 18-20, 2000. Track 1 awarded Grammy for Best Jazz Instrumental Solo 2001.

Michael Brecker

**** 2007 Pilgrimage

CD: Wa Records 0602517263512; Album length (77.42)

Musicians: Michael Brecker (saxophone), Pat Metheny (guitar), Herbie Hancock (keyboard), Brad Mehldau (piano), John Patitucci (bass), Jack De Johnette (drums)

Tracks: 1 The Mean Time (6.55), 2 Five Months from Midnight (7.40), 3 Anagram (10.09), 4 Tumbleweed (9.36), 5 When Can I Kiss You Again? (9.42), 6 Cardinal Rule (7.31), 7 Half Moon Lane (7.17), 8 Loose Threads (8.34), 9 Pilgrimage (10.02)

Notes: Awarded the Grammy for Best Jazz Instrumental Solo 2007 for Anagram. Awarded the Grammy for Best Jazz Instrumental Album, Individual or Group 2007 for Pilgrimage.

DVDs

Pat Metheny Group

**** 1996 We Live Here – Live in Japan

DVD Image Entertainment 14381-0581-2; Album length (110.00)

Musicians: Pat Metheny (guitar), Lyle Mays (keyboard), Steve Rodby (bass), Paul Wertico (drums), Armando Marcal (percussion), David Blamires (voice), Mark Ledford (voice)

Tracks: 1 Have You Heard, 2 And Then I Knew, 3 Here to Stay, 4 First Circle, 5 Scrap Metal, 6 Farmer's Trust, 7 Episode d'Azur, 8 Third Wind, 9 This is Not America, 10 Antonia, 11 To the End of the World, 12 Minuano (Six-Eight), 13 Stranger in Town

Notes: Recorded at Youport Hall, Gotanda, Tokyo, Japan, October 12, 1995.

Pat Metheny Group

***** 2001 Imaginary Day Live

DVD Eagle Vision 5-034504-926578; Album length (93.00)

Musicians: Pat Metheny (guitar), Lyle Mays (keyboard), Steve Rodby (bass), Paul Wertico (drums), Mark Ledford (voice), Philip Hamilton (voice), Jeff Haynes (percussion)

Tracks: 1 Into the Dream, 2 Follow Me, 3 A Story Within the Story, 4 Imaginary Day, 5 Heat of the Day, 6 Across the Sky, 7 The Roots of Coincidence, 8 Message to a Friend, 9 September Fifteenth, 10 Minuano (Six Eight)

Notes: Recorded live at the mountain winery, Saratoga Ca, July 21-23, 1998.

Pat Metheny Group

**** 2003 Speaking of Now Live

DVD Eagle Eye Media 8-01213-90239-2; Album length (135.00)

Musicians: Pat Metheny (guitar), Lyle Mays (keyboard), Steve Rodby (bass), Richard Bona (multi), Cuong Vu (trumpet), Antonio Sanchez (drums)

Tracks: 1 Last Train Home, 2 Go Get It, 3 As It Is, 4 Proof, 5 Insensatez (How Insensitive), 6 The Gathering Sky, 7 You, 8 A Place in the World, 9 Scrap Metal, 10 Another Life, 11 On Her Way, 12 Are You Going With Me?, 13 The Roots of Coincidence, 14 A Map of the World – In Her Family, 15 Song for Bilbao

Notes: Recorded live at Tokyo NHK Hall, 19-20 September, 2002.

Pat Metheny Group

***** 2006 The Way Up Live

DVD Eagle Vision 5-034504-959675; Album length (91.00)

Musicians: Pat Metheny (guitar), Lyle Mays (keyboard), Steve Rodby (bass), Antonio Sanchez (drums), Cuong Vu (trumpet), Grégoire Maret (harmonica), Nando Lauria (percussion)

Tracks: 1 The Opening, 2 Part One, 3 Part Two, 4 Part Three

Notes: Recorded in the LG Arts Center, Seoul, Korea.

Compilations

Pat Metheny

**** 1984 Works

CD: ECM 823 270 2; Album length (50.24)

Musicians: Pat Metheny (guitar), Lyle Mays (keyboard), Mark Egan (bass), Gordon Gottlieb (percussion), Steve Rodby (bass), Nana Vasconcelos (percussion), Charlie Haden (bass), Jack De Johnette (drums), Michael Brecker (saxophone)

Tracks: 1 Sueno con Mexico (5.57), 2 (Cross the) Heartland (6.51), 3 Travels (5.01), 4 James (6.43), 5 "It's For You" (8.18), 6 Every Day (I Thank You) (13.15), 7 Goin' Ahead (3.51)

Pat Metheny

**** 1988 Works II

CD: ECM 837 272-2; Album length (43.32)

Musicians: Pat Metheny (guitar), Jaco Pastorius (bass), Bob Moses (drums), Charlie Haden (bass), Jack De Johnette (drums), Dewey Redman (saxophone), Michael Brecker (saxophone), Billy Higgins (drums), Eberhard Weber (bass),

Lyle Mays (keyboard), Steve Rodby (bass), Danny Gottlieb (drums), Nana Vasconcelos (percussion)

Tracks: 1 Unquity Road (3.33), 2 Unity Village (3.38), 3 Open (14.22), 4 Story From a Stranger (5.48), 5 Oasis (4.02), 6 Sirabhorn (5.25), 7 Farmer's Trust (6.25)

Pat Metheny

**** 2004 Selected Recordings

CD: ECM; Album length (80.10)

Musicians: Pat Metheny (guitar), Lyle Mays (keyboard), Mark Egan (bass), Danny Gottlieb (drums), Paul Wertico (drums), Steve Rodby (bass), Pedro Aznar (voice), Michael Brecker (saxophone), Jack De Johnette (drums), Billy Higgins (drums), Charlie Haden (bass), Jaco Pastorius (bass), Nana Vasconcelos (percussion), Bob Moses (drums)

Tracks: 1 Bright Size Life (4.45), 2 Phase Dance (8.17), 3 New Chautauqua (5.19), 4 Airstream (6.20), 5 Every Day (I Thank You) (13.16), 6 It's For You (8.20), 7 Are You Going With Me (8.47), 8 The First Circle (9.16), 9 Lonely Woman (6.50)

Unofficial Releases

Pat Metheny Group

*** 1991 Blue Asphalt

CD: Jazz Door JD 1223; Album length (34.00)

Musicians: Pat Metheny (guitar), Lyle Mays (keyboard), Mark Egan (bass), Danny Gottlieb (drums)

Tracks: 1 Phase Dance (9.05), 2 Watercolors (7.40), 3 San Lorenzo (11.06), 4 Wrong is Right (6.31)

Notes: Recorded at the Great American Music Hall, San Francisco, CA, 31/8/77.

Pat Metheny Group

*** 1993 In Concert

CD: Jazz Door JD 1231; Album length (67.51)

Musicians: Pat Metheny (guitar), Lyle Mays (keyboard), Steve Rodby (bass), Paul Wertico (drums), Pedro Aznar (voice), Armando Marcal (percussion)

Tracks: 1 Have You Heard (7.18), 2 Every Summer Night (7.07), 3 Better Days Ahead (5.37), 4 Last Train Home (5.12), 5 If I Could (8.41), 6 Spring Ain't Here

(6.53), 7 Straight On Red (7.33), 8 Minuano (Six Eight) (9.18), 9 Third Wind (10.08)

Notes: Recorded live in the USA, 1992.

<u>Joshua Redman Quartet</u>

* 1995 Blues for Pat – Live in San Francisco

CD: Jazz Door JD 1282; Album length (70.11)

Musicians: Joshua Redman (saxophone), Pat Metheny (guitar), Christian McBride (bass), Billy Higgins (drums)

Tracks: 1 Blues for Pat (14.25), 2 Sketches (14.15), 3 Wish (10.45), 4 St. Thomas (18.26), 5 We Had a Sister (7.07), 6 Carla's Groove (5.13)

Notes: Recorded San Francisco, CA, 1994. Track 2 is actually Question and Answer.

Index

A

A Break in the Chain, 184
A Change in Circumstance, 171
A Hard Day's Night, 12
A Lot of Livin' to Do, 174
A Love Supreme, 93
A Map of the World, 106, 107, 174, 188
A Night Away, 132, 135, 176
A Place in the World, 119, 175, 188
A Story Within the Story, 99, 173, 187
A Study in Scarlet, 184
Above the Treetops, 68, 171
Acceptance, 174
Across the Sky, 100, 101, 173, 187
Across the Sky (Goldie Remix), 173
Acuff, Roy, 95
Adventures in Radioland, 60
African Skies, 89, 183
After the Rain, 94
Afternoon, 119, 175
Ahmid-6, 130, 176
Airstream, 32, 167, 189
Alabama, 94, 183
Alias, Don, 35, 88, 173, 183
All Across the City, 109, 185
All of Us, 169
All the Things You Are, 59, 109, 113, 170, 174, 185
Alone, 174
Always and Forever, 70, 141, 171, 177
Amelia, 36, 179
American Garage, 32, 34, 151, 167
Anagram, 129, 187
And Then I Knew, 84, 172, 187
And Time Goes On, 175
Andersen, Arild, 105
Angel Eyes, 73, 181
Another Chance, 120, 175
Another Hand, 95, 106
Another Life, 118, 141, 175, 177, 188
Antecedents, 184
Antonia, 70, 171, 187
April Joy, 29, 167
Aprilwind, 29, 167
Arc of the Pendulum, 186
Are We There Yet, 58, 170
Are You Going With Me?, 30, 43, 44, 45, 87, 116, 132, 140, 154, 168, 177, 188, 189
As a Flower Blossoms (I am Running to You), 70, 171

As Falls Wichita, So Falls Wichita Falls, 39, 151, 168
As I Am, 110, 173, 186
As It Is, 117, 175, 188
Asia, 39, 97, 121, 155
At Last You're Here, 176
Au Lait, 43, 168
Aura, 89
Autumn Leaves, 133
Avant-garde, 14, 16, 17, 18, 19, 23, 79, 94, 105, 153
Avatar, 41, 102, 104
Avatar studios, 102
Aznar, Pedro, 50, 58, 66, 169, 170, 171, 189
Azzolina, Jay, 159

B

B & G (Midwestern Nights Dream), 179
Back Arm and Black Charge, 176
Back in Time, 171
Badland, 173
Bailey, Derek, 79, 160, 184
Baker, Beverly, 181
Baker, Chet, 76
Balance, 79, 184
Ballad Z, 108, 185
Ballard, Jeff, 130, 175, 176
Baltimore, Maryland, 72
Barcarole, 43, 168
Bargeron, Dave, 171
Baron, Joey, 104, 105, 185
Basie, William Allen, 84
Bass Desires, 104
Bass Interlude, 183
Bat, 113, 174
Batterie, 178
Beale Street, 36
Beat 70, 58, 67, 170, 171
Beatles (band), 136, 157
Beau Rivage, 89, 183
Beauty is a Rare Thing, 48
Bennett, Tony, 105
Berklee College of Music, 13, 15, 17, 21, 76, 105, 159
Berlin, Irving, 73, 115
Berroa, Ignacio, 148, 186
Besançon, France, 66
Better Days Ahead, 57, 66, 170, 171, 189
Beyond the Missouri Sky (Short Stories), 184
Biel (Whiteness), 140, 177
Big Yellow Taxi, 34
Bigham, John, 181

Bill Evans, 24, 34, 39, 60, 104
Bitches Brew, 14, 71
Blade, Brian, 93, 94, 129, 183
Blamires, David, 57, 81, 170, 172, 173, 187
Bley, Carla, 17, 18, 20
Bley, Paul, 14, 178
Blue Asphalt, 27, 189
Blues, 48, 74, 75, 137, 169, 181, 182, 190
Blues for Pat, 48, 74, 75, 169, 181, 190
Blues for Pat - Live in San Francisco, 190
Blues for Pat (Live), 181
Blues M45, 182
Bona, Richard, 47, 116, 118, 119, 165, 175, 188
Borg, Tony, 181
Bossa Nova, 116
Boston, 13, 15, 21, 22, 67, 76, 150
Both Sides Now, 34
Bourgeois Tagg (band), 91
Bowie, David, 53, 81, 138, 169
Boyce, Christopher, 52
Brecker Brothers (band), 56, 61, 89, 96
Brecker, Michael, 35, 36, 37, 56, 67, 88, 90, 91, 93, 110, 114, 128, 134, 151, 158, 164, 167, 179, 180, 183, 184, 185, 186, 188, 189
Bright Size Life, 20, 21, 23, 59, 78, 113, 151, 152, 164, 166, 174, 189
Brooklyn Academy of Music, 147
Brown, Clifford, 134
Burrell, Kenneth Earl, 148
Burton, Gary, 13, 14, 15, 16, 18, 19, 20, 21, 23, 60, 76, 101, 151, 158, 162, 164, 178, 179, 180, 185
Bye Bye Baby, 73, 181
Bye, Bye, Birdie, 112

C

Cabin Fever, 89, 183
Calderazzo, Joey, 88, 183
Cantaloupe Island, 65, 181
Cape Wilderness, 90, 91, 184
Capricorn, 112, 174
Cardinal Rule, 187
Carey, Mariah, 61
Carnegie Hall, 129
Carrington, Terri Lynne, 181
Carter, Clifford, 34
Cathedral in a Suitcase, 68, 171
CERN, 133
Chairs and Children, 62, 180
Chambers, Dennis, 74
Change of Heart, 59, 170
Cherry, Don, 47

Childhood, 174
China Doll, 182
China Moon, 90, 91, 184
China Road, 90, 184
China Town, 90, 184
Cinelu, Mino, 173, 177
Cinema Paradiso (love theme), 184
Cinema Paradiso (main theme), 184
Circle (band), 50
Clapton, Eric Patrick, 12, 74
Clark, John, 171
Clarke, Stanley, 90
Claude and Betty, 20, 179
Cobham, Billy, 76
Cold Spring, 109, 185
Coleman, Denardo, 169
Coleman, Ornette, 23, 37, 47, 48, 53, 59, 65, 74, 150, 160, 169
Collier, J. V., 182
Collins, Judy, 34
Collins, Phil, 181
Coltrane, John, 71, 92, 96, 102, 111
Compute, 169
Concerto, 89
Conita, William, 181
Conte, Luis, 172
Contigo En La Distancia / En Nosostros, 186
Cook, Richard, 30, 164
Copley Square, 13
Corea, Chick, 16, 20, 85, 89, 101, 160, 162, 185
Coryell, Larry, 15
Counting Texas, 114, 174
Country Doctor, 76, 183
Country Poem, 31, 167
Country Roads, 103, 185
Court and Spark, 34
Coward, Lamont, 181
Cox, Anthony, 72, 73, 181
Coyote, 35, 179
Creamer-Dunville, Laura, 181
Crosby, Bing, 81
Crystal Silence, 101
Czarne Slowa (Black Words), 177

D

D'Earth, John, 182
Daulton Lee, 52, 53, 169
Davis, Miles, 11, 12, 14, 16, 18, 25, 27, 57, 59, 71, 72, 73, 76, 85, 88, 89, 93, 96, 97, 99, 102, 115, 125, 127, 159, 160
Day In – Night Out, 147

194

Day Trip, 77, 136, 138, 139, 176
Daybreak, 31, 167
De Johnette, Jack, 151, 167, 169, 180, 183, 186, 188, 189
Dear Lord, 93, 183
Decoy, 76
Desire, 158
Dewey, 37, 75, 151, 167, 188
Different Trains/Electric Counterpoint, 180
Dingy-Dong Day, 106, 185
Dismantling Utopia, 153, 173
Distance, 56, 170
Ditmas, Bruce, 14, 178
Donkey, 19, 178
Double Blind, 173
Downbeat (magazine), 164
Dr. Slate, 186
Dream of the Return, 58, 170
Dreaming Trees, 138, 176
Dreamland, 36, 179
Dreams So Real, 18, 179
Ducan, Dave, 181
Duet, 101
Duke, George, 76
Duster, 15
Dylan, Bob, 34, 104

E

Eagles (band), 106
Easy Listening, 62, 63
Ebb and Flow, 97, 183
ECM, 16, 17, 20, 21, 23, 27, 31, 37, 38, 48, 105, 166, 167, 168, 169, 178, 179, 188, 189
Edith and the Kingpin, 35, 179
Egan, Mark, 13, 24, 26, 27, 61, 167, 188, 189
Eighteen, 44, 168
Einstein, Albert, 133, 162
El Ciego (The Blind), 186
Eleanor Rigby, 81
Electric keyboard, 14
Electric Outlet, 76
Electric piano, 14
Elements, 34, 96
Elements (band), 34, 96
Elias, Eliane, 106
Elucidation, 103, 185
En La Orilla Del Mundo, 186
En La Tierra Que No Olvida, 133, 135, 176
Encontros e Despidadas, 147
End of the Game, 43, 52, 169
Endangered Species, 169

Epilogue Psalm 121, 169
Episode d'Azur, 85, 172, 187
Equinox, 93, 183
Erskine, Peter, 61, 104, 180
Escalator Over the Hill, 18
Estupenda Graca, 40, 168
Et Si C'Etait La fin (As If It Were the End), 171
Euclid, 184
Evans, Gil, 115
Every Day (I Thank You), 167, 188, 189
Every Summer Night, 57, 170, 189
Evidently, 184
Extent of the Lie, 53, 169
Extradition, 46, 168
Extrapolation, 153
Eyes Wide Shut, 130

F

Facing West, 68, 152, 171
Faith Healer, 114, 174
Faith in You, 105, 185
Fall from Grace, 174
Falling Grace, 109, 185
Farlow, Tal, 107
Fear and Trembling, 132, 135, 176
Ferla, Joe, 104
Ferrone, Steve, 171
Ferry Cross the Mersey, 175
Festival, 13, 39, 147, 167, 181
Fictionary, 104, 156
Fields of Gray, 182
It's Always Worth the Trouble, 172
Find Me In Your Dreams, 176
Finding and Believing, 69, 171
Findon, Andrew, 171
First Circle, 49, 66, 70, 136, 149, 151, 153, 160, 162, 169, 171, 187
First Song, 94, 184
Five Months from Midnight, 187
Fleck, Béla, 182
Fleming, Renée, 129
Florida, 13, 26, 129, 166
Florida Greeting Song, 26, 166
Follow Me, 98, 141, 173, 177, 187
For a Thousand Years, 104, 106, 185
Forman, Mitchel, 180
Fort Lauderdale Film Festival, 92
Forward March, 49, 169
Free Spirits (band), 15
Frère Jacques, 69

Frisell, Bill, 104, 105, 185
Furry Sings the Blues, 36, 179

G

Gailes, George A., 182
Gale, Eric, 16
Gambia, 91, 184
Garbarek, Jan, 105
Garcia, Jerry, 181
Garrett, Kenny, 92, 93, 182, 183
Geffen, David, 53
Germany, 16, 21, 166, 178, 179
Gershwin, George, 89, 104, 131
Getz, Stan, 15, 71, 75, 96, 102, 105, 134, 141
Ghost Town, 105, 185
Giant Steps, 93, 94, 103, 111, 113, 130, 174, 183
Gibson (guitar), 33, 41, 42, 148
Giddick, Charlie, 11
Gilberto, Astrud, 141
Gilberto, Joao, 141
Gillespie, John Birks 'Dizzy', 105
Go Ahead John, 164
Go Get It, 188
God Must Be a Boogie Man, 179
Goldings, Larry, 110, 115, 185
Goldman, Vivienne, 11
Goldstein, Gil, 67, 107, 114, 115, 128, 171, 174
Good for the Soul, 182
Good Vibes, 16, 103
Good-bye Pork Pie Hat, 36, 179
Goodman, Benjamin (Benny), 36
Goodrick, Mick, 16, 18, 19, 178, 179
Gottlieb, Danny, 13, 166, 167, 168, 171, 179, 189
Gottlieb, Gordon, 188
Grammy (award), 9, 12, 24, 40, 52, 56, 59, 66, 88, 89, 104, 114, 129, 168, 169, 170, 171, 172, 173, 174, 175, 184, 185, 186, 187
Graves, Peter, 13
Great American Music Hall, 27, 189
Grenadier, Larry, 111, 130, 133, 174, 175, 176
Grolnick, Don, 56, 89
Guitar Interlude, 97, 183
Guitar synthesiser, 5, 40, 41, 42, 64, 73, 94, 114, 133, 148, 151, 154

H

H and H, 170
Hackensack, 59
Haden, Charlie, 37, 47, 56, 67, 74, 77, 94, 114, 147, 148, 151, 160, 164, 167, 168, 169, 171, 180, 181, 184, 186, 188, 189

Hahn, Jerry, 16
Half Life of Absolution, 66, 171
Half Moon Lane, 187
Half Past Late, 186
Hall, Jim, 9, 77, 105, 107, 108, 132, 148, 150, 185
Hamilton, Philip, 187
Hancock, Herbie, 12, 16, 17, 63, 85, 89, 90, 96, 114, 117, 128, 147, 160, 180, 184, 186
Hand Jive, 105
Harbor Lights, 76, 181, 182
Harle, John, 55
Harlem Mist '55, 90, 184
Harpguitar, 25
Harple, George, 181
Harris, Julie, 92
Hart, William, 96, 183
Haslip, Jimmy, 76, 181, 182
Have You Heard, 57, 66, 170, 171, 187, 189
Hawkins, Coleman, 59
Haynes, Jeff, 187
Haynes, Roy, 16, 59, 102, 113, 170, 182, 185
Head Hunters, 16, 17
Heartland, 32, 167, 188
Heat of the Day, 187
Hejira, 36, 179
Henderson, Joseph, 42
Henry, Debbie, 182
Here To Stay, 172
Herman, Woody, 24, 104
Hermitage, 31, 167
Higgins, William (Billy), 47, 74, 75, 147, 168, 181, 188, 189, 190
Hill and Robison, 60
Hissing of the Summer Lawns, 35, 85
Holding Us, 174
Holdsworth, Allan, 39, 164
Holiday, Billy, 131
Holland, Dave, 21, 59, 64, 88, 102, 104, 113, 170, 180, 183, 184, 185
Hollywood, 68
Home, 65, 141, 174
Homecoming, 174
Hornsby, Bruce, 76, 158, 181, 182, 183
Hot House, 76, 182
House on the Hill, 62, 180
Howard, Ed, 72, 73, 181
Humpty Dumpty, 48, 169
Hurricane Katrina, 138
Hutton, Timothy, 52

I

I Can See Your Dreams, 115, 186

I Can See Your House From Here, 76, 105, 182
I Will find the Way, 175
Ibanez, 64, 65, 75, 110, 140, 141, 148
Icefire, 25, 166
Ictus/ Syndrome/ Wrong Key Donkey, 179
If I Could, 51, 53, 70, 100, 153, 169, 182, 189
Illinois, 42, 109, 157
Imaginary Day, 43, 54, 97, 100, 101, 113, 136, 152, 162, 173, 187
Imagine, 55, 62, 86
Improvisation No 1, 185
Improvisation No 2, 185
Improvisation No 3, 185
Improvisation No 4, 185
Improvisation No 5, 185
Improvisations for Expanded Piano, 156
Improvising Artists, 14
In a Quiet Place, 106, 185
In Concert, 101, 189
In France They Kiss on Main Street, 35, 179
In Her Family, 56, 170, 188
In Quest of a Solution, 79, 184
In the Shadow of a Miracle, 156
Incandescence, 115, 186
Indigo Dreamscapes, 64, 180
Infant Wilderness, 90, 184
Inori, 139, 176
Insensatez (How Insensitive), 188
Intermission Music, 19, 179
Into the Dream, 99, 109, 113, 152, 173, 174, 185, 187
Introduction to Naked Soul, 183
Intrude, 17, 178
Is, 52, 86, 99, 124, 128, 138, 140, 176
Is This America?, 138, 176

J

Jack Daniels, 114
Jackson, Anthony, 171
Jackson, Michael, 12
Jackson, Milt, 42
Jacksonville, 129
Jaco, 13, 14, 21, 22, 23, 29, 35, 36, 50, 59, 61, 164, 166, 167, 178, 179, 188, 189
Jacobs, Randy, 182
James, 34, 44, 73, 113, 114, 115, 168, 174, 182, 186, 188
Jarreau, Al, 105
Jarrett, Keith, 120
Jazz Door, 27, 75, 180, 189, 190
Jesus Maria, 19, 179
Jim Hall and Pat Metheny, 185
Jobim, Antonio Carlos, 141

Joel, Billy, 12
John Coltrane, 59, 71, 92, 96, 102, 111
John McKee, 182
John McLaughlin, 12, 16, 50, 60, 72, 89, 140, 149, 151, 153, 157, 164, 181
John Patitucci, 116, 128, 186
John Scofield, 76, 79, 104, 105, 131, 138, 158, 182
Johnson, Alphonso, 147
Johnson, J J, 73
Johnson, Marc, 24, 104, 157, 158, 185
Jones, Elvin, 110, 185
Jones, Quincy, 12
Joness, Wayne Scott, 41, 164
Jopek, Anna Maria, 140, 177
Joshua, 37, 72, 74, 75, 93, 123, 129, 158, 181, 190
Joshua Redman, 72, 74, 75, 93, 129, 158, 181, 190
Just Like the Day, 111, 174
Just the Two of Us, 82

K

Kanga, Skaila, 171
Kansas, 12, 31, 109, 155
Karcy, Bob, 97
Karyo, Tcheky, 92
Kaslow, Philip, 181
Kathelin Gray, 169
Kenny Kirkland, 56, 180
Kern, Jerome, 59, 109, 113
Kessell, Barney, 107, 150
Keys, 137, 176
Khan, Chaka, 76, 182
Kikoski, David, 182
Kind of Blue, 25
King Korn, 14, 178
Kirkland, Kenny, 56, 180
Kisor, Ryan, 171
Konrad, Cezary, 177
Korg, 156
Kowalewski, Wojciech, 177
Kubiszyn, Robert, 177
Kubrick, Stanley, 130

L

LA Express, 34
Lakes, 25, 166
Lament, 73, 93, 181, 183
Language of Time, 173
Large Hadron Collider, 133
Last Train Home, 55, 66, 116, 120, 152, 170, 171, 175, 188, 189

Latifa, 93, 183
Lauria, Nando, 122, 188
LaVorgne, Bill, 16
Law Years, 59, 170
Learning on the Road, 172
Ledford, Mark, 57, 69, 81, 170, 171, 172, 173, 187
Lee, Daulton, 52, 53, 169
Lee, Will, 61, 62, 63, 171, 180
Legend, 26, 131, 166, 176
Legend of the Fountain, 26, 166
Leroy the Magician, 103
Leswick, Adam, 181
Letter From Home, 57, 58, 66, 67, 123, 153, 162, 170, 171, 177
Level of Deception, 53, 169
Liberation Music Orchestra, 47
Liberia, 93, 183
Liebman, Dave, 26, 96, 160, 183
Like Minds, 101, 102, 103, 113, 158, 164, 185
Like Sonny, 94, 183
Like This, 182
Little, Levi, 182
Live in Tokyo, 176
Lofty Fake Anagram, 16
Lone Jack, 28, 30, 112, 167, 174
Lonely Woman, 48, 141, 169, 189
Long Ago Child/Fallen Star, 167
Long Before, 132, 135, 176
Long Tall Cool One, 182
Long Time No See, 169
Look Ahead, 171
Loose Threads, 187
Lorber, Jeff, 181
Lorenzo, 168
Louisiana, 31, 109, 131
Lovano, Joseph, 148, 186
Love Is, 73
Love Poem, 129
Ludwigsberg, 16, 21, 166, 178, 179
Lush Life, 73, 181
Lyle Mays, 13, 24, 26, 27, 28, 35, 36, 39, 43, 61, 104, 116, 121, 156, 166, 167, 168, 169, 170, 171, 172, 173, 175, 179, 187, 188, 189

M

Ma Femme Est Une Actrice, 130
Machu Picchu, 91, 184
Madonna, 12
Magnetic, 61
Mahavishnu Orchestra (band), 16, 31, 60, 153
Mainieri, Michael, 61

Make Peace, 131, 135, 176
Make Sure You're Sure, 181
Malone, Tom, 171
Mandel, Johnny, 95
Mantovani (orchestra), 57
Manzer, Linda, 48, 140, 149, 164
Marcal, Armando, 170, 187, 189
Maret, Gregoire, 45, 175, 188
Marsalis, Branford, 181
Marseilles, 66
Marta on the Bus, Marta in the Fields, 172
Maryland, 105
Mas Alla (Beyond), 52, 169
Maseli, Bernard, 177
Matrix, 92, 124, 125, 127, 128
Mays, Lyle, 13, 24, 26, 27, 28, 35, 36, 39, 43, 61, 104, 116, 121, 156, 166, 167, 168, 169, 170, 171, 172, 173, 175, 179, 187, 188, 189
McBee, Cecil, 96, 183
McBride, Christian, 75, 129, 176, 182, 190
McCartney, Paul, 12, 81, 156, 164
McClain, Jean, 181
McGraw, Martha, 92
McLaughlin, John, 12, 16, 50, 60, 72, 89, 140, 149, 151, 153, 157, 164, 181
McLean, Jackie, 97
McRae, Carmen, 105
Mehldau, Brad, 128, 129, 132, 134, 140, 175, 176, 186
Melody, 128, 134, 162
Memphis, 36
Mendoza, Vince, 61, 62
Merendino, Sammy, 171
Message to a Friend, 95, 184, 187
Message To My Friend, 182
Metalheadz (band), 101
Metheny Mehldau, 43, 77, 129, 132, 136, 138, 151, 175, 176
Metheny Mehldau Quartet, 43, 132, 138, 151, 176
Metheny, Mike, 171
Mevlevia, 17, 178
Meyer, Paul, 62
Miami, 13, 186
Michael Brecker, 35, 36, 37, 56, 67, 88, 90, 91, 93, 110, 114, 128, 134, 151, 158, 164, 167, 179, 180, 183, 184, 185, 186, 188, 189
Michael Franks, 34
Midnight Mood, 115, 186
Midnight Voyage, 88, 183
Midwestern Nights Dream, 20, 22, 166
Mikkelborg, Palle, 89
Miles Ahead, 71, 115
Miles Davis, 11, 12, 14, 16, 18, 25, 27, 57, 59, 71, 72, 73, 76, 85, 88, 89, 93, 96, 97, 99, 102, 115, 125, 127, 159, 160
Miles, Barry, 164

Milkowski, 14
Milkowski, Bill, 164
Minuano (Six Eight), 54, 170, 187, 190
Minuano (Six-Eight), 187
Miskiewicz, Henryk, 141, 177
Missouri, 12, 22, 31, 39, 47, 77, 94, 95, 164, 166
Missouri Uncompromised, 22, 166
Mitchell, Joni, 24, 27, 34, 53, 81, 85, 179
Mob Job, 150, 169
Mojave, 173
Molo, John, 76, 181, 182
Mona Lisa, 101, 155
Money in the Pocket, 115
Monk, Thelonius, 74
Montevideo, 173
Montgomery, Wes, 9, 89, 103, 107, 148, 150
Montreal Jazz Festival, 11, 60
Mood Swing, 129
Moonlight (Claro de Luna), 186
Moose the Mooch, 74, 181
Moose the Mooche, 74, 181
Moreira, Airto, 147
Moses, Bob, 13, 15, 16, 21, 166, 178, 179, 188, 189
Moss, Steve, 181
Mossman, Michael Phillip, 171
Mother Nature, 154
Motian, Paul, 105
Mozdzer, Leszek, 141, 177
Mr. Spring, 101
Mull of Kintyre, 81
Mulligan, Gerry, 76
Murphy, Tim, 72, 73, 181
Muth, Roy, 182
Mwandishi, 17
My Favourite Things, 71
My One And Only Love, 180
My Ship, 115, 186
My Song, 120, 175

N

Nacada, 20, 179
Naked Moon, 67, 171
Naked Soul, 89, 183
Napiorkowski, Marek, 177
Nascente, 114, 186
Nascimento, Milton, 147, 158
Native Dancer, 147
Native Sense, 101
Naturally, 50, 76, 97

Nearness of You: The Ballad Book, 186
Nelson Rangell, 51
Never Too Far Away, 59, 170
New Chautauqua, 30, 139, 167, 189
New Orleans, 73, 138
New York, 14, 39, 59, 96, 102, 114, 129, 130, 147
New York Counterpoint, 147
Night, 92, 113, 148, 174
Night Turns Into Day, 174
Nightfall, 186
Niles, Richard, 134, 152, 153, 164
No Matter What, 77, 182
No Te Empenes Mas (Don't Try Anymore), 186
No Way Jose, 77, 182
Noche De Ronda, 186
Nocturnal, 186
Nocturne, 148, 186
North, 24, 32, 104, 174, 175
North to South, East to West, 175
Not to be Forgotten (Our Final Hour), 71, 171
Nothing Personal, 180
Now He Sings, Now He Sobs, 102
Nussbaum, Adam, 76

O

Oasis, 25, 166, 189
Oceania, 173
Offramp, 34, 37, 40, 42, 44, 113, 136, 139, 148, 149, 153, 154, 162, 168
Oh! 128
Old Folks, 60, 170
Oleszkiewicz, Darek, 177
Omaha Celebration, 23, 166
On Her Way, 119, 175, 188
One Object, 184
One Quiet Night, 120, 175
One Way To Be, 182
Open, 38, 167, 189
Opening, 120, 124, 125, 127, 128, 175
Origin, 61, 180
Original Rays, 180
Orti, Polo, 61, 62
Oscars, 12
Oslo, 27, 166, 167, 168
Our Spanish Love Song, 94, 184
Out of the Loop, 89
Outcasts, 174
Outrance, 111, 186
Over on 4th Street, 120, 175
Overtoned, 178

Ozark, 39, 168

P

Panama, 62, 180
Paradise, 92
Paradiso, 92, 95, 107, 109, 172
Parallel Realities Live, 64, 180
Paris, 66, 91, 121, 179
Park, Laura, 181
Parker, Charlie, 38, 59, 71, 74, 102
Pass, Joseph, 148
Passage of Time, 123
Passengers, 20, 21, 179
Passing Through, 182
Pastorius, Jaco, 13, 14, 21, 23, 35, 50, 61, 164, 166, 178, 179, 188, 189
Pastures of Plenty, 182
Pat Metheny Group, 9, 11, 12, 24, 26, 27, 32, 34, 40, 45, 49, 52, 54, 57, 65, 80, 88, 91, 97, 101, 116, 120, 136, 157, 162, 167, 168, 169, 170, 171, 172, 173, 175, 187, 188, 189
Paterson, Alan B, 181
Patitucci, John, 116, 128, 186
Peace, 73, 120, 175, 181
Peace Memory, 120, 175
Penn, Sean, 52
Pepper, Arthur, 105
Perhaps, 9, 20, 38, 49, 68, 70, 80, 85, 107, 129, 135, 136, 157, 160, 162
Peter Erskine, 61, 104, 180
Peterson, Oscar, 12
Phase Dance, 27, 28, 29, 30, 45, 153, 167, 168, 189
Physics, 133, 162
Pikasso 42-string guitar, 25, 70, 97, 99, 108, 113, 132, 140, 149, 152
Pilgrimage, 128, 158, 186, 187
Pine, Courtney, 85, 121, 164
Poconos, 178
Poisoned Arrows, 184
Police People, 169
Polskie Drogi (Polish Paths), 177
Pooley, Wayne, 181
Porch Swing, 106, 185
Pospieszalski, Marcin, 177
Pospieszalski, Marek, 177
Pospieszalski, Mateusz, 177
Power Station, 59, 170, 172, 180, 182, 183
Praise, 52, 169
Presley, Elvis, 11
Pretty Scattered, 38, 167
Price, Clifford, 101
Price, Louis, 182
Private Eye, 92, 172
Proof, 117, 124, 175, 188

Psalm 121/Flight of the Falcon, 169
Purdie, Bernard, 16
Purim, Flora, 147
Pursuance, 92, 93, 94, 183

Q

Quartet, 15, 20, 75, 80, 88, 92, 132, 136, 173, 179, 183, 190
Question and Answer, 58, 59, 64, 75, 102, 113, 136, 170, 174, 185, 190
Quick and Running, 62, 63, 180
Quiet Rising, 78, 182

R

Rain River, 69, 171
Rainey, Chuck, 16
Raitt, Bonnie, 181
Rangell, Nelson, 51
Ransom, 147, 184
Read, Bobby, 182
Realization, 174
Red, 87, 172, 183, 190
Red Sky, 87, 172
Redman, Dewey, 37, 151, 167, 188
Redman, Joshua, 72, 74, 75, 93, 129, 158, 181, 190
Reflecting Pool, 97, 183
Reflections, 183
Reich, Steve, 147, 158, 164, 180
Rejoicing, 47, 48, 136, 141, 147, 168, 169
Relativity, 133
Remembering Home, Meeting the Kids, 172
Renaissance Man, 111, 186
Renewal, 174
Resolution, 174
Restless, 164
Return to Forever (band), 16, 31
Reunion, 60, 61, 63, 164, 174, 180
Reverence, 118
Richmond, 105
Right Track (studios), 114, 130, 173, 174, 175, 176, 184, 186
Ring, 16, 17, 130, 176, 178
Ring of Life, 130, 176
River Quay, 26, 166
Rivers, Sam, 97
Rodby, Steve, 34, 42, 47, 69, 70, 84, 114, 116, 126, 157, 164, 168, 169, 170, 171, 172, 173, 175, 187, 188, 189
Roland, 5, 41, 42, 114, 140, 148, 152
Rollins, Sonny, 75, 147, 156
Roots of Coincidence, 101, 173
Roots of Coincidence (Mr. Spring's Filter Kings 1.1 Mix), 173

Ross, Will, 181
Round Trip, 23, 166
Round Trip/ Broadway Blues, 23, 166
Rubalcaba, Gonzalo, 148, 186
Rufige Kru, 101
Ruiz, Frederico Britos, 186
Rush, Tom, 34
Russell, George, 18

S

S.C.O., 78, 182
Samuels, Dave, 173
San Francisco, 27, 75, 164, 189, 190
San Lorenzo, 27, 47, 167, 189
Sanborn, David, 61, 95, 106, 111
Sanchez, Antonio, 26, 116, 121, 122, 127, 165, 175, 176, 188
Sanchez, David, 148, 186
Santa Cruz Slacker, 133, 176
Say The Brother's Name, 182
Schlesinger, John, 52
Scofield, John, 76, 79, 104, 105, 131, 138, 158, 182
Scott, Tom, 34
Scrap Metal, 187, 188
Sea Glass, 180
Sea Journey, 20, 179
Sea of Wilderness, 90, 91, 184
Sea Song, 26, 166
Second Thought, 173
Secret Beach, 133, 176
Secret Story, 47, 56, 67, 71, 72, 92, 140, 150, 171
See the World, 70, 171
Selected Recordings, 189
September Fifteenth, 39, 168, 187
September Fifteenth (dedicated to Bill Evans), 39, 168
Seven Days, 115, 173, 186
Shadow Dance, 64, 180
Shadows and Light, 24, 34, 35, 36, 179
Shinola, 76
Shorter, Wayne, 61, 93, 97, 112, 122, 147, 156
Silent Movie, 133, 176
Silent Spring, 17, 178
Silver Hollow, 64, 180
Silver, Horace, 48, 73
Simon, Carly, 61
Sinatra, Frank, 12, 61
Sirabhorn, 22, 166, 189
Sivils, Gary, 13
Sketches, 75, 190
Skywalker, Luke, 79

Slings and Arrows, 88, 183
Slip Away, 58, 170
Slow, 31, 180
Small, Mark, 21, 164
Smith, Paul, 13
Smooth Jazz, 63
Snova, 137, 176
So May it Secretly Begin, 54, 113, 140, 170, 177
So What, 89
Solar, 59, 64, 170, 180
Soliloquy, 174
Solo, 171, 174, 179, 186, 187
Solo from More Travels, 171
Something To Remind You, 172
Sometimes I See, 115, 173, 186
Son of Thirteen, 136, 176
Song For Bilbao, 168
Song for the boys, 175
Song X, 38, 47, 53, 65, 150, 169
Twentieth Anniversary, 169
Song X Duo, 169
Sonor drum kit, 65
Soon, 15, 32, 104, 118, 124, 125, 185
Soul Cowboy, 112, 113, 174
Soul Dance, 74, 181
Sound Off, 111, 186
South Africa, 86
Spain, 100
Speaking of Now, 47, 100, 116, 120, 124, 162, 165, 175, 187
Speaking of Now Live, 116, 187
Spiritual, 95, 184
Spring Ain't Here, 57, 170, 189
Spyro Gyra, 159
Spyro Gyra (band), 159
St. Thomas, 75, 190
Stanley Clarke, 90
Star People, 76
Star Wars (film), 74
Steely Dan (band), 81, 83, 154
Steinway, 64, 156
Steps Ahead, 56, 61
Stern, Mike, 15, 61
Stewart, William, 76, 77, 78, 110, 111, 112, 174, 182, 185
Still Life (Talking), 54, 56, 65, 66, 67, 123, 162, 170
Sting, 12
Stitt, Sonny, 42
Stoltzman, Richard, 148
Storm, 97, 183
Storm Surge, 97, 183
Story from a Stranger, 48, 169

Straight on Red, 46, 168
Straight Up and Down, 104, 185
Strange Story, 184
Stranger in Town, 87, 172, 187
Strayhorn, Billy, 73
Streagle, Tim, 182
Street Dreams, 156
Streisand, Barbra, 12, 61
Strouse, Charles, 112
Stump, Paul, 30, 107, 164
Sueno con Mexico, 31, 167, 188
Summer, 105, 130, 176, 185
Summer Day, 130, 176
Summer Running, 105, 185
Summertime, 109, 185
Sunday, 107, 174
Sunlight, 69, 171
Sunrise, 174
Swallow, Steve, 15, 16, 19, 20, 76, 77, 78, 109, 178, 179, 182
Switzerland, 133
Synclavier, 40, 42, 49, 62, 64, 65, 66, 150, 152
Synthesiser, 25, 26, 40, 41, 42, 43, 46, 49, 60, 65, 68, 70, 87, 91, 92, 95, 97, 107, 119, 140, 149, 150, 152, 154, 156
Synthesisers, 46, 47, 52, 56, 57, 58, 62, 65, 69, 84, 89, 90, 100, 117, 128, 138, 141
Syzygy, 180

T

Take Me There, 173
Tales From the Hudson, 88, 183
Tao, 133, 135, 162
Taylor, David, 171
Taylor, James, 34, 44, 114, 115, 186
Te Vous / Praise, 182
Tears in Heaven, 74, 181
Tears Inside, 48, 169
Tears of Rain, 95, 103, 184, 185
Tee, Richard, 16
Tell Her You Saw Me, 71, 140, 171, 177
Tell It All, 169
Tesser, Neil, 60, 164
Texas, 24, 104, 114
The Adventures of Max and Ben, 106, 185
The Alternative Man, 60
The Aurora, 184
The Awakening, 101, 173
The Baptismal Font, 183
The Bat, 34, 37, 44, 65, 113, 155, 167, 168, 181
The Bat Pt II, 168
The Best Thing for You, 181

The Birds and the Bees, 185
The Blue Estuaries, 129
The Book of Hours, 129
The Calling, 49, 169
The Changes, 76, 182
The Chief, 62, 180
The Colours of Chloe, 17, 178
The Cost Of Living, 180
The Deserving Many, 74, 181
The Dry Cleaner from Des Moines, 179
The Elements - Water, 183
The Epic, 33, 167
The Falcon, 52, 107, 138, 169
The Falcon and the Snowman, 52, 107, 138, 169
The Fields, The Sky, 45, 168
The First Circle, 43, 116, 169, 189
The Gathering Sky, 118, 175, 188
The Girls Next Door, 84, 172
The Good Life, 65, 152, 169, 180
The Heart of Things, 72
The Heat of the Day, 43, 99, 173
The Jazz Workshop, 13
The Late Shift (TV programme), 11, 45
The Longest Night, 76, 183
The Longest Summer, 69, 171
The Matrix (movie), 125, 126, 127
The Mean Time, 187
The Moon is a Harsh Mistress, 184
The Moon Song, 95, 184
The Morning of This Night, 186
The Nearness of You, 115, 186
The New Crystal Silence, 102
The Night Becomes You, 140, 176
The Night You Were Born, 91, 184
The Opening, 123, 125, 188
The Precious Jewel, 95, 184
The Rain, 183
The Red One, 77, 138, 139, 176, 182
The Road To You, 66, 171
The Roads of Marche, 92, 172
The Roots of Coincidence, 100, 173, 187, 188
The Rule of Three, 184
The Search, 33, 152, 167
The Shape of Jazz to Come, 47
The Sign of 4, 79, 80, 160, 184
The Sound of Summer Running, 104, 158, 185
The Sound of Water, 132, 152, 176
The Sun in Montreal, 112, 174
The Talk of the Town, 182
The Tide Will Rise, 76, 182

The Truth Will Always Be, 70, 171
The Veil, 169
The Way Up, 5, 33, 56, 68, 81, 92, 101, 120, 121, 123, 124, 136, 162, 175, 188
The Who (band), 20, 179
The Whopper, 20, 179
Theme from Passaggio per il Paradiso, 172
Thielemans, Toots, 171
Third Wind, 55, 67, 170, 171, 187, 190
This is Not America, 169, 187
Thomas, Gary, 72, 181
Three Flights Up, 60, 170
Tiempos Felice (Happy Times), 62, 180
Till We Have Faces, 72, 181
Time, 110, 120, 177, 185
Time is of the Essence, 185
Timeless, 101
Timeline, 110, 186
To the End of the World, 84, 87, 172, 187
Tokyo Day Trip, 139, 176
Tomorrow is the Question, 48
Tony, 59, 89, 90, 91, 105, 164, 181, 184
Tony Williams, 59, 89, 90, 164, 184
Too Soon Tomorrow, 100, 173
Touchstones, 20
Towards the Light, 132, 135, 176
Townsend, Lee, 105
Transition, 174
Transparence, 186
Traut, Ross, 14
Traveling Fast, 176
Travels, 29, 34, 45, 46, 67, 111, 155, 168, 174, 188
Tres Palabras (Three Words), 186
Trichinopoly, 184
Trigonometry, 169, 182
Trinity (band), 133
Trinkle Tinkle, 182
Trio 99-00, 46, 174
Trio Live, 113, 136, 174
Tumbleweed, 187
Tunnel of Love, 17, 178
Turnaround, 74, 167, 181
Tuscany, 92
Two Folk Songs, 167
Two for the Road, 95, 184
Tyner, McCoy, 88, 93, 96, 183

U

Unfinished Sympathy, 17, 178

Union Pacific, 106, 185
Unity Village, 22, 113, 166, 174, 189
Universe, 49, 71, 80, 101, 133, 135
Unquity Road, 22, 166, 189
Unrequited, 130, 176
Untidy Habits, 184
Upojenie (Ecstasy), 140, 177

V

Vampira, 178
Van Gelder, Rudy, 59
Vasconcelos, Nana, 34, 43, 44, 67, 154, 168, 171, 188, 189
Vashkar, 14, 178
Vaughan, Sarah, 131
Vermont Counterpoint, 147
Vibrafinger, 16
Vidala, 58, 170
Video Games, 169
Village Vanguard, 74
Vince Mendoza, 61, 62
Virginia, 105
Visions, 89
Visions of the Emerald Beyond, 89
Vox Humana, 19, 179
Vu, Cuong, 116, 117, 119, 122, 125, 126, 175, 188

W

Waiting for an Answer, 49, 169
Waiting to Dance, 109, 185
Walk in the Sun, 76, 182
Waltz for Ruth, 94, 184
Wardenclyffe Tower, 164
Washington, Dinah, 131
Water, 96, 97, 155, 183
Watercolors, 24, 26, 27, 96, 151, 166, 189
Watts, Jeff, 185
We Had a Sister, 74, 112, 174, 181, 190
We Live Here, 80, 85, 123, 153, 160, 162, 164, 172, 187
We Live Here - Live in Japan, 187
Weather Report (band), 13, 17, 23, 24, 31, 61
Weaver, Sigourney, 107
Weber, Eberhard, 16, 20, 23, 24, 166, 178, 179, 188
Wechter, Abraham, 149
Wertico, Paul, 34, 50, 51, 55, 66, 69, 70, 79, 87, 169, 170, 171, 172, 173, 184, 187, 189
What a Time, 182
What Do You Want, 112, 174
When Can I Kiss You Again?, 187
When We Were Free, 138, 173, 176

Wherever You Go, 120, 175
Whitaker, Rodney, 93, 183
White, 27, 28, 32, 35, 45, 47, 76, 81, 97, 112, 136, 151, 153, 182, 183
White Caps, 97, 183
White Christmas, 81
White Wheeled Limousine, 76, 182
Why Do Fools Fall in Love, 179
Wichita, 13, 24, 39, 46
Wilderness, 89, 90, 91, 92, 184
Wilderness Island, 90, 91, 184
Wilderness Rising, 90, 184
Wilderness Voyager, 90, 91, 184
Will You Say You Will, 61, 63, 180
Williams, Anthony, 59, 89, 90, 164, 184
Williams, John McLaughlin, 181
Willie T, 89, 183
Wilson, Glenn, 181
Wilson, Ransom, 147
Windows, 103, 185
Wisconsin, 24, 107
Wish, 72, 74, 181, 190
With My Boots On, 106, 185
Withers, Bill, 82
Wolf Story, 92, 172
Wonder, Stevie, 74
Woodstock, 63, 179
Word From Bird, 169
Word of Mouth, 50, 61
Wrong is Right, 27, 189

Y

Yano, Akiko, 70, 171
Yellow Fields, 20, 179
Yellow Submarine, 136
Yellowjackets, 76
Yo Sin Ti (Me Without You), 186
Yolanda You Learn, 169
You Don't Know What Love Is, 181
You Speak My Language, 78, 182
Young, Lester, 102, 134
Young, Neil, 34

Z

Zarecki, Pawel Bzim, 177
Zawinul, Josef, 12, 85, 115, 116
Zero Tolerance for Silence, 79, 172
Zorn, John, 105